P9-DMQ-622

PARACHUTE INFANTRY

PARACHUTE INFANTRY

An American Paratrooper's Memoir
of D-Day and the
Fall of the Third Reich

DAVID KENYON WEBSTER

Introduction by Stephen E. Ambrose

LOUISIANA STATE UNIVERSITY PRESS
Baton Rouge and London

Copyright © 1994 by Louisiana State University Press
All rights reserved
Manufactured in the United States of America

Louisiana Paperback Edition, 1997
06 05 04 03 02 01 00 99 98 97   5 4 3 2 1

Designer: Glynnis Phoebe
Typeface: display—Novarese, text—Bembo
Typesetter: G&S Typesetters, Inc.
Printer and binder: Thomson-Shore, Inc.

Library of Congress Cataloging-in-Publication Data
Webster, David Kenyon, d. 1961.
    Parachute infantry : an American paratrooper's memoir of D-Day and
the fall of the Third Reich / David Kenyon Webster ; introduction by
Stephen E. Ambrose.
      p.   cm.
    ISBN 0-8071-1901-6 (cloth) ISBN 0-8071-2222-X (pbk.)
    1. Webster, David Kenyon, d. 1961. World War, 1939–1945—
Campaigns—France—Normandy.   3. United States. Army. Parachute
Infantry Regiment, 506th. Company E—History.   4. World War,
1939–1945—Personal narratives, American.   5. Soldiers—United
States—Biography.   6. Normandy (France)—History, Military.
I. Title.
D762.N6W43   1994
940.54'2142—dc20   93-33488
                                                             CIP

Unless otherwise noted, all illustrations are from the author's personal collection, now in possession of Mrs. Charles B. Embree, Jr.

Portions of Chapter 1 first appeared in somewhat different form as "The Night Before D Day," *Saga* (October, 1959). Portions of Chapter 4 first appeared in somewhat different form as "We Drank Hitler's Champagne," *Saturday Evening Post,* May 3, 1952, and are reprinted with permission.

The paper in this book meets the guidelines for permanence and durability of the Committee on Production Guidelines for Book Longevity of the Council on Library Resources. ∞

To my wife, Barbara,
who was fifteen years old at the time and not aware of D-Day,
and to the friends left in the green fields of Europe
who never came home to tell about it

CONTENTS

ILLUSTRATIONS

following page 166

ACKNOWLEDGMENTS

Most of this book is based on letters written during the war and on recollections put down at length right after the war. Whenever possible, the facts were verified in histories of the period, especially Leonard Rapport and Arthur Northwood, Jr.'s *Rendezvous with Destiny: A History of the 101st Airborne Division* (New York, 1948). The United States Army was quite helpful, providing maps, photographs, and historical works. Special thanks are due Pat Christenson, Bob Rader, Virginia and Leonard Rapport, Burr Smith, and Hans Wesenhagen.

PUBLISHER'S NOTE

In a few instances we have changed or omitted names in order to avoid causing possible embarrassment to a person or his family.

INTRODUCTION

Stephen E. Ambrose

David Kenyon Webster may have been the only Harvard "English lit" major who volunteered for the parachute infantry and who then fought through the campaign in northwest Europe as a combat infantryman. He didn't have to do it. His family was moderately wealthy and had influence, so he could have had a commission if he had wanted one, or a cushy job far behind the front lines. But he wanted to see the war firsthand, to be a participant, to do his part in crushing Hitler and the Nazis. He insisted on fighting from a foxhole rather than typing up reports at Company Headquarters or handing out footballs and baseballs at a rest area in the rear.

His motives for insisting on being a member of a parachute infantry regiment went beyond patriotism. Webster wanted to be a writer. Heavily influenced by the literature of World War I, he wanted to experience and then describe combat. He had a flair for writing, a keen sensitivity, and a well-developed ability to observe and comment. With those talents, and using the perspective of a paratrooper, he produced an outstanding memoir of the war, now happily being published for the first time by LSU Press. It is rich in detail and rewarding in its revealing anecdotes about men at war. Webster is scathing in his denunciation of officers who were "chickenshit," whether in barracks or on the front lines. He is full of heartfelt praise for noncoms and enlisted men who did their jobs. He is honest about the actions of his fellow soldiers, in camp, in combat, as conquerors.

Webster's book has all the features that make for a classic wartime memoir. He describes training; the relationships that develop within a squad, platoon, and company; the first combat jump into

Normandy; the experience of killing and getting shot at (and hit); attitudes toward civilians, whether friendly as in France and Holland or unfriendly as in Germany; grousing about the army and its ways; and more. Webster manages to show us the general and the particular, the universal experience and the unique detail, in a flow of words that the most professional writer would envy.

Overall, I recommend this memoir to anyone who wants to know more about World War II, about combat, about being a paratrooper, about discovering oneself and being involved when the whole world was being tested and threatened. It brings back a place and a time, a sense of commitment, the feeling of "we are all in this together" as the United States and her allies fought for freedom.

Most GIs in World War II found that their service in the army was a broadening experience. Webster was no exception. The soldiers met men they never would have known otherwise, men from all over America, men from different economic, social, and ethnic backgrounds. In the novels about the war, the typical squad is made up of a Jew from New York, an Indian from Montana, a Swede from Minnesota, a Pole from Chicago, a Cajun from New Orleans, and so on. At the beginning of the novel, they hate one another. The shared misery of training pulls them together, as does the common hatred of their drill instructors and junior officers. Combat strengthens the bond, to the point that they become a band of brothers, trusting and loving one another as they had never before trusted or loved anyone. And the truth is that this happened in fact before it was written up as fiction—in this case at least art truly imitated life.

Webster was a man of books and libraries, a reader and a writer, thrown into an intimate and life-dependent relationship with ill-educated hillbillies, southern farmers, coal miners, lumbermen, fishermen, and other typical paratrooper enlisted men—in short, with a group of men with whom he had nothing in common. He would not have particularly liked or disliked them in civilian life—he just would not have known them. Yet it was among this unlikely group of men that Webster found his closest friendships and enjoyed most thoroughly the sense of identification with others.

He was wounded in Holland, in October, 1944. He rejoined his squad in January, 1945, and later he recalled his feelings: "It was good to be back with fellows I knew and could trust. Listening to the chatter, I felt warm and relaxed inside, like a lost child who has returned to a bright home full of love after wandering in a cold black forest." He went on: "You felt like part of a big family. You are closer to these men than you will ever be to any civilians."

Webster and his fellow squad members had developed a bond that is unique to combat infantrymen. Just as there is no human experience to equal that of combat, so there is no human relationship to equal that of comrades-in-arms. Their relationships are closer than those of brothers, different from those of lovers, stronger and deeper than those of friends.

Philosopher J. Glenn Gray, himself a frontline soldier in World War II, got it exactly right in his classic work *The Warriors:* "Organization for a common and concrete goal in peacetime organizations does not evoke anything like the degree of comradeship commonly known in war. . . . At its height, this sense of comradeship is an ecstasy. . . . Men are true comrades only when each is ready to give up his life for the other, without reflection and without thought of personal loss."[1]

Private Kurt Gabel of the 513th Parachute Infantry Regiment described his experience in words that Webster might have written: "The three of us, Jake, Joe, and I, became . . . an entity. There were many entities in our close-knit organizations . . . core elements within the families. . . . This sharing evolved never to be relinquished, never to be repeated. [It produced] incredible results in combat. [Men] would literally insist on going hungry for one another, freezing for one another, dying for one another. And the squad would try to protect them or bail them out without the slightest regard to consequences, cussing them all the way for making it necessary. Such a rifle squad . . . was a mystical concoction."[2]

I have interviewed hundreds of soldiers from World War II—American, British, Canadian, German, French—ranging from the supreme commander of the Allied Expeditionary Force to the lowest privates. Virtually without exception, they tell me that their closest friends, the men from whom they have no secrets, the men with whom they would gladly share their last piece of bread, the

1. J. Glenn Gray, *The Warriors: Reflections on Men in Battle* (New York, 1959), 43, 45, 46.
2. Kurt Gabel, *The Making of a Paratrooper: Airborne Training and Combat in World War II* (Lawrence, Kans., 1990), 142.

men they call on the phone when they get drunk on New Year's Eve, the men they name their children after, are the men with whom they served in the war. No one could ever envy the combat experience—it is truly hell—but everyone has to envy the comradeship that is unique to the combat experience.

All armies, through the ages, have attempted to create that bonding that becomes an "ecstasy," a "mystical concoction," but few succeeded as well as the paratroop infantry of the U.S. Army in World War II, and none better than was done in Webster's rifle company, Company E of the 506th Parachute Infantry.

Professor Paul Fussell, a junior officer in a rifle company in the war, wrote in his book *Wartime* that the soldier going into combat the first time thinks to himself: "It *can't* happen to me. I am too clever/agile/well-trained/good-looking/beloved/tightly laced, etc.," to ever get hit. After a few hours or days or weeks of combat, that attitude gives way to: "It *can* happen to me, and I'd better be more careful. I can avoid the danger by watching more prudently the way I take cover/dig in/expose my position by firing my weapon/keep extra alert at all times, etc." Then comes the realization that "It *is going to* happen to me, and only my not being there [on the front lines] is going to prevent it."[3]

Webster could attest to the truth of Fussell's insight. After his combat jump into Normandy, when he had returned to England to prepare for the next jump, Webster wrote his parents: "I am living on borrowed time. I do not think I shall live through the next jump. If I don't come back, try not to take it too hard. I wish I could persuade you to regard death as casually as we do over here. In the heat of battle you expect casualties, you expect somebody to be killed and you are not surprised when a friend is machine-gunned in the face. You have to keep going. It's not like civilian life, where sudden death is so unexpected."

When his mother wrote to express her considerable alarm at this attitude (and her worries about her youngest son, John, who had just joined the paratroopers), Webster was blunt in his reply: "Would you prefer for somebody else's son to die in the mud? You

3. Paul Fussell, *Wartime: Understanding and Behavior in the Second World War* (New York, 1989), 282.

want us to win the war, but you apparently don't want to have your sons involved in the actual bloodshed. That's a strangely contradictory attitude. Somebody has to get in and kill the enemy. Somebody has to be in the infantry and the paratroopers. If the country all had your attitude, nobody would fight, everybody would be in the Quartermaster. And what kind of country would that be?"

For the combat infantryman, there is no way out short of the end of the war or the loss of a limb. Any other wound would be patched up and the soldier sent back to the front lines. So it was with Webster. In Holland, in October, during an attack on a German position, "what felt like a baseball bat slugged my right leg." Webster recalled that it "spun me around and knocked me down." All he could think to say was, "They got me!" which even then seemed to him "an inadequate and unimaginative cliché." (Like all writers, he was composing his description of the event as it happened.)

It was a clean wound. The bullet went in and out of Webster's calf, hitting no bone. A million-dollar wound. I got it made, he thought to himself. When the medic got to him, Webster had a big grin on his face.

The grin didn't stay. Webster was patched up, sent to a replacement depot, and listed as fit for combat. He insisted on rejoining his unit: If he had to fight, he wanted to be with the best, and E Company of the 506th PIR had no superior. "If I had my choice," he wrote his parents, "I'd never fight again. Having no choice, I'll go back to E Company and prepare for another jump. If I die, I hope it'll be fast." In another letter, he wrote, "The realization that there is no escape, that we shall jump on Germany, then ride transports straight to the Pacific for the battle in China, does not leave much room for optimism."

He wasn't volunteering. He never volunteered. He made it a rule of his army life never to do anything voluntarily. He was an intellectual, as much an observer and chronicler of the phenomenon of soldiering as a practitioner. He was there to do his duty, and he did it, but he never volunteered.

He also never let a buddy down in combat and was ready to go above and beyond the call of duty if necessary. In February, 1945, at Haguenau in western Germany, he and Private Bob Marsh got orders to set up a machine gun to provide covering fire for a patrol if needed. They were exposed in such a way that if they fired, a

German self-propelled gun directly across the river would spot them without the aid of observers. But they decided that if the patrol was fired upon, they would open up with everything they had, "because the lives of some twenty men might depend on us." Webster, the usually cool observer, commented, "This was one of those times where I could see playing the hero even if it meant death."

One characteristic of life on the front lines is that there is no past or future, only the present. Glenn Gray calls it "the tyranny of the present." He speculates that this is why soldiers will go to such extraordinary lengths to get souvenirs. In Holland, as he was crawling and limping his way to the rear after suffering his leg wound, under fire from a German 88mm cannon, Webster spotted a German camouflaged poncho and decided it would make "an ideal souvenir." He stopped to "scoop it up." Gray explains why Webster, and so many others, would take such chances for a worthless piece of uniform: "Primarily, souvenirs appeared to give the soldier some assurance of his future beyond the destructive environment of the present. They represented a promise that he might survive."[4]

Webster loved the Dutch people, thought the British people were quaint but dull, had serious reservations about the French, and began the war hating the Germans. He wanted them taught a lesson, so that they would never again try to conquer Europe. In July, 1944, he wrote his parents, "I cannot understand why you hope for a quick end of the war. Unless we take the horror of battle to Germany itself, unless we fight in their villages, blowing up their houses, smashing open their wine cellars, killing some of their livestock for food, unless we litter their streets with horribly rotten German corpses as was done in France, the Germans will prepare for war, unmindful of its horrors. Defeat must be brought into Germany itself before this mess can come to a proper end; a quick victory now, a sudden collapse, will leave the countryside relatively intact and the people thirsty for revenge. I want the war to end as quickly as anybody wishes, but I don't want the nucleus of another war left whole."

In April, 1945, after seeing his first slave labor camp, Webster

4. Gray, *The Warriors*, 82.

was furious. "There was Germany and all it stood for," he wrote. "The Germans had taken these people from their homes and sentenced them to work for life in a factory in the Third Reich. With cold deliberation the Germans had enslaved the populace of Europe." So far as Webster was concerned, "The German people were guilty, every one of them."

But after living in Germany for a few weeks, Webster found that despite himself he was drawn to the people. "The Germans I have seen so far have impressed me as clean, efficient, law-abiding people," he wrote his parents. They were churchgoers. "In Germany everybody goes out and works and, unlike the French, who do not seem inclined to lift a finger to help themselves, the Germans fill up the trenches soldiers have dug in their fields. They are cleaner, more progressive, and more ambitious than either the English or the French." Like other GIs, Webster identified with the clean, hard-working, disciplined, educated, middle-class Germans. Right here was laid the basis for the German-American alliance that flourished during the Cold War.

Webster hated the army. He hated its chickenshit ways, its bumbling bureaucracy, its privileges for officers and contempt for enlisted men. He wouldn't have done it again for one million dollars—but he wouldn't have taken a million dollars for the experience, either.

He got out of the army in 1945, thankful beyond words that he didn't have to make that "big jump" into Japan. He moved to California and worked at a variety of jobs as he wrote and submitted articles and the manuscript of his memoirs to various publishers. He placed many articles, the top being in the *Saturday Evening Post* on the taking of Hitler's Eagle's Nest in the Alps, but he could not find a publisher for his memoirs. (The publishers right after the war wanted novels with lots of sex, not authentic memoirs.) He became a reporter, first with the Los Angeles *Daily News,* then with the *Wall Street Journal.* In 1951 he married Barbara Stoessel, an artist and sister of Walter J. Stoessel, Jr., who later became American ambassador to Poland, the Soviet Union, and West Germany.

Webster had always been fascinated by sharks. Barbara explained: "The shark, for him, became a symbol of everything that is mysterious and fierce about the sea. He began gathering material for a book of his own. His research went on for years. He studied sharks firsthand, underwater, swimming among them; and caught many, fishing with a handline from his eleven-foot sailing dinghy, which he had named *Tusitala,* which means 'Teller of Tales.' "

Webster wrote his book and submitted it twenty-nine times, but could not convince a publisher that anyone wanted to read about sharks.

On September 9, 1961, Webster set sail from Santa Monica with squid bait, a heavy line, and hook for shark fishing. He never came back. A search the next day discovered the *Tusitala* awash five miles offshore. One oar and the tiller were missing. His body was never found.

Barbara was able to get his book on sharks published in 1963, by W. W. Norton and Company, under the title *Myth and Maneater.* There was a British edition and a paperback edition in Australia. When *Jaws* was released in 1975, Dell issued *Myth and Maneater* in a mass-market paperback.

And now LSU Press is publishing Webster's wartime memoir. Like *Myth and Maneater,* it has been worth waiting for.

For my part, I never had the privilege of meeting David Kenyon Webster, but I admire him without stint. He was a good soldier and a wonderful writer, one of those brave thousands of American combat infantrymen who helped win the war and thus preserve our freedom, and one of those very few with the talent and energy to write about the war in a way to help those of us who came later to understand it.

PARACHUTE INFANTRY

PROLOGUE

All my life I had wanted to go to England. I had wanted to ride in a big black boat with white cabins and red funnels across the Atlantic and bicycle through the British Isles to the places that I had read about in *Ivanhoe, Kidnapped, Robin Hood, Lorna Doone,* and *The Black Arrow.*

My poets were the English poets, and when I played with toy soldiers, they, too, were English: sturdy, kilted Scotchmen running with fixed bayonets; tall, bright-red guardsmen on parade in great black busbies. As a small child, I was dressed by my parents, who are of English and Scotch descent, like Christopher Robin, in button shoes, leggings that buttoned up the side, and a dashing little Black Watch cap with a checkered red-and-white band around its sides and two twirling black ribbons in back.

Finally, in September, 1943, I did go to England. I was a little boy no longer. The toy soldiers had come to life; I was one of them. Instead of a Black Watch cap with ribbons, I wore a steel helmet with a parachutist's chin strap. Jump boots were my leggings now.

We came down from Camp Shanks and crossed the black Hudson at midnight on a ferry from West New York. Welders were cutting up the capsized hull of the *Normandie* nearby, but there was no time for sightseeing, for all too soon the ferry banged into the river end of the Cunard Line pier and dropped its ramp and up we went. The shed that had seemed so vast and terrifying to me as a child was even more desolate now.

Gone were the stevedores and the taxis out front; gone the white-jacketed porters, the hurrying peacetime voyagers and their friends and relations. In their place we filed, a lone battalion bent under its barracks bags. Half a dozen Red Cross women handed us coffee and doughnuts and little green sewing kits, but we could not linger to chat with them. Instead, we marched quickly by with a faraway look in our eyes, snatched cards marked with our sleeping quarters and eating time from an officer at the front of the gangplank, and, without stopping, clutched our steep, sweaty way onto the old gray *Samaria* and went aft to the sheets of canvas stretched between iron pipes that were our bunks.

We left in the morning. There was no confetti, and there was no "All ashore who are going ashore!" because *nobody* was going ashore. Our sole audience was a handful of bored stevedores standing by the hawsers. They cast us off, and the hawsers splashed and wriggled back up into the ship. Then the tugs pushed us out and left us, and we turned slowly, without a band or a wave of good-bye, and went down the river with the tide.

I was going to England at last, but not quite as I had envisioned.

1

The Jump into Normandy

It was the end of May, 1944. We had been in England eight months while others fought, and now our time had come. A last inspection, a last short arm. Clean the barracks and police the area. Every man gets a new jump suit and an orange smoke grenade. We move out at noon.

OK, let's go. Mount the buses and say good-bye.

We were hot and crowded on the ride south but not unaware of the beauty around us, a beauty made more lovely by the knowledge that many of us would never see it again. Loaded with gear and ammunition and sweating terribly in woolen winter uniforms, we drove under the tall green trees south of camp, past Wittenditch and the back hill to Ramsbury, past the cozy tea room at Chilton Foliat and the water meadow and cattail bog that fronted on the pink Elizabethan magnificence of Littlecote Manor, home of the legendary wild Darrells and more recently of our regimental commander, Colonel Robert F. Sink.

We rode to Hungerford and through it to the Great Western Railroad station, where we must have waited for hours. At least it seemed like hours, for the sun was so hot, our gear so tight, our clothes so airless and itchy. Gradually the talk died down, and more and more men lay back on their musette bags and fell asleep. Tension passed into boredom.

It was supposed to be a secret that we were setting off for the Invasion of Europe, but the secret was hard to keep from passersby. Our fresh bandoliers, new ammunition pouches, and full musette bags; the camouflage netting on our helmets; the bundles of orange cloth and identification panels that almost every man carried; the trench knives sewn on our boots; the tense, excited way we talked; and the distant look in our eyes meant only one thing: invasion.

I, however, was still skeptical, for I had imagined that our last move would be at least as well disguised as our arrival in Aldbourne. It would be proper, correct, and traditional, I thought, to fade away from Aldbourne on a cold dark night in a sealed convoy. After all we had been told about security, it seemed downright foolish to move us out for D-Day so openly, at hot high noon. I looked at the orange cloth and the orange smoke grenades and, wise guy to the end, loudly proclaimed: "Hell, this is just another goddamn maneuver. This time we're the orange team."

Our train slid in and stopped. We piled aboard, a squad of twelve to each compartment designed for six civilians, threw our excess gear on the floor, and put the machine guns and mortars in the luggage racks overhead and the musette bags under the seats. Down came the broad leather window straps and with them the windows, and soon everybody had settled back quietly with his thoughts and memories and forebodings to rest awhile and enjoy the trip. Our tiny engine tweet-tweeted, and we slid off down the tracks.

Fast and smooth we rode, shooting through the green landscape in our sealed tube, faster, faster, faster, as if we were trying to make up for all the waiting we had done overseas. We rattled south and west, through pocket villages and little towns we had never heard of before and past sights till now unseen. Through Pewsey and Westbury and Bruton and Cas Cory, Yeovil, and Axminster. Through tunnels and across rivers that would be brooks and creeks in our own land (the Avon, the Wylye, the Stour, the Frome, the Axe). As we got sleepier and sleepier, we came nearer the Channel and saw, like rusty relics of an ancient battlefield, scores of overgrown 1940 pillboxes, their sagging barbed wire draped with wild vines.

"Tweet-tweet!" our engine shrilled as we rattled through the stations without a pause. "D-Day calling," the wheels replied, "D-Day calling, D-Day calling, D-Day calling."

We dozed or talked softly, smoked or looked out the windows, opened our K rations and ate them. The hills got bigger and greener, with great shadowy belts of trees on their tops, and the train increased its speed. Whistling shrilly at tunnels that blew soot back at us through the open windows, it carried us like a tidal wave toward the dark shore of combat for which we had been so long preparing. On and on: "D-Day calling, D-Day calling, D-Day calling."

At twilight time, when the air was hushed and flashing birds twittered and glided home to their hedges and shadows cut purple gashes in the huge hills, we rattled into a village way station and stopped. HONITON, the sign said. Men got out of the forward cars, cursing and hanging their gear, and soon an officer shouted in our window: "Everybody outside! This is it!"

Machine guns and mortars on our shoulders, we staggered up a steep incline, turned a corner, climbed aboard a column of trucks waiting for us with tailgates down and motors running, and drove slowly out of town.

"Where are we going?" someone asked our driver.

"To this airfield five miles out."

"Oh."

And that was that.

The long brown convoy snaked and whined and grated uphill with drily shifting gears on a narrow, twisting, dusty road. Higher and higher we went, until at last we reached the topmost plateau, a man-made butte for runways. We stopped in a country lane bordered by stout hedgerows sweet with honeysuckle.

I looked over the tailgate and saw a half-timbered cottage down the way and a line of green pyramidal tents on the other side of the north hedge and suddenly recognized the place. We had bivouacked here before the last night jump a few weeks ago. It was simply a bivouac area then and a very good one, but nothing more. Now it was the marshaling area.

Entertainers and newsmen on deadline can talk all they want to about tension, but they wouldn't know tension if you dipped it in a bucket of water and hit them in the face with it—unless they had spent five days in a marshaling area waiting to start the Invasion of Europe.

Finally there isn't anything more to do. You eat your last meal and put on your clothes and walk down the corridor to the big flash. You go out of the world the way you came in—surrounded by people and utterly alone.

That's the way it was in the marshaling area.

Ours included both the runways from which the C-47s and gliders were to take off and the tent cities pitched on their outskirts for the accommodation of waiting parachutists and glidermen. Troops were assembled here for greater control, absolute secrecy, and more intimate instruction in the tasks before them. They were briefed and issued maps and whatever special equipment or ammunition was necessary to complete their wardrobe. They loaded the bellies and doorways of C-47s with parapaks of bandoliers, mortar shells, and machine-gun ammunition, with K rations and D rations, medical supplies, and 75mm pack howitzers. Jeeps, trailers, and fully assembled 105s were lashed down in British Horsa and American CG4A gliders. Nobody visited other companies; nobody left the area for a mild-and-bitter. We walked in the shadows of the hedgerows and amused ourselves without the Red Cross or the USO.

Since SHAEF, or something equally academic and Olympian, feared the consequences of German observation planes' noticing new paths beaten across the meadows to the slit trenches, we were ordered to follow the U-shape of the hedges to the latrine instead of cutting straight across. SHAEF never explained how the Luftwaffe could miss hundreds of planes and gliders and scores of tents and still pick up a threadlike Indian trail through footlong grass. But then, SHAEF never explained a lot of things.

The trucks drove away and left us in the peaceful silence of a country twilight. The sun was fading, swallows glided home, and still we stood, hot, tired, sooty, and churlish. Our ODs itched. We were bleary from naps on the train and dusty from the truck ride. The snaps on our musette bags bit and twisted into our collarbones. Be done with it, be done with it! our patience cried. We've hurried up and waited for two long years. Now let's go!

"Is the coffee ready yet?" someone called in a loud voice to our right. A cuckoo whispered down the lane by the timbered cottage, and there was a clatter of pans out of sight behind the north hedge. Its wings and fuselage marked with broad white identification bands, a great brown C-47 rustled over us with its flaps down and glided to a landing out of sight several hundred yards away.

Our captain, who had disappeared through an opening in the hedge, popped up again and took a stand on a mound in the opening. "On your feet, Headquarters Company!" he shouted. "Let's go!"

The food situation was incredible. No sooner had we relaxed on our camp cots in squad tents as close and hot as New York in August than a shrill cry of "Chow!" brought us out on the path with a clatter of utensils. Friendly, obliging Air Corps KPs loaded our tin dishes like garbage scows. It was a beautiful load: white bread (our first overseas), great gobs of melting butter, marmalade (from an open keg swarming with yellowjackets, but who cares?), rice pudding and cream, all the coffee you can drink.
"Seconds? Why sure, help yourself, buddy."
"You kidding?"
"No, no, we got orders to give you guys all you want."
The millennium had arrived.
While we were smoking and chatting and thinking about thirds in the hushed, drowsy lull afterward, the CQ put his head in the tent flaps and shouted something about a movie in fifteen minutes.
A rumor, we said. White bread and movies on the same day? Impossible. But this was the marshaling area, where Air Corps engineers did all the chores and nothing was too good for paratroopers, so movies it was.
They were held in the base theater near the runways half a mile away, with the whole regiment in attendance. The atmosphere was more like a cruise to Bermuda or a high-school graduation party than a prelude to invasion. Friends shouted to friends in other companies and battalions. Officers visited back and forth. Colonel Sink stood benignly up front like a headmaster, smiling at his boys, or people, as he called us.
The movie started with a Gothic title starkly emblazoned on a gigantic swastika. This was soundly hissed. The camera lowered its focus to a battalion commander below the swastika who was addressing his men in frantic, Hitlerian fashion from a platform in a hangar. He wore a parachutist's rimless bowl helmet and a long, spotted jump jacket. His pants were perfectly bloused over his boots. The sound track, which was in German, carried his guttural ravings to us. We hissed again and again.
In the long silence before the lights came on again, we thought

about the burly German paratroopers we had seen in the film, and wondered if they would be waiting for us wherever we were going. Sensing our subdued mood, Colonel Sink got up and made a little speech.

"Men," he said, wiping his face with his hand, "we've shown you this picture because we wanted you to see how the Germans fight. Did you watch them closely? Did you see how fast they moved? How they used every bit of the available cover and concealment? Remember those things when you go into combat.

"You remember what General Montgomery told you. He said he'd seen the German troopers and he'd seen you, and by God, he said he felt sorry for the Germans. You're bigger than they are and a hell of a lot better. You can whip 'em and, by God, you *will!*

"Now go get a good night's sleep. We have a lot of things to do in the next couple of days."

The rumor blew through the tents. "The news is out!" men called from field to field and hedgerow to hedgerow. "They've chosen the drop zone."

The CQ came around shortly afterward, and we left the area in formation and assembled, one platoon at a time, in the closely guarded battalion briefing tent. Our platoon leader told us that a real beauty was waiting for us there.

Two large sand tables stood on yard-high legs in the center of the tent. Maps and diagrams hung from the rear wall. Our instructor, the S-2 captain, watched us come in and look around. Yale men, his face seemed to say as he stared at us dully with a studied air of unshaven indifference, must remain poised and blasé in the presence of the unwashed. When the last man had ducked in, the guard secured the door flap and the captain started to talk.

"I have something here," he said, "that may interest you: a sort of field problem. These are sand tables, one for the big picture and one our own size. You've seen other sand tables before at other airfields before other jumps, but these are different.

"Oh, yes. Before I go any further, maybe I'd better tell you where we're going. You might be interested. We're jumping behind the enemy lines on the peninsula of Normandy. Don't look so blank. Surely you've heard of Normandy? It's a large peninsula on the coast of central France about a hundred miles southeast of here."

He stepped to the back wall, unrolled a map of southern England and central France, and, taking a pointer, indicated Normandy.

"Here's where we are, and here's where we're going. Normandy's rather a large peninsula, but we're not going to take it all—at first. We're going to jump behind the beaches ahead of the infantry. We'll go in about midnight. They'll hit the beach at 7 A.M., so we'll be all alone that night. I hope none of you men are afraid of the dark.

"There are two beaches: Utah, here, and Omaha, here. We drop behind Utah. The 4th Division is supposed to pass through us on D-Day. If they take the beach.

"The 82nd's jumping up here around St. Mere Eglise, and the British 6th Airborne Division will go in ahead of their infantry here. But let's not worry about those people. We'll have enough worries of our own."

The captain stepped from the map to one of the sand tables. No one breathed. Normandy? Normandy? I said to myself. All I know about Normandy is William the Conqueror, and that was 1066.

"Gather around me so everybody can see. If I point it out to you on the sand table, then perhaps you'll be better able to visualize the operation. See this bend, where Normandy joins the mainland? See the flat green land at the bend? That's the estuary of the Douve River. It divides the two beachheads. Carentan is the key city. We have to take the bridges to it and the high ground along the Douve, but we'll land north of the river behind Utah Beach, here.

"The main purpose of jumping at night, aside from the obvious ones of dodging flak and surprising the Germans, is to give us plenty of time to clear the roads to the beach so the 4th Division can get in. The 101st has to take the four southern causeways from Utah Beach to the high ground and hold them open at all costs. We'll also have to take the key villages and strongpoints and knock out a couple of gun batteries and any odd Jerrys who get in our way.

"Our regiment must take the two causeways, Exits 1 and 2, here. The Germans may flood the low ground behind the beach and confine the infantry to these causeways, so they are A1 on our list of objectives. They have to be taken and *held!*

"Those gun batteries I just mentioned have to be wiped out. If they're not fully destroyed, we may be all alone in Normandy, because they can stop the infantry right in the water. Somebody will also have to blow up the communications lines to the beach, and somebody else will have to take these little villages—St. Marie du Mont, St. Martin de Varreville, Foucarville, St. Germain de Varreville, Audouville, La Hubert, Pouppeville, and a couple of others you needn't worry about.

"As far as we know, not too many Germans are waiting for us down there. We have information coming in from the underground every day and photoreconnaissance planes over the area right now, and we don't think the Germans are expecting us. There's a tank school in Carentan, which is the biggest city in our sector and one that we'll probably have to take later, but they're training with beat-up old 1939 Renault tanks and shouldn't cause us too much trouble.

"The other Germans are mostly static-defense troops, low-grade Poles and White Russians with German officers and noncoms. Most of them were forced into the Wehrmacht after they were captured on the eastern front, so they shouldn't put up much of a fight. They're formed into two divisions—the 709th and the 243rd. The 243rd has a lot of veterans who were transferred from the Russian front to Normandy for a rest. We won't give them much rest, I can assure you. Oh, and G-2 says that elements of the 716th Infantry Division are also roaming around down there. But don't worry about any of those divisions. A German division is lucky nowadays if it has three thousand men in it.

"Just a few more words before you go. Our mission, as I said before, is to jump behind the enemy lines on the peninsula of Normandy. Now for the timing. We'll leave at 11:30 P.M. The 2nd Battalion will drop and assemble on radar and a string of three white lights set up by the Pathfinders in an orchard near a crossroads village named Hébert. We'll march to the two southern causeways from Utah Beach and hold them. We'll kill any Germans who get in our way.

"And don't forget that word *kill!* Hitler has ordered the Wehrmacht to treat all Allied parachutists as spies and shoot them on the spot. So you know what to do with the Germans. We're not playing with flags and umpires anymore."

The regimental riggers who always packed our chutes were waiting for us at the hangar's mouth with a mountain of green canvas kit bags containing our main and reserve parachutes. We threw our bags on our shoulders and staggered indoors, where our company commander lined us up and bade us fit on our harness.

And so we sweated with leg straps, main lift webs, bellybands, and chest buckles, loosening here, tightening there, until all were evenly secured and so tight that we were bent over like arthritic old men. We checked the fishline lacing on the outer cover of our backpacks, for this alone held the canopy in until our falling body weight ripped off the cover, and we made sure that our anchor line was tucked securely into its rubber bands on the top of the cover. Click, snap; click, snap: Make sure the anchor-line snap fastener works smoothly. We are jumping at midnight. There will not be time or light enough to check these things then. So check and recheck and check again and again.

When the chutes had been adjusted, we put them back in the kit bags, zipped them shut, marked the bags with our names and company, and lined them up in a company file, so that we could march in at departure time, pick them up without delay or confusion, and go straight to the planes.

High overhead, a twenty-four-hour cover of P-47 fighter planes crossed and recrossed the blue sky, lacing it with cottony vapor trails. Nine C-47s circled the airdrome, peeled off, and landed one by one. They were coming in from all the troop carrier bases in southern England. At almost every parking space along the runways a great brown plane now stood silent and ready for us.

Our general was intellectual, fervent, and believing, but he was not one of the boys, like slim Jim Gavin of the 82nd, who carried a rifle and bore the nickname the Two-Star Platoon Leader. Our general spoke as he thought and acted, and I will do my best to reproduce his speech as it was given. It was a good speech of its kind. I regret to say that it left his audience quite unmoved.

The general was a promising young man, tall, taut, and handsome, who had gone far in his chosen field. He spoke four (or was it six?) foreign languages fluently. He had made a brilliant record at West Point and married well. At this time, he was best known for a cool and daring feat performed in Italy, where he had served as a brigadier in the 82nd.

"Men," he said to the regiment, assembled above him on a grassy slope west of our tents, "we have ahead of us the biggest job of the invasion. The 101st has been chosen to kick off. We're the first team, the best division in the army, so we've been picked to go in first.

"The Germans are good, but you are better. You're fighting for a good cause; his cause is rotten. As soon as you've gotten the upper hand, he'll come running to you with his arms in the air, crying 'Kamerad!' I've seen it happen. But don't think it happens easily. Don't think you're just going to walk in and take over. You're going to have to fight for every yard of ground and fight night and day to hold it.

"The Germans will counterattack again and again, because that's their specialty. As soon as they lose a position or a battle, they reform and counterattack while you're digging in. They try to catch you off balance. I want you to throw them back every time.

"We're jumping between twelve-thirty and one in the morning. H hour for the infantry is six. That gives us approximately five hours to clear the causeways and destroy the gun batteries. We've *got* to clear those causeways and hold them open! The 4th Division is counting on us. We can't let them down!

"I've just seen General Eisenhower. He says it will be two days before we'll know for sure whether the invasion will succeed or fail. After two days, the balance will be in our favor. So what I want from you men is *two days!* Two days and nights of violent effort, two days and nights of ceaseless, savage fighting. Drive yourselves! You've done it before. Force yourselves! Hold on and fight like the world's best soldiers, American paratroopers! The whole invasion depends on you.

"I have one last request to make of you: I want every man who jumps on D-Day to go out the door shouting 'Bill Lee!' General Lee has heart trouble, and he's sitting at home by the radio now, waiting for the invasion to begin. He raised this division from an idea. As a tribute to a great parachutist and a great leader, I want every man to shout 'Bill Lee!' when he jumps. Don't count 'One thousand, two thousand, three thousand.' Yell 'Bill Lee!' instead."

Now it was certain. Now the day was set. Of all the planes that had landed on the runways, not one had left. The 1st, the 4th, and the 29th infantry divisions were seaborne in vast gray fleets, and the

Germans had already started parachute and panzer reinforcements from Brittany and northern France to meet them. Savernake Forest and all the roads in southern England were lined with green wooden cases of mortar and artillery ammunition, and the later waves of Bradley's 1st Army clattered and clanked their dusty way south through the ancient Devonshire villages to the medieval ports that held their barges. London was empty. There were no troops on pass in Edinburgh or Birmingham. Half the trains suddenly disappeared from the British timetables. The future was rising in the green country to sweep across the narrow sea and smash the hateful nation that worshiped war. D-Day was scheduled for tomorrow. It blew icy fumes of fear in our faces as we gathered in the S-2 tent for the final briefing.

"At ease, men," the captain snapped, all indifference gone from his voice and attitude. "I have something important to tell you that you may already know: We're leaving tonight. This is final. The Pathfinders take off at 9:50, the 1st Battalion at 11:05. We go at 11:15. The whole regiment will be airborne by 11:30.

"Once each battalion is airborne and formed in a V of Vs, it has sixty minutes' flight time to reach the drop zone. This is a combat mission. Everybody jumps! Nobody, but nobody, goes back to England. The pilots have orders to jump every man in their planes. If they miss the drop zone—and it's happened before, even in broad daylight—they'll drop us on the Douve bridges. The bridges are second in importance only to the causeways.

"There will be forty planes in a serial, each serial a battalion, and six minutes between serials over the DZ. So wherever you land, clear that jump field *fast!* Get the hell out of the way of the next serial because they're dropping pack 75s and a lot of other heavy equipment with the men.

"You'll have two means of identification—the password and this dime-store metal cricket. The password is 'Flash . . . Thunder.' If you hear somebody coming towards you, cover him and challenge him with 'Flash.' He should reply 'Thunder.' If he doesn't answer your 'Flash' and doesn't use his cricket, then you'd better speed him on his way with a bayonet or a hand grenade.

"This cricket is an ingenious idea. Sometimes I'm convinced that the army thinks of everything. Who else could conceivably have thought of using a child's toy for combat identification? This cricket will probably surprise the Germans as much as our presence in his beloved West Wall. One click, like this, to be answered by two. Simple, isn't it? You hear somebody coming and you go click-clack, and he'll answer click-clack, click-clack. Hold on to these crickets! They're lifesavers. Get some string and tie them around your necks so you won't lose them.

"Remember, your life depends on two things, this cricket (click-clack . . . click-clack, click-clack) and the password 'Flash . . . Thunder.'

"We want to take the Germans by surprise. In order to do so, we'll have to move as quietly as possible. Nobody jumps with a loaded rifle. Nobody shoots if he can possibly avoid it. Use your bayonet! Use your hand grenades!

"This will be night work, silent and deadly. Once you get free of your chute, whip out your bayonet and ram it on your rifle. Don't give away your position by shooting at strange noises. Sneak up on 'em! You have the psychological advantage—you're attacking. They're sitting passive in their holes and billets, scared to death. They don't know where you are or who you are or how many of you are after them. Crawl up on 'em in the long grass and kill 'em with your trench knives. Cut their throats. Strangle 'em if you can. But don't shoot!

"Above all, kill 'em! We can't be dragging a lot of prisoners around with us at night. You know where they are and what to do with them: the officers' mess and billets and company of infantry at St. Marie du Mont, the platoon on the gun batteries at St. Martin de Varreville, and all the others.

"Go down there and get 'em and kill every last sonofabitching German you find."

The colonel was our last speaker and our best, and when he finished talking, I felt better about going. I knew we would make it all right. For some strange, unaccountable reason, the wearing of wool-knit caps in the 101st Airborne Division was apparently considered a crime more heinous than rape. If the general caught a man taking a break in one of these knitted affairs with stiff little visors, he stopped the problem and personally scolded the bewildered miscreant and his immediate superiors. British commandos might raid Dieppe in socklike caps and British parachutists might wear red berets to Sicily, but we slept in our helmets and hid our wool-knit caps under their iron lids. It was a source of constant friction, with men continually trying to wear them and the officers, goaded from on high, on the lookout to snatch them off. Wool-knit caps became a command phobia of such proportions that the colonel had to devote a large portion of his final talk to this tender subject. D-Day was tomorrow, and he was talking about wool-knit caps. The thought of it made me laugh.

"Now men," the colonel said, rubbing his hand over his face and moving his overseas cap back and forth, "I don't care what else you do, but for God's sake, don't let the general catch you in a wool-knit cap! Steal a tank, rob a German payroll—anything but a wool-knit cap. He caught one of you wearing one on the last jump and gave me hell for it. Now, I don't like to catch hell, and I know you don't, so if you have to wear a wool-knit cap, keep it under your helmet all the time. The general's hell on wool-knit caps."

Weaving slightly back and forth, he smiled at his men, moved his hat around his head, wiped his face a few more times. He spoke of the enemy's avowed intention of killing every paratrooper they caught where they caught him and of our reciprocal intentions toward their infantry. He spoke of the need for silence, of bayonets and hand grenades, of the flak expected above and the Germans below. He dwelt at such length on the general's demand for two days' violent effort that he left the impression in our minds that this was the limit expected of us. Gas might be used in a desperate attempt to stop the invasion, so keep your masks handy. Don't drink the water; the Frenchmen don't. Keep your wool-knit caps under cover. Watch out for mines and booby traps. Don't jump with any identification but your dog tags. We want to keep this thing secret so they won't know how many of us there are, and if you're captured and interrogated, just tell them your name, rank, and serial number—nothing else. There will be no saluting in Normandy, and officers are not to be sirred. When he had covered all the contingencies, the colonel looked around, relaxed his stance, and reminisced.

"Men," he said, shoving his cap to the back of his head, "we've been together a long time. You're probably as sick of it all as I am. You're sick of field problems and so am I. We're ready to go to combat.

"Anybody who doesn't want to fight can get up and leave right now. This is your last chance. Anybody want out? We won't hold it against you. Anybody want to quit?"

He stared at his audience with a smile on his face.

"Nobody? Not a hand raised? I knew it. OK then, everybody jumps! That's a direct order. From now on it's twenty years. Refusal to jump in combat is desertion under fire."

The colonel paused and smiled again, a smile of pride. His confidence in us gave us confidence in ourselves. He put his hands on his hips, leaned back, and said: "I feel sorry, I feel mighty sorry, for those Germans. God help 'em all when we get to Normandy."

The audience laughed, and he raised his hand and shouted: "I want you men to go over there and *kill* those people and get us a Presidential Citation! You can *do* it. Good luck and God bless you!"

West of our tents, where the wind came from, a mighty shouting filled the air. Men whooped and hollered and gave the rebel yell. The joyous sound swept over the marshaling area like a tidal wave.

I sat bolt upright. Could it be? Can it be? Oh God, I hope so!

The CQ stuck his head in the air and screamed deliriously: "They called it off, they called it off! No jump tonight! Too much wind. Yippee!"

Yelling and laughing like idiots, we leaped from our cots, incoherent with joy, and danced wildly on the sod floor. Men ran from tent to tent shaking hands and slapping backs and screaming at the top of their lungs. The reprieve had come to the death house.

You can put off a shave for a week or more. You can break a date and postpone a wedding. Doctors can even delay death.

But you can't put off an invasion—not for more than a day. Not when three airborne divisions are waiting in marshaling areas and six infantry divisions are already at sea. You can't delay the Invasion of Europe more than a day when the landing depends so much on a full moon and a minus tide that comes only three or four times a year.

Now it was final and irrevocable: We were jumping tonight, wind or no wind, one German or ten thousand. The S-2 captain said that the enemy had just moved his 91st Infantry Division into the area behind Utah Beach and that we were going there regardless.

The wind had blown itself out while we slept. We woke up, late and rested, on a still summer morn, noted the lack of wind, and immediately knew that our reprieve had been good for only one day.

In the little hundred-yard-square meadows bounded by dense walls of intertwined earth and stone and hedge and tree, the separate companies, hushed by the finality of departure, lay silent in their tents and waited to go. Men who had celebrated so loudly the night before could barely talk today. They bit their lips and worked their bolts and spent the longest day of their lives in semi-idleness, waiting, waiting, waiting. There was no laughter, no singing or shouting. The most inveterate gambler couldn't get a crap game started. A deadening stillness hung in the warm, sweet air.

Late in the afternoon, when swallows glided over the great round hills whose separate ridges thrust long fingers to the sea, the supply sergeants began to circulate cans of camouflage greasepaint and handfuls of burnt cork, and we streaked our faces and darkened the backs of our hands for the night ahead.

They gave us stew before we left. The Air Corps said we were lucky to get that, for it was all that was left. "We hadn't counted on feeding you another day," they explained. We filed through the chow line at four o'clock in blackface and listened dully as the KPs apologized for the fare—C rations, leftover scraps of bread and coffee—and cursed the army for sending us over on such a meal.

At five o'clock, the CQ went from tent to tent, warning us that we were moving out in half an hour. Put on your gear and stand by.

First you put on your cotton underwear. Then you wriggled into your woolen long johns. OD shirt and trousers were next, and over all, a shrunken, impregnated jump suit. It was a stifling ensemble for seersucker weather, and I prayed, as I buckled on my musette bag and hung my cartridge belt with a canteen, a bayonet, a trench knife, a first-aid packet, and a pair of stolen wirecutters, that I would not have to make a water landing. I zipped up my jump jacket to the collar and could barely breathe.

Hot, itchy, stiff, and extremely confined, I broke my rifle down with trembling fingers and put its three pieces into the padded canvas case that would be buckled under my reserve chute. Then I lay down stiffly, like a knight on a sarcophagus, and closed my eyes and tried to think of other things. But I couldn't.

There was no way out, no escape. The miracle happened yesterday. It won't happen again. We're going regardless. Ten thousand

Germans. This is fantastic. I must be having nightmares. Summer is vacation time. God, it's so quiet. What a lousy way to leave the world. Nobody to say good-bye. Nobody who loves you waving from the dock. No friends or relatives at the bedside. How quiet it is—and godforsaken lonely. In the old days the soldiers had drums and bugles. The English still have bagpipers. Nobody gives a damn for us, nobody cares. We'll fight their war, and they'll all make money and get good jobs and gripe about the butter shortage and chisel on the gas ration.

We started off at route step, four abreast, filling the sunken lane with our bulging bodies and the heavy tramp-tramp of our boots. Nobody joked or sang or whistled; nobody laughed or counted cadence. Our gear made the only sound—a muffled clatter of shovel, gas mask, and bayonet against moving legs—our gear and our heavy boots, tramping, tramping, tramping. A hundred and twenty men, no shouts or cries, nothing but a dull tramp and a muffled clatter.

We crossed the parking strip where we had tried on our chutes and went into the hangar, now become a seething, dark hell of shouting, wild-eyed men in blackface. Soldiers who had lost their chutes scrambled among the rows of bags, seeking their own, while officers shouted directions and noncoms ran up and down the line in an effort to organize the chaos. The hue and cry rang and echoed in the girders overhead, changing our mood from sullen quiet to noisy excitement.

The line ahead of us started to move. As we followed them inside, Apache-faced savages ripped open lead-lined cases of hand grenades and rifle bullets and offered extra ammunition to passersby. GI trucks backed into the far end, which opened on the airfield, and hauled load after load of parachutists off to their planes. Headquarters Company lined up on its bags.

A rigger who was helping with the chutes and the movement went down the column, talking to the men. He was cursing the outfit for not letting him go over with a line company.

"I told the colonel I wanted to go," he said. "The hell with flying resupply! I didn't join this goddamn outfit to be a messenger boy. I want to jump. Colonel said I had to stay here and fly the ammo over. Piss on that! Fuck the ammo! Fuck resupply! If I can get a chute, I'm going."

You jerk, I thought. You goddamn jerk.

A GI truck picked us up and took us to our plane. Both sides of the runway on which we drove were lined for half a mile with full-bellied C-47s with clinging loads of equipment bundles and armed crews lolling in the doorways. The truck turned left a quarter of a mile from the hangar and stopped beside one of the planes. "Everybody out!" our lieutenant cried.

While we were unloading, another truck drove up with a three-man naval fire-control party from Division Headquarters, a runner from Company Headquarters, and two demolitions men whose waists were encircled with primacord and whose pockets bulged with blocks of TNT.

Our lieutenant lined us up in jumping order and made us count off. There were twenty-one of us altogether. He placed Sergeant Graham, a calm, stocky middle westerner, at the rear and himself first as jumpmaster. We counted off again, and then he gave us a direct order to jump and told us to refit our chutes.

This took about fifteen minutes, for almost every strap and buckle had to be readjusted for a girth increased by clothing, gear, and supplies. When we were finally satisfied with the fit, we put the main chute on the ground, tilted with the top resting on the reserve, and, using it as a backrest, lay down to wait for darkness.

Porter the medic, who had been put in our plane and who always joshed me by referring to me as a Groton man (which I was not), got up with me and walked to the edge of the strip, where we relieved ourselves. The splash of urine sounded by every plane.

"Must have been the coffee," Porter said. Usually bouncy and noisy, he seemed rather subdued tonight.

"Yes," I replied. I did not feel like talking. The enthusiasm that had stirred me to join the paratroops and the challenge that had kept me going were gone forever. In their place I felt a numbness, a blank, heavy, all-filling numbness. "Beautiful country," I said at last, zipping my fly.

Porter nodded, and we stood together and stared in silence at the hills.

We were on the rim of the parking strip, where the airfield's butte dropped off steeply into fallow green fields, and we could look down a long slope of high grass and waving buttercups to a wide, winding valley that followed the course of a dark brook three or

four miles through strips of forest. There were light-green patches
of meadowland and pale-brown fields of grain on the slopes on both
sides of the valley, with here and there an isolated farmhouse.

A few moments later I pulled out the mimeographed sheet and
read it. My head bobbed up and down as I frowned at the clichés
that covered the page. "Christ," I muttered. I crumpled the paper
and threw it away. Oh, hell, I said to myself, why throw away a
souvenir? I retrieved it, smoothed it on the concrete, and put it in
my breast pocket. "Crusade," I thought. "Liberty-loving." "Home
front." "Victory." Ugh. This was written by the Prince of
Platitudes.

"It's from Eisenhower," Nash, an ammo bearer, said defensively.
He had been watching me.

"God, those generals . . . They don't talk our language. There
isn't a one of them knows why we're here. Do you know why
we're here?"

Nash shrugged his shoulders. How could a man desecrate a letter
from Eisenhower?

"We're here because the outfit's here. This crap has nothing to do
with it. If we fight, it's because the outfit's fighting, it doesn't matter
who, not because we're a bunch of knights on a goddamn crusade.
This war doesn't mean a thing to me beyond this outfit. I never met
a GI who knew what the war was about or who believed in it,
did you?"

Nash sighed. This was no time to admit that the war and the
jump to come had no meaning.

"Piss on SHAEF!" I said, and yanked out my trench knife and
began to strop it on my boot.

8:30.

"Hurry up and wait," Porter sighed. He was lying on my left.
"Goddamn army'd rather be four hours early than two seconds
late." He flipped his cigarette butt down the runway and lit another.

I grunted, got to my feet, and relieved myself again. Nash sat
huddled up, his arms around his knees, and watched me. When I
returned, he shifted his stare to the cold yellow sun, which was
sinking rapidly toward the horizon. He wanted to stop it, to reach
out with me and all the others and hold it up in the sky. Only a dish
edge of distance separated us from darkness.

9 o'clock.

All over the airfield, the quiet groups of men by each plane turned their eyes to the west and watched the sun bulge suddenly large and then drop out of sight. Their hearts sank with it, and the light went out of their eyes.

I went to the edge of the strip and relieved myself for the third time. Four other men followed suit. A few planes start to roar, then died out. "Just checking their motors," one of the men said. His face was dripping with sweat.

9:30.

I shiver and sweat at the same time. My head is shaved, my face darkened with charcoal, my jump suit impregnated for gas. I am carrying over a hundred pounds of equipment. I have two bandoliers and three hand grenades for ten thousand Germans, and yes, I am ready.

10 o'clock.

More and more men got up and relieved themselves. Someone said it was the coffee we had for dinner, but that didn't get a laugh anymore. The smokers lit one cigarette off another and lost themselves in the smoke, but there was no escape for the nonsmokers. They could only think.

My mind whirred and clattered with all the things I had learned in the briefing tent. Flash . . . Thunder. One click of the cricket in challenge, two in reply. Check your sleeve detector for poison gas. Loosen your trench knife in its sheath. Take the villages, the causeways, the Douve bridges, the high ground. I'm going nuts. Hébert is the drop zone, pronounced Aybarc. A crossroads village surrounded by apple orchards. Kill 'em all; they're not going to be taking *us* prisoner at night. Use your bayonet and your trench knife and creep up on 'em in the long grass. Everybody jumps, nobody goes back to England; we need all the firepower we can get. No, the Air Corps says the Germans haven't flooded the low ground behind Utah Beach. The 2nd Battalion jumps at one. There are ten thousand Germans waiting for you down there. Go get 'em!

10:45.

The crew chief climbed down the short metal ladder from the plane and stopped at its foot. "Let's go, men," he said. "It's time to load up."

We put on our chutes and snapped the buckles and, with our rock-heavy musette bags banging against our knees, shuffled to the ladder and were helped up by our lieutenant and the crew chief. Once aboard, we groped our way through the close darkness to the cold aluminum bucket seats that lined both walls and sat down.

I waddled forward to a spot between Porter and Nash. My body was steaming hot. I sat down and closed my eyes and tried to go to sleep, but the weight of my chute and my equipment was too oppressive. I thought of the water we would pass over and of my chances of getting free of my harness in time to prepare for a water landing. I hope I don't land in the Channel or the Douve River, I thought. I'd drown before I could get free of my chute.

The plane filled up. The crew chief took in the ladder and lashed it beside the door. Some men smoked, others went to sleep, the majority sat and blinked at the darkness. The crew chief, a heavy man with a bald head and a fatherly air, came up the aisle with packets of airsickness pills and quart ice-cream cartons for vomit, then returned to his stand by the door.

Our lieutenant joined him. He glanced nervously at his watch and then looked outside. The darkness for which we had been waiting two years had finally come. He turned away from it and said: "Remember what the colonel told you: Everybody jumps! Sergeant Graham will enforce this order. He's the last man out of the plane. If the man ahead of you falls, grab him and push him out! If we get knocked down in the Channel, be sure to take off your chute before you inflate your Mae West; otherwise you'll be strangled. Good luck, men, good luck to everybody!"

10:55.

All of the planes warmed up at once. The thunder was deafening. I opened my packet of airsickness pills and downed the contents in one gulp, hoping that their sedative would numb me completely.

Nash grabbed my forearm. "Jesus, Webster," he said, "we're going."

Sergeant Graham, who was next to the bulkhead by the radio room, raised his voice and yelled, "Say good-bye to England!" I nodded, trying to smile.

The motors died down to a throbbing rumble. The crew chief leaned out the door and quickly pulled his head in as a plane went by. "There they go, there they go!" he shouted. "They're off!"

11 o'clock.

The tail swung around in a dizzy arc, almost throwing us from our seats. "This is it," the crew chief said, buckling on his flak vest. The C-47 trundled up the runway with squeaking wheels and a heavy, coughing, all-powerful rumble until it reached the line of departure, where it stopped and waited for the signal to take off. The pilot gunned the motors and then let them idle.

11:15.

The signal flashed from the control tower. Go! Go! it blinked. Kill 'em all!

There was a last, terrible, rattling, all-pervading roar, and the plane began to move ahead. Then, gaining speed, it raced down the runway, faster, faster, faster. We held our breath and clung to our seat belts. The tail rose slowly until the cabin floor, which had been aslant, was level with the ground. Just when it seemed as if we would never leave the runway, the plane's nose lifted and we were airborne.

The motors' roar faded to a steady drone. With a collective sigh of relief, we relaxed and undid our seat belts. The invasion had begun.

"Cigarette?" Porter asked, on my left.

"No thanks," I smiled. With the lift from the ground, I had experienced a sudden, total change of feeling. The load of brooding worry had dropped off, leaving me light, reckless, resigned, and almost detached. Part of this feeling was due to the drowsy effect of the sleeping tablets, but most of it was sheer relief at the end of all the waiting.

I looked around to see how the others were reacting to the take-off. Only the smokers, who were faintly lighted by the firefly glow of their cigarettes, were visible. When they inhaled, the flaring tips lit up their shadowy, blackened faces. They did not look happy.

The engines roared louder, as if for a grip on the sky. We were bucking and slamming around now in the rough air currents above the big Devonshire hills that had once seemed so lovely.

I turned stiffly and, staring out the window, saw, far below in the shifting moonlight, the dotted white perimeter lights of the field and the tiny red-and-green wing-tip lights of other C-47s taxiing and taking off and getting into formation. My God, I thought impatiently, we're still circling the airfield.

We banked again and continued round and round in a great, droning loop until the whole 2nd Battalion was formed in a long V of Vs, nine planes wide.

While I watched, a red light crept up on us in the darkness outside. It was our wing plane moving into position. When it was almost abreast, it throttled down and rode alongside with a bouncing, yawing motion.

It's too close, I said to myself, my eyes fixed on the light. One dip, one twist, and we'll come together and both go down. But hell, why worry? There's nothing I can do about it.

The moon went behind a cloud, and I twisted back into position. Suspended in a rackety darkness lit only by cigarettes and a tiny blue ceiling light in the pilot's passageway, I felt as if I were in the wildest of bad dreams, riding a nightmare to a Goya hell. A night jump was always eerie, but this one seemed so utterly unreal and incredible and yet so final that it wrung the feeling out of me and left me passively indifferent. Impatience was now my greatest emotion.

The crew chief left his stand near the door and, stopping here and there to chat with the men, slowly worked his way back toward the bulkhead, where Sergeant Graham was sitting. Soon he made a return trip to the tail, clutching the anchor line that ran down the plane's ceiling, and stood by the open door. He beckoned to our lieutenant, who rose clumsily from a seat nearby and looked out, then nodded and smiled. Facing down the aisle, the lieutenant yelled, "Look, men, look! It's the fleet."

I turned stiffly to the window again, like a rusty robot, and gasped, "Man, oh man." Five hundred feet below, spread out for miles on the moonlit sea, were scores and scores of landing barges, destroyers, cruisers, and attack transports. They were bearing the infantry slowly east, like a flood of lava, to a dawn assault on the shingle shore of Normandy.

As the battalion passed overhead, a lamp blinked up at us from a command ship. All the planes' wing-tip lights flashed off. The blue lights went out in the pilots' passageways.

My shoulders swung away from the window. I stared at the men opposite me in the racketing, vibrating, oil-reeking, vomit-scented darkness. "Isn't it great?" I said to Nash. "Those guys are going in!"

There was no reply, so I turned and looked at Nash, who had said for months that he was going to die on D-Day and who by comparison made me seem like an optimist, and saw that he had not heard me. He looked very scared.

I started to tell him that everything was going to be all right, but as I shouted the first words, my ears tingled and the engines' pitch changed as they strained for altitude. It wouldn't be long now, I knew, and suddenly lost interest in Nash. My stomach tightened and filled with ice, and a voice told me to get ready. "It's coming," the voice said, "it's coming."

The red light flashed on in the jump panel beside the door.

The plane lurched and roared as if in answer, and our lieutenant staggered erect, grabbed the anchor line with one hand, and snapped his static line to it. "Stand up and hook up!" he shouted.

These were the Channel Islands, Guernsey and Jersey, between which we were now flying. We knew they were the Channel Islands because we had been told that we would stand up and hook up when we reached them. With only twenty minutes to go, we stood up and hooked up over a hostile land of flak batteries and antiaircraft machine guns. As we passed between the islands, tiny red dashes of tracer fire floated up at us lazily from both sides.

The men rose woodenly from their seats, felt blindly for the anchor line, clicked their static-line snap fasteners to it, and held on. How did I ever get into this? we asked ourselves, and why?

Now we stood in one line, facing the tail, so crowded together that we could scarcely breathe. This was the line of departure—the Channel Islands.

"Push me," Nash said. "Push me when we go." He was clinging to the static line with both hands.

The plane went slower and slower; the motors got louder and louder. From the strain on them, I could tell that we were still climbing, gaining altitude for the run to the drop zone. A stream of tracer bullets floated up at us, speeded up as they passed the windows, and disappeared with a rattling burrat.

We had reached the mainland. It was a little after midnight. The infantry was due at six—"if they take the beach."

Someone threw up and cursed, and Porter had to catch me to keep me from falling in a sudden lurch as the pilot took evasive action to avoid another flak nest that had opened fire on the planes ahead.

Ten thousand Germans.

Oh God, I prayed, get me out of here. I don't want to blow up in the sky and burn to death. I don't want to die like a mouse in a can on a garbage dump fire. I want to die fighting. Let's jump, let's jump. Let's go, go, go!

"Check your equipment!" the lieutenant shouted.

I felt the snap fasteners on my leg straps. They were closed tightly and in place. How about the reserve snaps? Also good. And the bellyband? In place. I knew the chest buckle was snapped, for it had been digging into my ribs ever since I had put on my chute.

Now I checked Nash, who stood in front of me, while Porter checked my pack, for each man was responsible for himself and the man ahead. Yes, Nash's backpack was all right; the chute was in its cover, the rubber bands still held most of the static line in position.

Burrrrat! Another machine-gun burst crackled around the plane.

"Sound off for equipment check!"

Up by the pilot's passageway, where Graham had been crowded into the entrance, the lieutenant's command sounded like a child's whisper. The pilot gunned the engines and threw the craft from side to side.

An 88mm shell burst outside with a quick flash and a metallic bang. The blast tilted the plane, throwing men onto the seats. They clutched their way back up again.

"Sound off for equipment check!" the lieutenant shouted again.

"Number twenty OK!" Graham roared. "Like hell I'm OK," he confided. "I'm scared speechless." He slapped Porter's shoulder.

"Number nineteen OK!" cried Porter, slapping my shoulder as a signal for me to shout.

I yelled that I was OK, and then Nash took up the cry and passed it on. The plane dived toward the ground, passing under a string of three white flares that hung malevolently motionless in the sky. The pilot twisted and yawed and raced back up again.

I smelled the smoke and oil and puke and gagged on my supper as it rose in my throat. Nash whispered the Lord's Prayer, and Graham goddamned the pilot for using evasive action.

"Number fourteen OK!"

"Number thirteen OK!"

I shook my head and clamped my teeth shut. I was beyond all hope. If you have to die, you have to die—and what a way this is! If you have to jump, you have to jump. A man's life and death are decided by forces that he cannot fight. He can only question them and rebel against them, but in the end, he has to go with them. For Chrissake, let's get out of this firetrap!

The plane slammed up and down, zigzagged, rattled and roared, threw us from side to side with such violence that several of us fell down again, cursing the pilot. The muscle and fiber melted from my legs. It was all I could do to remain upright and not dissolve into a gutless, gibbering blob of fear. Too weak to stand, I clung to my static line with both hands. I felt like crying, screaming, killing myself.

A flash of light came in the window, and I glanced outside and saw wisps of cloud streaking by. Now and then a pale full moon, mocking in its serenity, appeared briefly among the long, thin, scudding black clouds. This is a night for murder, I thought. God must have planned it that way.

"Close up and stand in the door!" the lieutenant yelled. Left foot forward in a lock step, each man pushed hard against the man before him. The plane bounced up and down and gasped for altitude.

I could feel Graham crowding Porter and Porter crowding me, but I had forgotten all about them. I had forgotten all about everything and everybody but Private David K. Webster, who wanted to get out of this plane more than anything else in the world.

The motors faded out somewhat, and the plane rustled through the air more slowly.

We're over the drop zone, we're over the drop zone! Let's *go!* I had an insane urge to jump.

"Go!" the lieutenant shouted. He bent over and lifted the ends of the parapaks, slid them out the door, and jumped after them. The line of men surged forward.

Two men fell down on the threshold. There was a wild, cursing tangle as others fought to lift them and push them out, and then the line moved again, sucked out the door like a stream of water. I shuffled up, glanced down, and stopped, dumbfounded.

All I could see was water, miles and miles of water. But this was D-Day and nobody went back to England and a lot of infantry riding open barges seasick to the low-tide beaches were depending on us to draw the Germans off the causeways and gun batteries, and so, as Porter hurled himself against me, I grabbed both sides of the door and threw myself at the water.

I fell a hundred feet in three seconds, straight toward a huge flooded area shining in the moonlight. I thought I was going to fall all the way, but there was nothing I could do about it except dig my fingers into my reserve and wait to be smashed flat. I should have counted "one thousand, two thousand, three thousand"—the general would have had me shout "Bill Lee," but that was expecting too much—and yet all I could do was gape at the water.

Suddenly a giant snapped a whip with me on the end, my chute popped open, and I found myself swinging wildly in the wind. Twisted in the fall, my risers were unwinding and spinning me around. They pinned my head down with my chin on the top of my rifle case and prevented me from looking up and checking my canopy. I figured that everything was all right, because at least I was floating free in the great silence that always followed the opening shock.

For several seconds, I seemed to be suspended in the sky, with no downward motion, and then all at once, the whole body of water whirled and rushed up at me.

Jesus, I thought, I'm going to drown.

I wrenched desperately at my reserve chute's snap fasteners as the first step in preparing for a water landing. I also had to undo two leg snaps, my chest buckle, and the bellyband. The next step would have been to drop the reserve and work myself into the seat of my harness, so that I could fling my arms straight up and drop from the chute when I was ten feet above the water. I didn't even have time to begin the procedure.

We had jumped so low—from about three hundred feet, instead of the scheduled seven hundred—that while I was still wrenching at the first reserve snap, I saw the water twenty feet below. I've had it, I thought. Goddamn Air Corps. I reached up, grasped all four risers, and yanked down hard, to fill the canopy with air and slow my descent. Just before I hit, I closed my eyes and took a deep breath of air. My feet splashed into the water.

I held my breath, expecting to sink over my head and wondering how I was going to escape from my harness underwater—and hit bottom three feet down. My chute billowed away from me in the light wind and collapsed on the surface. I went to work to free myself from my gear. Immensely relieved at the safe landing, I undid the reserve and discarded it, yanked loose the bellyband, unsnapped the leg straps and chest buckle, detached my rifle case, and let the harness sink into the swamp. I was on my own at last.

The silence ended abruptly with a long, ripping burst—burrrrrrrrp!—that made me look around in fright. That's a German machine gun, I told myself. They've seen me. The bullets cracked and popped in the air above, and as I stared open-mouthed and paralyzed with fright, I saw whiplike tracers darting at me from some faroff place. I dropped to my knees in the cold, black water, which tasted old and brackish, as if it had lain still for a long time, and passively waited to be killed.

Somebody wants to kill me, I thought. So this is what war is really like? I couldn't believe that somebody wanted to kill me. What had I done to them?

I wanted to go up to them and tell them that I didn't want to kill anybody, that I thought the whole war was a lot of malarkey. I don't want to hurt anybody, I would say. All I ask of the world is to be left alone. Why do you want to kill me? You've never seen me before. Why do you want to kill me?

The machine gun fired again, a longer burst that held me motionless. I shook my head to make sure it was all real, and it was. The bullets were not in my imagination. They were real, and they were seeking me out to kill me. The gunners wouldn't even let me get close enough to talk it over with them. They wanted to kill me right here in the swamp.

The machine gun searched the area again. Faroff in the night, others burped and spluttered. Enemy rifles added their pop, pop-pop.

I waited about five minutes for someone to walk up and kill me. Then my courage returned when I noticed that the shooting was all quite far away. I rose from the water, assembled my rifle and loaded it, and rammed on my bayonet. I was ready to go.

Burp . . . burrrrp . . . burrp . . . crack-crack . . . pop . . . pop-pop.

Lost and lonely, wrestling with the greatest fear of my life, I stood bewildered in the middle of a vast lake and looked for help. They've wrecked the invasion, I thought, hearing only enemy fire. Where are Porter and Nash and the lieutenant and the rest of my friends? Where is the drop zone? Where are the other regiments? Six regiments jumped tonight, and I am alone in Normandy.

I shivered convulsively and started to cry, then thought better of it. The hell with everything! I'm here for keeps; make the best of it. At least I can try to get out of this swamp before sunrise. But where will I go? Which way is out?

I took the little brass compass from my pocket and looked at it in the next spell of moonlight. The needle was frozen in position. I shook the compass and cursed and, holding it close, saw that it was filled with water. "Son of a bitch," I hissed, throwing it away. A wise guy probably made a fortune off those compasses in the States. And now men will die because somebody gypped the government. Sons of bitches.

A flare burst over the water several hundred yards away. I bowed my head and waited for the bullets to hit me like a baseball bat, but there were no bullets. The flare died out with the afterglow of a burnt match, and I looked around in the moonlight. I sought an orchard, three white lights, a crossroads village named Hébert, and five hundred men from the 2nd Battalion, and all I saw was water and flares and tracers. I listened for our bugle call, and all I heard was enemy rifle and machine-gun fire.

Suddenly the whole thing struck me as ludicrous: all the preparations and briefings, all the maps and sand tables, and for what? Why had they bothered? For all the good they did, the army might as well have yanked us out of a pub and dumped us off helter-skelter to find our own way to the Germans. Instead of a regiment of over fifteen hundred men carefully assembled on a well-defined drop zone, D-Day was one man alone in an old swamp that the Air Corps said didn't even exist.

The angry clatter of a plan gone wrong filled the air. Zigzag tracers arched through the sky, and there were red flares, green flares, white flares. Grenades and mortars thumped and blammed, while small arms continued their serenade to liberation. From inland came the strange tolling of a church bell. "Invasion, invasion," it seemed to clang to the Germans still in their billets. I stood transfixed, as at a great spectacle of nature. The uneasy moon shifted behind some dark, racing clouds, and black night fell again, but there was no peace.

My courage, which had flared up briefly, died down again. My God, I thought, only the Germans are shooting. They must have been expecting us. We're done for. The invasion will fail. We'll be rounded up and butchered by the SS.

Now a new noise came—the distant rumble of a massed flight of planes—and my spirits rose. The planes were coming toward me. I followed their progress by the fountains of tracer that splashed up at them. It's the 501, I thought excitedly. They're due now. Come on down and we'll get 'em together!

They jumped in a moonlit moment in a Fourth of July sky laced with great fans of tracer bullets. The bullets lit the planes and the shadowy parachutes of the men tumbling out of them like strings of ball bearings and followed the men to the ground, fanning back and forth with a ferocious rattling. Sick at my stomach, I watched the men swing helpless in the heavy fire. I wanted to help them, but there was nothing I could do but watch with mounting anger and hate.

"Those freaking Krauts!" I whispered. I wanted to kill them all.

I threw away my gas mask and adjusted my musette bag on my back. The box of 30 caliber ammunition I had carried on the jump was dropped at my feet. Where was the machine gun that would use it now? I took my Hawkins mine from a big pants pocket and threw that away too, for there were no tanks in the flooded area. I had to travel light to reach the Germans before dawn.

Swish . . . swish . . . swish–swish: I heard the sound of wading. I held my breath and sank slowly into the water with my rifle ready. A flare rose in the distance, but it was no help, for all I could see was black night and black water. The swishing came closer.

With my finger tight on the trigger of my M–1, I reached for the cricket hanging from a string around my neck. The wader was very close now, but I still couldn't see him. I had a slight advantage, however, in that a person at night can see better looking up from ground level than looking down from a walking height. I squeezed the cricket, click–clack, and waited.

The wader stopped. I held my breath until it was ready to burst from my chest in a gigantic pop. Bayonet, hell! I'm going to shoot this son of a bitch. One more step and I'm shooting.

Click–clack, click–clack.

"Who is it? Jesus Christ, who is it?"

"Lachute, Headquarters Company."

"Polecat! It's me, Webster." I jumped up with a splash, walked to him, and hugged him and pounded his back and told him how glad I was to see him. "I thought there were only Krauts down here," I said.

"Sure sounds like it, doesn't it, buddy?" He was as glad to see me as I was to see him. "Looks like they got us by the ass. Seen anybody else from the plane?"

"No. I've only been out of my chute ten or fifteen minutes. One more step and I would have shot you."

A small, slender young man from New Orleans, with liquid black eyes and a lively sense of humor, Lachute said that he hadn't even seen me, not even after he had heard my cricket. "What'll we do now?" he asked.

"Go to the high ground. There's no cover here. We have to get out of this swamp before daylight. Goddamn Air Corps sure made a mess of this one, didn't they? How's your compass?" Lachute searched his pockets and handed me his compass. It, too, was waterlogged. I threw it away with a curse.

We had to orient ourselves before we could go anywhere, and so I crouched at water level and waited for the moon to reappear. In its light, I looked around slowly in a complete circle. There was a big, dark ridge about a mile away that was dotted with flares and gun flashes. Parallel to it, on the other side of the flooded area, was a lesser ridge. The flooded area was about a mile and a half wide. There was no action on the lesser ridge. "That must be the sand dunes behind the beach," I said.

I closed my eyes and tried to re-create the sand table in the S-2 tent. Evidently we had been dropped between Utah Beach and the mainland, in the low ground spreading out from the estuary of the Douve River. The thing to do now was to head for the big ridge and help shoot the Germans off it. The infantry was due at six. They couldn't cross the flooded area with Germans still on that ridge.

"Let's go," I whispered, standing up and starting off.

"Where to?"

"The high ground. That big ridge where all the shooting is. See those flares? See the trees? Man, they're killing troopers up there. What a sound those church bells make! It gives me the creeps."

"Yeah, it sounds like a funeral—our funeral," Lachute laughed.

We waded fifty yards, then stopped abruptly when we heard a number of men talking in the loud tones of irritated soldiers on a tedious field problem.

"Christ," one said. "Let's get out of here."

"Nah," another replied. "Stick around till morning. Then we can see where to go."

I clicked my cricket. The talking stopped, but there was no answer to the challenge, so I clicked again.

"Flash," someone whispered.

"Thunder," I replied. We walked up to a grassy hummock twenty yards long and almost a yard high.

Six men squatted there like chickens flooded out of their roost. There was a first sergeant from a 2nd Battalion line company, a Headquarters Company machine gunner who had lost an older brother at Anzio and had joined the paratroops to avenge him, two men from the 501, one from the 502, and an 82nd Airborne man from the 508. Four of the six regiments that had jumped were represented. Nobody knew where they were or what to do next. They had been debating the issue for almost half an hour, according to the machine gunner, a hotheaded eighteen-year-old from a large Italian family in Trenton, New Jersey. He told us that he was sick and tired of the whole damn bunch.

I went to the first sergeant, the senior noncom and theoretical leader, said hello, and asked if he knew where we were.

"Beats the hell out of me," he said cheerfully. "Nobody's compass works. I'm going to stay here till daylight, then take off."

I gaped at him. "You're crazy," I said. I had never liked him before, and now I wanted to spit on him. "They're killing troopers up there. We have to get those Krauts."

"Oh, hell . . ."

"On top of that, if you wait till daylight, the Krauts on the high ground will nail you before you go a hundred yards. There's no cover in this swamp. I'm going up to that big ridge. You can come if you want to, but I don't really give a damn, because I'm going anyway. But first I'm going to junk these ODs. They weigh a ton."

I removed my webbing and spread it carefully on the ground. A flare arched through the sky and burst almost directly over the hummock, lighting us all in its fierce glow. A machine gun followed the flare, and once again I had the sensation of being watched. "Jesus," somebody gasped, "they see us." The flare died out, and the machine gun, which had been shooting high, stopped firing. Everybody commenced arguing again, louder than before, over whether they should leave the island or stay and what direction they should take when and if they left and what they should do when they arrived wherever they were going.

Group action, I thought, undressing quickly and throwing away my water-soaked woolen shirt and pants. I'll do better on my own.

I took off my woolen underwear, wrung it out, rolled it up, and put it in my musette bag. I cut off the bottoms of my jump pants to keep them from holding water. Then I put my jump suit and webbing back on again. I threw away my jump rope and two cartons of cigarettes that I had brought along to trade with the friendly natives.

"Let's go," I said to Lachute. "The hell with these guys."

"OK, buddy."

"I'm with you," the young machine gunner said. He turned to the others and asked if they wanted to come along. They all rose except the first sergeant. He remained seated and told us to be careful and not get hurt. As we moved off, he rose uncertainly and watched us go, then sat down again.

A flare rose over the big ridge, and the Germans started shooting under it. A Thompson submachine gun pututted, and an M-1 joined its solid bamming in reply. I smiled. The troopers on the high ground were coming out of it. There was hope for us all.

Listening intently, freezing under flares, crouching and eyeing the night with distrust, our little column waded slowly across the flooded area. The lone M-1 and the Thompson died out, the enemy firing increased, the hope that had flared in us flickered low again. We all felt tired and depressed and discouraged, the usual reaction that set in an hour or so after a jump. I wanted to lie down and go to sleep, but there was no place to lie down.

Wading slowly across a field two feet in water, I pushed through a line of reeds and suddenly stumbled headlong into a hidden ditch six feet deep. Throwing my arms high to keep my rifle dry, I held my breath and drove forward underwater. After ten feet, I staggered up a steep bank and back into the air again. Lachute, who had stopped bewildered when I had vanished, stood on the far shore, awaiting developments.

"Watch it!" I whispered, as the other men came up. "That ditch is six feet deep."

"I can't swim," Lachute said.

"I'll help you," I replied. "Be right over." I took a deep breath and held it and went back underwater. He climbed on my shoulders, holding both our rifles, kicked his heels in my side, and yelled, "Giddyap!" I walked down into the ditch, staggered across, and forced my way up the other bank, where we waited, shivering, for the rest of the men to join us. When everybody was over, we set out again, hoping that our ammunition had not been dampened.

There was a deep drainage ditch like this on the edge of almost every field, and we had to make such a crossing every hundred yards or so. The process exhausted us, and we had to stop more and more frequently to lean on our rifles and gasp for air.

The sound of American firing grew more widespread, as scattered paratroopers on the high ground gradually came together and sought out the Germans in the fields and villages. The church bell rang no more, the flares diminished, and slowly the moon, which saw it all begin, dropped down in the west.

Two men from the 82nd waded up on us quickly from the right, accompanied us for several hundred yards, then drifted off as casually as they had come. Lachute threw away his gas mask, and the others discarded all their superfluous equipment. The ridge got bigger and longer and higher, the air suddenly turned very cold, and finally the sky lightened and dawn came with a gray drizzle.

Our group began to break up. The two 501 men, who were carrying all their company headquarters' maps, said good-bye and went off to seek their captain, and the others went to the side or continued forward. Lachute and I headed for a patch of young trees that offered some concealment in the final approach to the ridge. Finally we were the only ones left. We stopped and ate breakfast among the trees.

While we were eating, a massive group of A-20 light bombers came up behind us, following the coastline, and laid a string of bombs a mile long on the sand dunes behind Utah Beach. It was the preliminary bombardment; the infantry was ready to come ashore. The smoke rose a thousand feet into the air. We stood up and cheered as the kettledrum booming of the bombing came to us.

Lachute noticed a column of men wading parallel to the big ridge and decided to join them, even though they were dangerously exposed and appeared to be going into a firefight. I decided to follow the little trees closer and then cut across a tree-covered mound about fifty yards from the base of the ridge. We wished each other luck and set off on our separate ways.

As I came up to the tree-covered mound, I heard someone call my name. "Webster, Webster!" I looked around and saw Nash lying on the ground.

"What's the matter?" I inquired, kneeling beside him. He appeared to be hurt and in shock. "Are you wounded?"

"No, I wrenched my ankle on the jump. I can't move. God, it hurts."

I looked around at the ridge. It was only about fifty yards away. A channel of deep, black water about twenty yards wide lay at its base.

"Come on," I said. "I'll help you reach dry ground."

"No," he replied. "I'm going to die here. I'm hurt. I can't go any farther."

I looked at him and thought of what fun he had been in Aldbourne and of the time I had met him in London and of the raucous little songs he used to sing, and I felt like crying.

"Come on!" I said. "For Chrissake."

He shook his head. "I said this jump was going to be my last, Web, and it was. You go on. I'm staying here."

"They'll kill you. Better get out of here while the coast is clear."

"So long, buddy." He gave me his hand, and I shook it hard. I couldn't understand what had come over him.

I left the mound and, slinging my rifle over my back, swam to the edge of the big ridge. Nash waved to me when I got out, and I waved back and started off on a forest path with the safety catch off my rifle and my eyes scanning everything ahead. A hundred yards later, I came to a road that led out of the swamp. A band of men was milling about on its edge, near a little stone stable. They had just cleaned out a pocket of Germans, they said, and were about to follow after another group of paratroopers who had gone over the ridge. I sat down in the stable and fell asleep. An officer roused me in a few minutes and told me to go up the road with the rest of the men.

The road passed through a dense forest of trees so thick and lush with undergrowth that it looked like a jungle. After a while, it topped the ridge and came out in a little village. No civilians were on hand, but the place was full of life, as dozens of wild-eyed paratroopers in blackface ran about in the streets. One group found a German truck and piled into it. They immediately drove down a side street in search of the enemy. An E Company man passed by on a captured motorcycle, and two others from the 506th came up in a farm cart drawn by a fine brown horse. A lone paratrooper stood in the center of the village square, firing his rifle at the bronze rooster weathervane atop a very old church.

Stopping to watch the fun, I noticed men running up a side street with bottles in their hands. "Where'd you get the liquor?" I asked as the men came together and began to move out of the village in parallel columns.

"Third house down that way, buddy," one of them replied. "Door's open. Help yourself." I ran down and went in. The liquor cabinet, which had been broken open by an earlier liberator, stood in one corner of a dark living room with lots of lace and old furniture. Ashamed of myself for housebreaking and yet chilled through, I selected a fifth of Hennessy cognac and ran back to join the column.

I tried to dig the cork out with my bayonet, then smashed the top of the bottle against a rock and drank. The column I had joined was mostly 2nd Battalion—I was home again. Glad to be back with the outfit and bound I knew not where, I swallowed a huge mouthful of liquor. It seared its way down my throat and whirled around in my stomach like a blowtorch.

The warmth spread through my body, making me smile with pleasure. I was alive, and I intended to stay that way.

Memorial services, I mused as our bus left Aldbourne for Littlecote, are usually civilian affairs. The hometown turns out, the American Legion marches, a handful of graying mothers lay wreaths on scattered graves while a high-school bugler blows taps. Very seldom does a fighting outfit hold formal services for its dead in wartime. And yet that is what we are going to do.

We had returned to England after thirty-one days in Normandy, and we could look forward to a long memorial service, for the losses on the jump had been heavy—dead paratroopers scattered like blown leaves over all the roads, fields, hedges, and villages— and they had been followed by equally heavy losses in later fighting for places like Carentan, St. Marie du Mont, and St. Come du Mont.

In the end, and with the assistance of men from other units, the regiment's D-Day objectives had been taken and consolidated. On June 11, after fighting farther and farther in from the beaches, we moved at night down a long causeway strewn with the dead bodies of more than five hundred men lost in a frontal attack, and then, in the flickering light of a burning factory, cut cross-country to flank the key city of Carentan, juncture of the Omaha and Utah beachheads.

Now we were back in the hills near Aldbourne, where our overseas story had begun. Our ranks had been filled with replacements in whom nobody was interested. We had received a week's furlough, new green jump suits, and machine guns with bipods for hedgerow fighting. Our training schedule had been jammed night and day for more than a month with infuriating field problems. We were ready to go again, but we did not look forward to it, for the adventure was over, the battle was joined, and the rest would be brutal.

It was midmorning, August 28, 1944, two months and twenty-two days after D-Day, and the sky, which had been surly gray at reveille, was blue and clear and filled with hope. We moved slowly onto a soft green field behind Littlecote. A reviewing platform had been erected in the center of the field. Colonel Sink, his staff, and several civilians (probably the owners of Littlecote) stood on the stand and watched us pass. A band from a parachute artillery battalion played us into position with the strains of the death march that goes, "Once in the dear, dead days beyond recall."

When the regiment was formed, Chaplain McGee stepped to the front of the stand and made a short speech to the effect that the dead had not died in vain, that they were really heroic, that we should be inspired by them, etc., etc. The general was the next speaker, but he didn't come through very clearly, for a flight of C-47s chose this moment to circle overhead in memory of the men they had carried to their death. They circled and roared at a low altitude, dipping their wings in salute, and shout as he would, the general could not be heard.

The planes left the area just before he finished. A lieutenant from Regimental Headquarters stepped forward and read the roster of men killed in action. He called the roll in a loud, clear voice and paused between each name, so that every man would be remembered.

The list was very long—231 names—and aroused a flood of memories. As it went on and on, I looked at the pink Elizabethan magnificence of Littlecote, stretched out on the site of a Roman villa, at the mullioned windows and scores of picturesque gables, the beautiful rose garden and ivy-covered brick walls, and I thought of all the fine young men who were no longer alive to enjoy the beauty of a great sixteenth-century house.

"Private William E. Nash," the lieutenant shouted.

Nash was many things: a voice that was sort of southern; a song, "Galway Bay," which he sang soft and sentimentally, sometimes with tears in his eyes; a favorite saying—"We's goin' tuh coombat, and we ain't *never* comin' back." He was right about that, for in the end, as I had feared when I left him behind in the swamp, Nash stayed in Normandy, Nash and 230 others.

I looked for him the first night, when the 2nd Battalion, which was the first to be organized—150 men out of more than 500—set up a defensive position and dug in, but he was not there. He still had not shown up a week later. Well, I thought, maybe he made it back to England on a hospital ship.

But a month later, when I asked the men returning from Normandy what had happened to him, I learned that his luck had run out only a few yards from the place where we had met. Apparently he had changed his mind about staying on the hummock and had forced himself to swim to the big ridge. That move was his undoing, for there were still plenty of Germans left in the woods after the rest of us had gone on. Nash went to the stone stable where I had rested briefly, and he lay down with the wounded men collected there in an impromptu aid station. The Germans found him and the others and, swarming in without mercy, killed them all.

Nash had a small, sad, prematurely wizened face to match his small body. He was one of the few men who knew that they were going to die on D-Day, knew it just as we all know that we are going to die but not exactly when. He said his first combat jump would be his last, and so it was. I missed him very much; the machine-gun platoon was not the same without him.

After a long time we get to the *R*'s—Radeka, Radovich, Ramirez, Repine, Rigaux, Riggs, Riley, Risner, Robbins, Roberts, Ronzani—and now the *S*'s. This is a very long list. The sun is so hot that two men have fainted already.

"T-4 Benjamin J. Stoney."

I wanted a drink of hard cider. The bottle of Hennessy that I had acquired in first village up from the swamp had long since evaporated, and I was tired of water. So I got up from the ditch and started back to a farmhouse where an old man (for the old men were always good to us) was giving away his homemade stock of wonderful, tingling Normandy cider. But I never reached the farmhouse.

This was Vierville, about June 8, on the road to Carentan. Two rifle companies had already passed through town without opposition. Headquarters Company was diverting itself for some brief, ecstatic moments, shooting every weapon it had at a lone sniper in the church steeple. I had lain in the gutter, watching the marksmen, until a bullet from the belfry spatted the dust in front of my nose, and then I had moved across the road to a deeper ditch in the shade of a thick stone wall. Shortly after this, our lieutenant had shifted us forward to some other ditches just beyond town and a rumor spread that there was free cider in the farmhouse at the last crossroads.

Always the conservative soldier, I waited until the rumor was confirmed by the sight of men with full canteen cups coming from there before I buckled my gear, slung my rifle over my shoulder, and strolled leisurely toward the farmhouse courtyard, where Sergeant Hoagy and other machine gunners were sunning and sipping.

"Krauts!" someone yelled.

I stopped in my tracks and whipped my rifle off my shoulder, clicking it off safety.

Pututut! . . . Pututututututut! An M-3 "greasegun" submachine gun spat angrily near the intersection, twenty yards ahead of me. Sergeant Hoagy's sunbathers vanished into the courtyard, while Captain Cox, our company commander, leaped back from the corner of the nearest hedgerow, cursing and yanking at his M-3 in an effort to clear a stoppage.

"Kraut troopers!" he shouted. "They're dug in along the road here. Kill 'em, kill the sons of bitches!"

Tech Sergeant Stoney, from Battalion S-2, ran up the ditch and took the captain's place at the corner with another M-3. Just as he leaned out to fire, a German leveled a machine gun on him and caught him in the face with a short burst. He spun around and lay still, his gun clattering to the pavement behind him.

Sergeant Hoagy's men took up firing positions at the courtyard gateposts and began to shoot back at the Germans. A rifle grenade tumbled through the air end over end toward them and exploded in the courtyard. Sergeant Hoagy reeled out of the cloud of oily black smoke, blood streaming down his face, and staggered up the road to the medics.

Its cider siesta over, Headquarters Company abruptly came to life. Everybody who had been relaxing in the ditches took up firing positions behind the hedges. A cloud of white smoke drifted toward us from the other end of town, and when I looked over the top of my hedge, I saw dozens of Germans running through some woods in the low ground three hundred yards to my direct front. They were working their way up a wall to my right, evidently planning to cut us off from the rest of the battalion. I started shooting like mad.

Colonel Strayer ran down the ditch, took a quick look at the low ground, and shouted, "Get those goddamn tanks back up here!" A runner departed at high speed to overtake a column of 2nd Armored Division tanks that had passed through shortly before.

"Krauts in the graveyard!" someone yelled near the church. The cry kindled a spluttering, banging firefight.

At the far end of town, from which we had come half an hour before, the white smoke rolled closer and closer. I imagined a Tiger tank creeping up on wide, clanking treads to blast us with its 88 and hose the ditches with machine guns.

While I watched the smoke, a German jeep popped out of it and whirled boldly through the village. It was flying a big Red Cross flag and carried two wounded Germans on stretchers in back, and it was such a startling phenomenon, with a big, husky German paratrooper at the wheel, that nobody made a move to stop it. It drove down the middle of the road until it was finally stopped by an officer with more presence of mind than the rest of us. The jeep was commandeered. The driver, a medic, was shot for carrying a pistol, and the two wounded men were left by the side of the road to die.

Now a big blond private from the communications platoon shoved a tall, terrified young German parachutist along the road at the point of his carbine. The German walked quivering, his hands folded on top of his bowl helmet. His eyes rolled from side to side in fear and curiosity as he blinked down at the men watching him from the ditches. When the shooting flared up, his captor halted him and tried to make him lie down, but the German, who was afraid he was going to be shot, pretended not to understand the order. Pittman, an ex-boxer who had drifted back from D Company, jumped up, ran over to the prisoner, and slammed him savagely down on his face.

"Cut it out!" someone yelled. "Lay off the son of a bitch!" Pittman returned sulkily to his ditch, and a GI who spoke the language told the German to lie flat till the shooting was over.

Cheered on by the riflemen, three dusty tanks clattered back down the road. Their commanders studied the situation in a maddeningly leisurely fashion and then went into action. I was so absorbed in my own shooting that I failed to notice one of the tanks move up behind me, stop, and swing its 75 across the hedge near my ear. It fired, and the blast almost blew me off my perch. I jumped down with a curse and took up a more distant position.

That was Vierville, a town nobody ever heard of. The skirmish there was typical of the early fighting in Normandy. Groups of paratroopers would inadvertently bump into wandering bands of Supermen, there would be a brief firefight, and one side would get superior firepower and move in for the kill.

As it was, the tanks won Vierville for us with their high-explosive shells and 50 caliber machine guns. The main body of Germans, which I had seen running through the woods, bogged down in a swamp there and were piled up dead two and three deep by the tanks' cannon. It was a battalion of our enemy counterpart, the 6th Parachute Regiment, and this was its first time in action. When he surrendered, the battalion commander crawled out of his CP on his hands and knees with tears in his eyes, begging not to be shot, for a particularly vicious and not overly brave person in our company was killing some wounded prisoners nearby. It was reported that the German commander lost more than two-thirds of his men in that one short action.

Stoney was our only casualty. Stoney, the quiet, stocky Indian from S-2. But every village had a Stoney—or two Stoneys, or many more—because that is how wars are finally fought and won, not by rich factories and the coddled air force, but by the infantry, who take the ground and kill the enemy, and the infantry is made up of Stoneys.

*   *   *

I returned to Littlecote with a start when the lieutenant ended his list abruptly with a private named Zoltz. For a few seconds the regiment stood sad and silent in the lovely Wiltshire dale under the big white summer clouds that were so peaceful, and then, before we could start coughing and shifting our feet, Chaplain McGee stepped to the front of the reviewing stand and said: "Let us pray. We will read aloud the 506th Parachute Infantry prayer that is printed on your program sheets."

We had been handed these programs as we marched onto the field. The prayer, a fine example of the "Gott mit uns" spirit of the paratroops, was written by Lieutenant James G. Morton.

"Almighty God," we began, "we kneel to Thee and ask to be the instrument of Thy fury in smiting the evil forces that have visited death, misery, and debasement on the people of the earth. We humbly face Thee with true penitence for all our sins, for which we do most earnestly seek Thy forgiveness. Help us to dedicate ourselves completely to Thee. Be with us, God, when we leap from our planes in the dark abyss and descend in parachutes into the midst of enemy fire. Give us iron will and stark courage as we spring from the harnesses of our parachutes to seize arms for battle.

"The legions of evil are many, Father; grace our arms to meet and defeat them in Thy name and in the name of the freedom and dignity of man. Keep us firm in our faith and resolution, and guide us that we may not dishonor our high mission or fail in our sacred duties. Let our enemies who have lived by the sword turn from their violence lest they perish by the sword. Help us to serve Thee gallantly and to be humble in victory."

There was a pause and then through the still, warm air came the clear notes of a lone bugle playing taps. The regiment said amen and lifted their heads. Colonel Strayer spun on his heel, threw back his shoulders, and called the battalion to attention. We straightened our backs, raised our heads, clicked our boots together, slapped our hands to our sides. The band played "Onward, Christian Soldiers," and the 1st Battalion went by. We wheeled about and followed them off the field.

The invasion was over. The memorial service had ended. In Normandy, the dead lay forever silent in the dappled-green parachutes that had carried them to earth. We were ready to go again, because we could only go forward, never back.

Somebody had to do it; we were not ashamed of the task. We

were the infantry. The truckdrivers could do their part and get our battle stars, and the manufacturers could get rich on "cost plus 10 percent" and shout that wars are won by production. But we knew that nothing was solved and nothing accomplished until the infantry had killed the enemy and driven him from his ground. We were the infantry and proud of it.

And so we went forward, one regiment, filled up with replacements, the dead as fine and strong a part of us as the living men, so fresh and new, who had come to take their place.

2

THE WINDMILLS WERE WONDERFUL

I was reading a book. It was not a very well-written book, but it interested me at the time because I was the first scout in a rifle squad and the book was about my trade. I wanted to finish it before we jumped.

It was September 17, 1944, a beautifully clear Indian summer day, and we were circling Membury Airdrome, forming up for the flight. The time was noon, our destination Holland.

I glanced out the window and saw Aldbourne off to our right. We were still circling. Nobody had said good-bye to us in Aldbourne when we marched out this time, because we had already marched out twice since our return from Normandy, and the villagers thought this was just another dry run. But it was final, very final. I didn't particularly mind, for I was fed up with training and ready to go in again and take my chances. In fact, I was so bored that I had transferred from Headquarters Company to E Company in search of the action I had missed in Normandy.

I tried to read some more of my book, but it failed to hold my interest. My mind wandered to the jump ahead.

This was the largest airborne mission in history, the three-division jump of the 1st Allied Airborne Army. The 101st Airborne Division was leaving England simultaneously with the 82nd and the

British 1st. We would all land astride a highway in southern Holland that ran fifty miles from Eindhoven in the south to Arnhem in the north, capture the canal and river bridges, and hold the road open for tanks of the British 2nd Army to burst through the enemy into the broad plains of north Germany and flank the Siegfried Line.

Everything depended on the bridges. If they were taken and held, the armor could go north. If even one bridge was lost, the whole operation would be delayed and might even fail. Many men would die, because we were very deep in enemy territory, and there was no way out for us but on the British tanks.

The British 1st Airborne Division ran the greatest risk, for they were farthest north, over seventy miles from the present battle lines in Belgium near the Albert Canal. A fine, spirited outfit with whom we had become acquainted in joint maneuvers in England, the 1st had never been in action before as a unit. Its cadre, however, was composed of quiet, older men who were veterans of Africa, Sicily, and Italy, and so it would not go in wholly green. We had watched a battalion of the 1st start back for their barracks on a fifteen-mile hike in a driving rain that would have had us all cursing aloud, and had marveled at their snap and spirit as they had moved off briskly in step, whistling "I've Got Sixpence." Now their spirit would be tested on the bridges at Arnhem, where the Neder Rhine formed the last obstacle to the armor heading north. A pretty resort city of about ninety thousand population, Arnhem was said to be near a large German panzer training area. Enemy tanks were expected.

Veterans of Sicily, Italy, Normandy, and of great bar brawls with the 101st, the 82nd Airborne Division would land ten miles south of Arnhem at Nijmegen, a city of about ninety-four thousand, and seize its bridges, which spanned the Waal River. Another branch of the Rhine, the Waal was a formidable obstacle with two giant bridges, one for cars and another for railway trains. The 82nd also had to capture the Maas-Waal Canal bridge at Grave, a long, curving highway bridge over the Maas River, and the pine-covered hills at the edge of the Reichswald, about five miles east-southeast of Nijmegen. This was the highest ground in Holland.

The 101st had three main canal bridges along the road to Arnhem. They were located at Veghel, Zon, and Eindhoven, a city slightly larger than Nijmegen, which the 1st and 2nd Battalions of the 506th had been ordered to capture the day of the jump. In a sense, we were the luckiest of the three divisions, because we were the farthest south and would be the first to meet the British tanks—if they broke through to us. There was always the question of whether the tanks would or would not break through.

Trying to forget what lay ahead—the German tanks operating in perfect tank country, a drop zone that could be flooded, the British armor held up far away, our extreme vulnerability on a daylight drop—I returned to my book.

Oh, hell, I thought as the plane leveled out and began a steady drone, I can't concentrate on this today. It was easy to concentrate in the marshaling area, where there was nothing but mud and tedium, but too much is on my mind now. I looked out the window again.

The 2nd Battalion was formed in a long column nine planes wide. Headed due east, we were rapidly approaching the north suburbs of London.

I was calm and almost unworried, for the daylight was considerably more reassuring than the night had been on the way to Normandy. I could see P-47 and P-51 fighter planes swarming all around and above us. They would escort us to the drop zone to beat off enemy fighters and strafe any flak batteries that opened fire on us from the ground.

All in all, it was a good plan, proceeding smoothly. Colonel Sink had said that it would. In the best form yet, he had given us a colorful farewell the day before.

"You'll meet British tanks," he had said, "some of them Cromwells, others Shermans. The Cromwells look like a cheesebox on a raft. They mount a 76mm cannon with a muzzle brake that makes them look like Kraut tanks, but for God's sake, don't shoot 'em because they're there to help you.

"And those Guards divisions," the colonel had continued, wiping his face and moving his hat back and forth across his head, "they're goddamn good outfits. Hell, you can't get in 'em unless you have a 'Sir' in front of your name and a pedigree a yard long. You'll see the Royal Household Cavalry and the 17-21st Lancers, fighting mad 'cause they're not on horses. But don't laugh at 'em. They're good outfits.

"This time take *lots* of prisoners!" the colonel had shouted. "With luck, we might even be out of there in ten days."

A laugh had rocked the marshaling area. Too many of us remembered the "two days' effort" asked of us before Normandy—two days that had somehow stretched into thirty-one. We weren't buying that again.

Colonel Sink had smiled and held up his hand for silence. After the cries of "Oh, Christ!" and "Shit!" had died down, he had given us a direct order to hide our wool-knit caps in Holland. "General Taylor spotted one of you people in a wool-knit cap in Normandy, and men, he really raised hell about it. Now, I don't want to catch hell, see, and I know you don't, so for God's sake, if you have to wear a wool-knit cap, hide the damn thing under your helmet and don't let the general catch you with that helmet off! That's an order, men, goddamn it. The general can't stand those little hats."

Delightful as ever, the colonel had rambled on, carrying the regiment with him on waves of laughter. "This is a good outfit," he had concluded, "good enough to win a Presidential Citation in Normandy. I know you people can do all right, so I don't have to talk about fighting. You old men look after the replacements, and we'll all get along fine together."

The colonel, I mused with a smile. If only all the officers were Colonel Sinks. Someday I hope to meet him and shake his hand and tell him how much we liked him.

We were over London now. It was Sunday morning, and the streets were empty. Here and there, a few people stood on the sidewalks and waved up at us. London clutched my heart and tried to pull me down. I wanted to relax, to go with it, all the way to the nearest Underground station, but I couldn't move. Jammed in with twenty other men, I could only watch the familiar streets fade slowly away from us far below and wish that I were walking on their hard surface instead of riding a noisy, bouncing airplane to combat and possibly to my death.

It was too pretty a day to go to war. Those civilians, I thought, how lucky they are! They'll go to church and then have a big Sunday dinner. The family will be around the table, and they'll talk about the planes that passed overhead. By that time we will be in another world.

"See the water?" somebody asked. "We're over water already."

God, I thought, looking down. The city had disintegrated into scattered houses on large lots that ended at the banks of a yellow-brown body of water. As we crept on, the water deepened to pale green, turquoise, and then midnight blue.

We're done for, I thought in despair. Good-bye, England.

Suddenly a jagged brown headland appeared. My spirits soared: more land. But it was only a jagged finger of coast, and we flew over it in an instant to the far side, where a line of white cliffs made our departure final. This was the Channel coast for sure.

My stomach tightened. I hoped that our plane would break down, that we would have to turn back, but the engines' roar was as steady as ever. The white cliffs faded away. I tried to find distraction in my book, but I couldn't resist looking out the window.

Down below, miniature waves molded on a deep blue sea slapped against motionless model boats anchored at regular intervals to mark our course. The sea, which reflected the sky, seemed very strong and deep, a Maxfield Parrish blue.

I returned to my book, but before I could really concentrate, we were over land again, roaring with gathering speed above the high white cliffs of the French coast. There was rolling farmland behind the cliffs. Soon the country flattened out. We passed many wrecked villages and came to a huge flooded area so still and motionless that it seemed as if life had been suspended there. Nothing moved in the trees or among the houses or in the little Flemish villages where the water stood six feet deep. I hoped that the Germans had not flooded our drop zone.

We dipped lower. The final run would be made in at six hundred feet, to minimize the danger of flak. This was the start of it. The knowledge twisted my stomach and turned it cold.

I went back to the book. Soon someone jostled my elbow and pointed ahead. "Looks like the front," he said.

A big canal lay across our path. A column of tanks and trucks a quarter of a mile long inched forward on a highway almost directly below us to a Bailey bridge partially obscured by clouds of white smoke. Orange smoke pots burned nearby as identification of friendly forces. This was the front—the Albert Canal. The Guards Armored Division had forced a crossing and were fighting to widen the bridgehead. They were supposed to break out of the crossing today and drive north to Holland. A handful of British soldiers waved to us from the banks of the canal and then disappeared in the smoke.

We swooped over the German lines in a brief rattle of small arms fire. This was enemy country now, and it was a beautiful day for flak.

"Stand up and hook up!"

I lunged at the anchor line and snapped the end of my static line to it. The book was still in my hand. There was no flak yet. I dropped the book on a seat so the Air Corps could read it.

"Check your equipment!"

My chest and leg straps were properly centered in the new British quick-release fastener in the middle of my chest. My reserve-chute snaps were snug. I moved the .45 I had bought from a crew chief after Normandy for fifty dollars close to my front, where I could reach it quickly. A bullet was already in the chamber. No German was going to bayonet me or cut my throat on *this* jump field.

"Sound off for equipment check!"

The door was open and the motors roared so loudly that I could barely hear the men behind me shout their numbers. Someone prodded me, and I yelled and slapped the shoulder of the man ahead of me. As the lead scout, I was closer to the door than I had been in Normandy, but my impatience to leave was not less. All I wanted now was out. My legs were weak, and I swallowed again and again. There was no flak.

"Close up and stand in the door!"

The flat green fields of Holland flashed by a few hundred feet below. I saw a windmill, a small pine forest, a canal crossing. In the distance, the spire of an immense church rose from a cluster of tile-roofed houses.

No flak, I said to myself, no flak. Maybe this won't be so bad after all. We were jammed together so tightly that I could hardly breathe. Our left legs were all forward in a lock step, ready to go. The jumpmaster was crouched by the equipment bundles in the door. The pilot lowered the flaps, and the plane slowed down.

Still no flak. Come on, let's go! No flak.

"Go!"

The line of men surged forward, flinging their static lines at the tail as they jumped. I followed them. Stopping all thought, my mind went blank, and I ran out the door without taking the proper stance.

I fell without knowing that I was falling, without even seeing where I was headed. Suddenly the opening shock unsnapped me.

I was spinning furiously, for my poor exit, combined with a

badly packed chute, had twisted my risers and suspension lines so much that, as sometimes happened, my chin was thrust down onto the top of my rifle case. I couldn't look up to check my canopy, but I didn't particularly care. Why worry? I thought, glad to be out of the plane and on my own. I'm alive and floating free.

Everything looked fine on the ground. There were no trees, rocks, roads, or houses on the mile-square brownish green field that was our drop zone. Flat and smooth, the field was cut here and there by low barbed-wire fences and shallow drainage ditches. No enemy were in sight. There appeared to be no hostile ground fire.

The drop zone was alive with men. Hundreds of spotted-green parachutes dotted the grass, while still more floated down in a beautiful spectacle alive with shouting. This was a big jump—a regimental combat team on one field—and we were all landing together. It was a thrilling sight.

My risers had untwisted by the time I was ready to land. I reached up, grasped all four, pulled down hard, and landed standing up. This was a sin in combat, but I couldn't resist the temptation, for the jump was so perfect. My chute collapsed, and I lay down quickly and got free of my harness. With amazing swiftness, the other men were already clearing off the field. I did not want to be left behind.

A C-47 came over low, streaming fire from a wing. I watched with gritted teeth as the men tried to get out. One, two, three, four, five, six, seven, eight . . . They were still jumping when the plane slammed into the ground and blew up half a mile away. God, I thought, that could have been me.

But it wasn't. I'm still alive, and as long as things are so quiet, I think I'll get a souvenir. I had always wanted a piece of parachute silk for a scarf but had never dared cut a chute on a training jump. Now was my chance. I pulled out my trench knife and went to the canopy.

Ku-rump!

I dropped the chute and looked up with a frown. A puff of black smoke hung over the jump field several hundred yards south. Airburst.

Ku-Rump!

Another shell burst considerably closer.

88s. Time to leave.

I put my trench knife back in its sheath, picked up my rifle, and ran toward a column of white smoke that was rising from a pine forest a quarter of a mile east. This was the assembly point for the 2nd Battalion. Another shell went off, and I increased my speed. Of the hundreds of men who had been on the field five minutes before, only a handful were left.

"Hey Webster, help me, will you!"

I slowed down and saw West limping toward me. We had been in the machine-gun platoon together. He had hurt his ankle on the Normandy jump and had been evacuated almost immediately after daylight. Now he said that his ankle was broken.

"Medic! Medic!" I shouted, not wishing to linger in the open. "For Chrissake, medic!"

A casual individual with a Red Cross armband sauntered toward us in a drainage ditch. "Keep your shirt on, buddy," he said. "I'm coming."

"Take it easy, West," I said, and ran for the cover of the pine forest.

Suddenly I came on three corpses—two paratroopers and an Air Corps crew chief. They had evidently been killed by the same airburst, for they were within a few yards of each other and still in their chutes. The crew chief had a bloody gash three inches long and an inch wide in his temple. I looked at him closely, for he seemed vaguely familiar.

Oh, I thought, suddenly remembering him, he was such a nice guy.

We had met him one night after Normandy in the Shepherd's Rest. He had blond hair and an open, friendly face, and he had treated us to some beers while we talked of the Air Corps and the paratroopers, for he was stationed with a troop carrier unit at Membury and often carried us on jumps. We had thanked him by trying to steal his jeep afterward for a ride back to Aldbourne. We were drunk, and the Air Corps was always fair game, for they were rich, spoiled, carefree, and undisciplined. But we couldn't get the motor started, and so we had had to walk back to camp. The crew chief was young, innocent, and friendly. Now he was dead on the drop zone.

Ku-Rump!

The airburst was only a hundred yards away. Ducking low, I ran for the woods, where I could make out scores of men lying low among the young pine trees.

A man passed me on the run.

"Hey," I shouted, "is this the 2nd Battalion?"

"Goddamn if I know."

I went into the forest and found myself in the 3rd Battalion. An officer suggested that I try farther north, and so I kept going until I found E Company. Spread out in brambly ditches beside a sandy road, they were waiting for the last stragglers to come in. I lay down with the rest of the squad and began to discuss the jump. It was, we agreed, our best jump overseas. The drop zone was perfect, the planes in formation, the wind light, the field flat and soft. England had nothing like it. As far as we could tell, no one in the company had been killed on the landing.

Five P-51 fighter planes circled a far corner of the field, peeled off one by one, and strafed an object on the ground there. A column of greasy black smoke rose in the sky.

"Tank," a man said who was watching them with field glasses. "They just got a Kraut tank."

The planes re-formed and flew away. I watched them go with a sinking feeling in my heart, for we needed their firepower. The thrumming sound of their engines faded into silence in the south. The ditch seemed very still and lonely.

I sighed and shrugged my shoulders. What the hell, I said to myself. We're off to a good start. Maybe Holland won't be so bad after all. I opened a K ration and began to eat lunch.

It was very hot and anticlimactic lying in the ditch and waiting to move out. In fact, it was almost our hottest day overseas. The sun glared down from the clear sky, and there was no wind to deflect the heat, which seemed to settle in the ditch. A few men drifted up and down the sandy road. Then everything was quiet. Although the stragglers had apparently all come in, still we waited to go. Our initial excitement and enthusiasm, which had reached its highest pitch as we floated down with hundreds of other men released from the planes that had held them captive, dried up in the heat and the waiting. It would have been better psychology to have set off as soon as we were assembled, but no, the army had to wait—and wait—and wait.

Sooner or later, I knew, the waiting would end. Eventually we would meet the Germans. How would the other men react? I had never been in action with any of them before. I wondered about them.

Rader and I were bound to argue. We had started already. Leader of the third squad, he was tall, thin, and rather sarcastic, but steady and not easily excited.

Hoobler was his assistant. An exuberant boy from the same part of Ohio as Rader, he was Rader's complete opposite—raucous, hearty, laughing, disputatious. I had wrecked his Thompson on a field problem in England when I had tried to mow down a giant jackrabbit, but he had taken the accident as a joke, saying that he preferred an M-1 anyway. Hoobler was young, cocky, and sturdily built. Nobody had to fear for him in combat.

He loved to josh thin little Pace, the second scout, who had come in as a replacement after Normandy. A wild crapshooter, Pace had a small paratrooper's natural cockiness that, combined with his southern spirit, forecast a fine combat soldier. He was a good man to work with as a scout.

Two replacements, Massaconi and Lyall, manned our 30 caliber light machine gun, which had been equipped with a bipod for the operation. More-experienced gunners had also taken a tripod into Holland for greater accuracy (the bipods were meant for Normandy-type fighting, in which the machine guns often had to be fired from the top of walls and hedgerows), but neither of our men had thought to take this precaution, since both were new to action. Massaconi was a worldly, talkative man from Massachusetts who had trained in the 26th (or Yankee) Division. He was full of comments, jokes, and nicknames. His assistant, Lyall, was very young, likable, and chatty. He talked extremely fast and not always with complete accuracy. Ten minutes after he had arrived in the company, he was borrowing clothes and money from his new acquaintances. Slender and with a sharp, clean profile, Lyall would tell you one minute that he was married and the next that he was not. Sometimes he said his brother had been killed with the 504 at Anzio and other times claimed he was alive with the 502. Our platoon sergeant, Talbert, looked on Lyall as a bright and eager younger brother who, with the proper guidance, would turn into a great soldier. Massaconi called him Knothead.

There were two ammo bearers, Janovek and Miller, who were also new to the outfit. Janovek, who was always humming or singing "Racing with the Moon," was dour, stubborn, and sarcastic but generally reliable—if he liked you and thought your ideas made sense. For some reason, he and I got along well together, and I preferred to have him nearby over almost anyone else in the squad. How he would react under fire remained to be seen. No man could possibly predict how any other man would act in combat.

Miller had a brush haircut and a missing front tooth that gave him an engaging, boyish appearance. Less than twenty years old, he had come to the ETO as an infantry replacement, then volunteered for the paratroops. So far, he had drawn only one month's jump pay. Quiet and friendly and well-mannered, he did not seem to have the independence required for the parachute infantry, where every man, in the words of a British writer, is an emperor. Each of us had to be ready to act on our own, without the least briefing, orders, or advice, and I feared that Miller was too disciplined for this kind of action. He was an ideal soldier, quiet and obedient, and I hoped that these qualities would not work to his disadvantage in the first free-for-all.

We were lying down in marching order, with Rader at the head of our twelve-man column and the others strung out behind. Hoobler brought up the rear. I looked from Miller to the next man, Rice. No need to worry about Rice; he did enough worrying for ten men. A stocky southerner, he was our grenadier. He had started as a machine gunner in F Company in Toccoa, had transferred to the kitchen, and had joined E Company after Normandy. Rice was somewhat of a busybody, especially to the replacements, whom he was forever telling what to do and how to do it. As a soldier, however, Rice would, I was confident, be an asset.

Whitesill, Wiseman, and Josephson were the three remaining riflemen. Whitesill was quite young and friendly, full of talk and wisecracks and a great friend of Wiseman's, whom he called Goldie. Wiseman called him Slick, for he had a very short crewcut, and palled around with him most of the time in Aldbourne and the marshaling area. Whitesill appeared to be quite a good soldier.

I liked Wiseman the best of all. A burly miner from Colorado, he was the oldest man in the squad—about twenty-five—and the roughest. He was strong and durable and highly independent, yet intelligent, well-trained, and understanding. Nobody feared for Wiseman.

The same could not be said for Josephson. He was eager. He had volunteered to come along, when he could well have stayed back in the rear, but he was not a trained, hardened, or experienced soldier. Short and plump, with a Brooklyn accent, he had spent most of his army career as a cook. One cook had, however, jumped in Normandy and had lorded it over the other cooks on his return, so most of them, to save face, had volunteered to jump in Holland. We didn't want them—they were not trained soldiers—but they were along, and so we had to help them. I had been with the other cook in Normandy, and I knew what we were in for. Josephson was, however, quite likable and earnest.

"On the road, on the road!" Rader cried. "Let's go." I stood up, buckled my cartridge belt, and put the bayonet on my rifle.

"Five yards between men. Get a move on, Webster!" I fell in behind some men from F Company who were moving out ahead of us. It was nice to have somebody between me and the enemy.

We walked briskly east on the sandy path through the pine trees until we reached the main road, which ran north and south from Eindhoven to Arnhem. Half a mile away, we saw the tile roofs and big steeple of the village of Zon, our initial objective. The 1st Battalion had to secure the jump field for glider landings and aerial resupply and hold the bridge over the Wilhelmina Canal at Zon while the 2nd and 3rd Battalions went south to Eindhoven.

Nobody came out to greet us at Zon. Silent and deserted, the village had an ominous air about it that made me click my rifle off safety. I eyed all the windows of the houses ahead. A rustling of paper flashed through the air high above me. Ignoring it, I continued to follow close after F Company.

"Jesus Christ, Webster!" Rader exclaimed. "Don't you know what this is?"

I shook my head without taking my eyes off the houses. Something was going to happen very soon, I could tell, and I didn't like it.

"That's an 88."

"Oh? Didn't sound like one to me."

"Wise up, boy."

"Hell."

Evidently the same cannon that had sent the airbursts, killed the crew chief, and knocked down one or two planes was still in action, probably near the canal bridge. The thought of it failed to worry me, for I was intent only on staying close to F Company. As the lead scout in E Company I was now the connecting point between the two units. I was more afraid of an ambush in the village than of the 88. I knew that the civilians wouldn't be lying low if they didn't expect a battle. They knew before any soldiers when a battle was brewing. I began to sweat freely. We approached an intersection in the middle of town.

"Go left, go left!" my platoon leader shouted. A former noncom who had won a battlefield commission in Normandy, he was dark, sturdy, and sensible. His name was Lieutenant Hudson. "Go left!" he shouted again.

F Company went straight down the road. I turned left with no-body in front of me. Edging over close to the houses, with my rifle at my hip, ready to fire, I slowed down to an invalid's walk.

"Faster! Get a move on!"

Oh, goddamn you, I thought. Goddamn all you officers. I'm out here to draw fire, and you want me to run right into it. I stepped out at a quicker gait and, following the road as it curved to the left and then to the right, passed beyond the village. A bridge over a small creek called the Dommel River lay ahead. I looked at it and around it and then beyond it—and stopped cold. There, a hundred yards beyond the bridge by the side of the road, near a stone barn, were three Germans. The one in the center squatted behind a machine gun, with the others close beside him. All of them waved to me in greeting.

You'll be sorry, I thought, you sons of bitches.

Grasping my rifle by the upper hand guard and the small of the stock, I flung it above my head parallel to the ground as a signal for the men behind me: Enemy in sight! In one second, I had made the motion, yanked the rifle down to my shoulder, and aimed at the machine gunner. I wanted to kill him first, because he was the most dangerous.

The Germans continued to wave. Evidently they thought we were German paratroopers who had come to reinforce them. My eyesight was better than theirs, for I could tell a German right away by his stance, which was utterly unlike that of an American soldier, but I was not as relaxed as they were. Tense with nervousness, I leveled on the machine gunner's chest, winced, and pulled the trigger.

The bullet cracked above the German's head, and before I could fire another round, all three men had disappeared behind the barn. I cursed myself. An enemy machine gun fired a short burst to my left. It was not aimed at me, I knew, but my brief heroics were over. I jumped behind the bridge. Some shooting, I thought, crouching close to the earth. I am the world's worst shot. Never could shoot worth a good goddamn.

Lieutenant Hudson ran up and got me back on the road and across the bridge. A shout rippled up the column behind us: "Hold it up! Hold it up! Hold it up!" I stopped and sidled over to the cover of the embankment.

"Come on back," Lieutenant Hudson said.

Some men from Company Headquarters had already started off through a field on the right, heading toward the canal. Vastly relieved to be a follower again, I fell in with the column. We waded a filthy ditch filled with scummy water that smelled like the distilled essence of barnyard and sewer, scrambled over some barbed-wire fences, cursed our way through patches of briars, dodged across a few backyards, and suddenly came out on the broad cobblestone embankment of the Wilhelmina Canal near a brickyard with piles of sand and a water tower on steel legs.

There had been a tremendous explosion only a few minutes before. Now we saw the result—a blown bridge. The Germans had wrecked our first objective. We scattered out in the brickyard, taking good care to have cover between us and the enemy side of the canal, and lay down to await developments. Half a dozen empty 88 shell casings lay in the vicinity, but the cannon had evidently departed.

Now what? I wondered as time went by and nothing happened. Hurry up and wait: It never changes. I sighed and, because I was hot, removed my wool undershirt and stowed it in my musette bag, then rolled up my sleeves. The officers made us look for logs or boats or boards to get across on, but since there was nothing suitable in the vicinity, we lay back down again. There was no sign of life in the half dozen little houses across from us.

A German rifle popped far away, and soon a barn began to burn about six hundred yards to our direct front. Small figures ran out of the barn and tumbled down from a poplar tree close to it, where they had evidently been watching us. A Headquarters Company machine gunner on the bank of the canal ran a belt through his 30 caliber, but the bullets were high and hurt nobody. A few rifle-men joined him. I held my fire. If I couldn't hit a man at a hundred yards, I certainly couldn't hit one at six hundred. Why waste the ammunition? It might come in handy later.

This is dull, I thought, yawning. It certainly can't compare with D-Day. I leaned back against a foot of the water tower and blinked my eyes. It's afternoon already, I mused, and there's a good five miles to Eindhoven. We were supposed to take the city today. Hope the British tanks beat us to it.

A naked figure streaked past, dove into the canal, and swam twenty yards to the other bank, where two waterlogged rowboats were moored.

"Johnny Weismuller!" Hoobler cried. "That goddamn Carson." He yipped with delight. The whole company laughed and yelled as Carson, a first-platoon runner, climbed into one of the rowboats and paddled it back to our side. A group of men from the first squad helped bail it out, then went over to investigate the houses.

While this drama was unfolding, a less heroic but more practical unit of the 326th Parachute Engineer Battalion, which had jumped with us, was gathering boards and building a rough footbridge over the ruins of the blown bridge. Carson put on his clothes, and after a long wait, we started over, rushing down the planks one by one into the arms of an engineer, who caught us and steadied us for the run up the other side. A slow process, the company crossing took almost an hour.

By now it was almost twilight. We had traveled two or three miles in five hours.

Fortunately, our company had not encountered an 88. Rumors came to us that several cannons had been posted around Zon as protection for the bridge. Dual-purpose antiaircraft, antipersonnel guns, the 88s had fired on the planes and gliders and then leveled on the men coming down the road, killing almost a dozen.

A 3rd Battalion captain had been shot through the head in Zon by a German rifleman. Burr Smith, a big Californian, and another man from Company Headquarters had carried him into a little cafe and laid his body on the bar. The German gun crews' packs were still lined up neatly along the walls of the cafe, where they had had lunch, and the Dutch family who ran the place, bewildered by the sudden fighting, had stared at the dead captain and wept and sobbed, "Gott, Gott, Gott," and wrung their hands. The Company Headquarters men had divided the contents of the captain's musette bag and gone on their way, leaving the body with the civilians.

The sun was down by the time we had crossed the canal. The air turned cool with surprising speed as we lay in the ditches beside the highway and waited for the rest of the battalion to come over. A twilight hush fell on the countryside. There was no sound of war or nature. Men began to fall asleep. It was obvious to all that we would not take Eindhoven today.

Never able to nap on the bare ground, I shivered in the gathering mist and wondered what was going on. As usual, we had been elaborately briefed before the takeoff—and told nothing once we were in action. I always felt better when I knew what was taking place.

Just when the stars grew bright and low and the cold twisted into my muscles and made me get up and exercise to keep warm, an officer came down the road and moved us into an adjacent field, where we posted two men as guards and settled ourselves around a haystack. Our bivouac was so congested, however, that Janovek and I decided to seek more comfortable quarters in some nearby farm buildings. Stumbling through the darkness, we came to a little shed. It looked good, but the first squad, which was very sly and first in many things, had already taken possession. They shouted us off the premises.

As we moved through the backyard toward the main farmhouse, we heard German voices coming out of the mouth of a sod-covered underground air-raid shelter to our left. We stopped.

"Cover me," I whispered to Janovek. He unslung his rifle, and I cocked my .45 and tiptoed to the entrance, crouching low.

"Heraus!" I yelled. "Hände hoch! Mach schnell!"

A man crept out on his hands and knees, mumbling, "Niederländer, Niederländer." I yanked him up, frisked him, and pulled him close. He was a Dutch civilian. Quivering with fear, he told us that he was the owner of the farm. He had taken refuge with his

family in the shelter as soon as the first planes had come over and
had been below ground ever since.

"Wir sind Amerikaner," I told him, adding that we were paratroopers, Fallschirmjäger. We had come to shoot the Germans, I
explained. Were there any around?

"Nein, nein," he replied. He shook our hands and told us that he
was glad to be free again. Welcoming us to Holland, he invited us
into his house. Hoobler, ever restless and alert, had drifted up in
the meantime. "Ask him if he has any food," he said.

"Ja, ja. Komm!" He led us into a barn where a platoon of men
from Headquarters Company had settled. We passed through their
jealous mutterings and opened the door to his kitchen, then shut it
to keep out the machine gunners. Hoobler lit a candle.

Chattering away happily about how much he hated the Germans
and wanted to help us, our host, who was a thin, strong, middle-
aged man in a dark suit and cloth cap, went to some shelves lined
with Mason jars filled with preserves, and gave us an assortment of
beef, peaches, and cherries. Hoobler and Janovek offered some of
their cigarettes in return, while I donated a D-ration chocolate bar.
The farmer was overwhelmed. These were the first decent cigarettes he had had in five years, he said. As for the candy, he would
save it for his little boy, who had never tasted chocolate.

We thanked him again for the food, suggested that he lock the
door to keep Headquarters Company from cleaning him out, and
went back to the squad. The preserves were a delicious treat, and as
we passed them around in the cold starlight near the haystack, we
agreed that Holland was indeed a fine country.

We set off at dawn, two battalions of a thousand men on foot, without tanks, trucks, artillery, or air support, to capture a city of a
hundred thousand. The city, Eindhoven, was supposed to be lightly
held. It was presumed that the Germans could not bring in enough
reinforcements to stop us. The 3rd Battalion led the way.

At first we moved swiftly down the road, which was raised, like
all the other roads in southern Holland, about a yard above the
surrounding farmland and lined at regular intervals with tall, stately
trees. Soon, however, there were scattered shots ahead. A firefight
developed, and the column came to a halt. The firing continued,
then died out. We got to our feet again.

On flank guard a hundred yards out on the right and pushing hard to keep up with the column, which was moving smoothly down the highway, I came upon a big, dark paratrooper lying wounded in a ditch. A thick forest of high trees lay about two hundred yards farther on, to our right, and I hated to stop and offer myself as a target to a sniper who might be hiding in the forest.

"Help me, buddy," the man said. He looked like Trujillo from the mortar platoon, and so I stopped beside him with one eye on the woods. The men on the road continued to move on.

"Get going!" Rader shouted, waving at me.

"Medic!" I called. "Medic!"

"Jesus, buddy, don't leave me. I can't move."

"Medic!"

A first-aid man left the column and ran toward us.

"Don't go."

"I have to go. I'm on flank guard. The medic's coming now."

He gave me the look of a helpless man abandoned by the one person who can aid him. Hoping desperately that I wouldn't be wounded on flank guard and left behind as he had been, I ran off, feeling like an utter heel. God help anybody who is hit now, I thought. The outcome is so uncertain, and there are no ambulances or hospitals.

We passed some more wounded men, all from the 3rd Battalion, which had run into the first outposts of Eindhoven, and then stopped again.

"3rd Bat's held up," Lieutenant Hudson informed us. It looked like they had run into the Main Line of Resistance, he added. We cut left into open farmland to flank the enemy positions. Under a hot summer sun, we struggled through truck gardens and freshly plowed fields toward the city, which rose abruptly from the green meadows a quarter of a mile away. A German machine gun fired a long burst at us.

"Hit it!" Rader cried. I dropped behind a small tree and wriggled around to cover the buildings. The machine gun fired again, but I couldn't locate it.

Several guns in E Company returned the fire. Manned by veterans, they carefully sprayed the windows of a long row of two-story apartment houses that faced us. Their toom-toom-toom mixed very pleasantly with the wonderful noise of breaking glass. I smiled. Everybody liked to shoot at windows.

"In that line of houses!" Rader shouted at Massaconi and Lyall. "Spray 'em, spray 'em!" They joined the shooting. In a few minutes, however, everybody lost enthusiasm and the firing died out.

Still safe behind my little tree, I decided to abandon my gas mask, which kept banging against my legs in an irritating fashion. It was too hot to bother with nonessentials.

"On the road! Moving out." We started down a sandy path that paralleled the buildings. The enemy gun fired another burst.

"Hoobler, take Webster and Pace and get that guy!" cried Lieutenant Brownlow, an assistant platoon leader and to me the most infuriating officer in the regiment. "I think he's in that farmhouse out there." The place he referred to was about two hundred yards to our right front. A small dwelling, it stood all alone in a big, bare field without any covered approach whatsoever.

I gave the box of machine-gun ammunition that I had carried ever since the jump to the man nearest me and ran after Hoobler, with Pace beside me. It was a long run over deep, sandy furrows, but we covered the distance in about ten seconds—or so it seemed, for I never ran faster in my life. While the others covered me, I beat on the door and bade the occupants come out with their hands high. A very old man obeyed the summons. So terrified that he could only stutter, he made no sense to us, so we pushed him aside and looked indoors. There were no Germans. We ran back to the company.

"Lieutenant Hudson got hit," Rader informed us. "Burp gun knocked him down."

"The good officers always get hit," I remarked, dreading what this would mean to us. "Now we're stuck with Brownlow."

"You know it, boy, you know it."

A right swing across the field a few minutes later brought us into the streets of Eindhoven, a bright new city built around the giant Phillips electrical plant. The first sight that greeted us was the body of a 3rd Battalion captain who had been shot through the head by a sniper in a windmill down the street. This is a bad country for captains, I mused, wondering why they always threw a covering over a dead man's face. I looked at the windmill. It had been liberally shot up with small arms and bazookas. I hoped that the sniper had been killed.

People came out of all the houses as we marched past the windmill. "So nice to see you," they said in perfect English, for the

Dutch were extremely well-educated. "We have waited so long."

The column stopped, and the civilians brought us chairs to sit on, milk and tea to drink, and fresh fruit to eat. Thoroughly enjoying the role of liberators, we chatted with them gaily, for it was wonderful to feel wanted and welcome, to meet someone (for the first time) who appreciated what you were doing. Nobody had ever welcomed us to France.

A German rifle popped down the street.

"Sniper!"

I dropped my peach and fell behind a stone gatepost. In an instant, all the soldiers were flat and the civilians indoors.

Pop. Pop. Pop.

"Get him! Get him!"

"Come on, Web," Hoobler yelled. "Better cover in the schoolhouse."

We darted across the road, climbed a high wire fence, and ran behind the sturdy brick building. After examining the premises for Germans, we sat down in the sun with the schoolhouse between us and the sniper.

Hoobler took off his helmet and sighed. "This is the way to fight a war, isn't it?"

I nodded.

Colonel Sink came into the yard with Lieutenant Colonel Chase, his quiet, friendly executive officer, and a retinue of enlisted men.

Hoobler slapped on his helmet, and we struggled to our feet and tried to look alert and eager, but Colonel Sink merely smiled at us, glanced around, and went out. We returned to our sunbath.

"Let's go, Hoobler!" Rader shouted. "Moving out."

We walked all the way through Eindhoven, from north to south. Our march quickly changed from a tactical exercise to a triumphal progress as the last Germans and their machine guns and cannons were knocked out by other platoons and companies. Orange flags and armbands appeared everywhere, and the cheering, clapping crowds soon thickened so much that we could barely move. The civilians wanted to help us, to shake our hands, to pat our backs and thank us for driving away the Germans. The applause and din of gratitude was so deafening that we had to shout to each other to be heard. It was the most sincere thanksgiving demonstration that any of us had ever witnessed, and it fixed Holland forever in our hearts.

Our objectives, several bridges over the Wilhelmina Canal in the southeastern corner of Eindhoven, were taken without resistance. Guards were posted (and almost immediately blew up a truck filled with escaping German soldiers), and Lyall, Massaconi, Janovek, and Miller set up the machine gun on the roof of a liquor warehouse, which they promptly inspected via a broken skylight. Pace and I were sent down a side street to watch for Germans approaching from the east. Heroes for the day, we posed for snapshots ("I want a picture of the first American soldier I've seen"), signed our autographs, drank cognac and wine that had been hidden away to celebrate the Liberation. A Dutchman named Hans Wesenhagen served us a splendid meal of vegetable broth, roast veal, Brussels sprouts, boiled potatoes, applesauce, and fresh milk. The girls stared at us in admiration, the small boys fingered our gear, the older civilians mobbed us as if we were movie stars. Although most of them understood my Linguaphone German, they preferred to exercise their English. Our language, we were told, was a required subject in Holland, where the educational level of both young and old was far higher than in America and where almost everybody also studied German and French.

"We are so glad to see you," the people said. "The Germans were terrible."

"Holland is a wonderful country. Very good people, beautiful windmills."

"You are good boys."

"Your girls are very pretty. Yes, thanks! Good cognac."

Eindhoven was a lovely place.

"Where are we going?" I asked.

"Goddamn if I know," Rader replied. "Brownlow told me to have the squad on the road in ten minutes."

"Oh Christ. This was such a nice deal."

We had moved into a new position early in the afternoon, after the first British scout cars had bypassed heavy resistance in the south and come into the city. Located in the eastern outskirts on the bank of the Wilhelmina Canal, our new position was tactically stupid—in an open beet field below the level of a large factory that the enemy could use as a likely avenue of approach—but it was very pleasant. The owners of a nearby house brought us soup and tea and hot buckets of water for shaving, and we scrounged rabbits and fresh fruit and vegetables from other neighbors. Our holes were deep and lined with straw, the sun was pleasant, and even the steady booming of a battle farther south failed to disturb our tranquillity. Hoobler became so well-known to the civilians that he adopted the name of Count Von Hoobler, much to their delight. Now we were moving out.

We bade the civilians farewell and marched off at a hurried pace to join the rest of the 2nd Battalion, which was assembling near a large church on the main road east. Nobody knew where we were going—only that this was an emergency. The rumor said that our destination was Helmond, a city about fifteen miles northeast that was supposed to be a German strongpoint.

We marched at top speed for about three hours. The Dutch cheered us as we passed through their villages, and they hung out orange flags and offered refreshments and generally acted as if the war was over, but we were no longer enthusiastic. Our feet hurt, our clothes were wet with sweat, and the handles of the 30 caliber ammo boxes cut deeper and deeper into our hands. Carrying all our gear and ammunition by hand (Company Headquarters, as usual, was hogging all the captured vehicles), we marched faster and with fewer breaks than in basic training. The sun started to go down after we had traveled about twelve miles. Suddenly the column stopped.

"Dig in here," Lieutenant Brownlow said. It was another bad position, dominated by a railroad embankment, but we dug in as ordered. Our front was a small brown field and a farmhouse. Nobody liked the location or the air of mystery that surrounded the whole expedition. As we continued to dig our holes and complain of our feet and officers, a German rifle cracked beyond the embankment. A single tracer arched overhead, and Lieutenant Brownlow ran back to us.

"Krauts, men! Krauts!" he cried. "We're pulling out of here. On the double! We're going back to Eindhoven."

I was livid. A single tracer and everybody turned and ran. Some outfit. As I wriggled into my harness, put away my shovel, and grabbed my rifle, I wailed aloud and wondered when the army was going to make up its mind. "Why don't they tell us something?" I yelled at Rader as we ran away from the embankment. "What the hell is going on?"

He laughed.

Back we went, as swiftly as before and in as great ignorance. Our feet burned, our throats were dry, our patience was exhausted. Lamentations of five hundred men filled the air with four-letter words. No longer trying to be tactical, we closed ranks and slowed down in the gathering dusk. Wiseman and I kept hitching rides on a horse-drawn cart that belonged to the machine-gun platoon, and Lieutenant Brownlow kept peeling us off. "Goddamn it," he said, almost in tears at the disorder, "if I can't ride, nobody else can either."

Just as darkness fell, a new sound rose above the general cursing—the short throbbing of enemy airplane motors. We stopped and looked up.

About eight twin-engined JU-88 bombers were circling overhead. God, I thought, they've seen us. Now they'll come down and strafe the column. And there's no place to hide—no ditches, no houses, no nothing.

We made a perfect target. The riflemen were closed up almost in parade-ground order, and the captured vehicles—horse carts, handcarts, German jeeps, trucks, and command cars—were bumper to bumper in a wild tangle that halted all movement. As the drivers swore and shouted at each other, a lone officer ran up and down the line, trying in vain to restore order. The only thing that saved us was the camouflaging branches of the tall trees on both sides of the road.

The airplanes continued to circle, as if getting their bearings, then went west. In a few moments, we saw them drop flares and heard their bombs whistle down. Great fires began to burn in Eindhoven.

Considerably chastened, we spread out and started to move again. The villages that had greeted us so wildly on the way out quickly hid their orange banners and closed their doors and windows when they saw us come back. Nobody waved to us or patted our backs or offered apples and pears. They were afraid the Germans would follow us in.

While the fires crackled and popped and flared up, we stopped east of the city and dug into the backyards. We settled down for the night to the sound of the flames and the British armored columns rattling north.

Though we had cursed the march to Helmond and back, we now

discovered that it had been our salvation, not only from the airplanes, which had set afire a British ammunition convoy in the streets of Eindhoven and killed several hundred people, but also from an enemy armored column from Helmond.

Mounting the railroad embankment, Captain Nixon, Battalion S-2, had spotted a long line of German tanks and halftracks going down a road at right angles to our front, evidently in hopes of cutting us off. Then the tracer had gone by, and a withdrawal was ordered immediately. By good fortune, we had outmarched the armor. The Dutch Underground, which was extremely conscientious and reliable, had reported, according to the rumor that we heard, that there were fifty tanks and five thousand Germans in Helmond.

I was no longer sorry that my feet were sore.

A column of tanks from the Guards Armored Division came up to us at dawn the next day and stopped on the road beyond our position with their radios crackling and an air of readiness about them that made me shiver. A mixture of Cromwells, with long, boat-shaped hulls, and American Shermans, the tanks mounted high-velocity 76mm cannons and bore on their sides the desert rat insignia of General Montgomery's North African veterans.

There was no time for briefing, no time for anything but a hurried breakfast of apples and German rations, which we cooked over a little fire near our hole, for word had come in the night that the Germans in Helmond had moved up on our flank. The dew was heavy on the grass as we got ready to go, and the air was chilly from a ground mist that reduced the rising sun to a dull white ball. Other tanks came up and moved into a nearby field, filling the air with barks and clanks and squeaks. In jaunty black berets, the men in the turrets talked quietly to one another as we went by. We halted at the head of the column on the road.

"Ride these tanks till you're hit," an officer cried, "and then start fighting!"

Six men to a tank, the first and second squads mounted the lead vehicles. We climbed on the fifth and sixth.

I did not look forward to the ride. Tanks drew artillery fire like magnets, and the difficulty of communicating with the crews inside, once the shooting started and they had buttoned themselves in, more than outweighed any good they might do. Blind as they were, tanks had a strong tendency to hang back in action and let the infantry go ahead, thus losing touch with them altogether.

We jolted forward, twenty yards behind the fourth tank. The sun came out, and the mist began to dissipate, but I felt cold and tense. I put my bayonet on and knelt behind the turret, where I could see everything, have some protection, and still be ready to jump off at the first shot. Aloof in his turret, the tank commander nodded to us but made no effort to chat. None of us was very talkative.

"Where are we going?" I asked Rader.

"A place called Nunen. They think the Krauts have moved in. We're going to find out."

We swung around a corner and headed east by north. The air was quite clear now, and we made a lovely target as we clattered along the raised road into the open country.

These British are pretty casual, I thought, noticing that all their guns were pointed forward. They think the war is over. They talk about Patton running wild and act as if they can coast from here on. American tankers would move out with the lead gun forward, the next pointing right, the third left, and so on down the line. Thus, if an enemy target appeared on the right, it was covered. At the same time, the column was protected against ambush by the guns pointing left.

"Take it easy, Web," Wiseman grinned, noticing my nervousness. Perfectly relaxed and self-confident, he sat beside me with his back to the turret.

I laughed without taking my eyes off the road and flat fields ahead. Pace stood nearby, and Lyall and Massaconi were ready with the machine gun. Lyall had already draped a belt of 30 caliber over his shoulders. I took two hand grenades out of my pockets and hooked them on to my suspenders. The air smelled very clean and cool and country-fresh. I loved the open country. We swung north, with the sun on our right quarter.

After going about four miles, we stopped abruptly by a cluster of three or four houses at a crossroads. A British armored reconnaissance car stood behind one of the houses. Two men with Sten guns were peeking around the corner at the road ahead, where a large village with the usual big church of southern Holland, which was Catholic, stood sharp and clear in the morning sun almost half a mile away.

"Where's Nunen?" I yelled.

One of the guards pointed down the road. "Straight ahead of you, mate," he replied. "Jerry!"

We moved off, and everybody on the tank stood up and got ready. No one said anything. The lead tanks proceeded as fast as before.

When we were halfway to the village, Jack Matthews, a lively, witty rifleman in the first squad, yelled and pointed to the right. "Hey, look over there!" he shouted. "Kraut tank, Kraut tank!"

The column stopped, and all the turrets swung right. Less than three hundred yards away, parallel to our course, a large yellow-brown German halftrack was slithering through the brush like some evil beast.

We jumped off the tanks and ran for the roadside ditches. The British opened fire: Bam! Bam! Bam! Bam!

The first shell was short. It hit the ground in a cloud of dust and, skipping like a stone on water, smashed into the side of the halftrack. The other shells hit it square. The halftrack stopped, and a handful of men jumped out. Men on that side of the road shot at them.

Without waiting for orders, we moved down the ditches toward Nunen. The first and third squads were on the left, the second and mortar squads on the right. The tanks stayed behind to finish off the halftrack.

We were among the houses in a few minutes. Scouting for the first squad, Marsh, a big, rough steelworker, and McCreary, a plump tailor who was all guts, saw a German medium tank hiding behind a house farther in. The tank eased out to see what was going on, then withdrew and eased out again. A German got out of the turret and walked toward them with his hands up. They waved him on, but someone in the rear shot at him, and he disappeared. The tank backed away.

"Bazooka man up front!" Marsh yelled. "Bazooka man up front! Kraut tank."

We passed the word along, for the bazooka men usually traveled with Company Headquarters, well in the rear. Marsh and McCreary ran back to the first British tank, which had crept up behind us, and told its commander to shoot through the house and knock out the German tank.

"Sorry," the Englishman replied. "We can't fire now. We're waiting for orders."

They goddamned him and ran back up the ditch. "Freaking Limeys," Marsh muttered as he went by. "Come on, let's go in without them."

No orange banners greeted us in Nunen, and nobody came out to wave or give us a glass of milk. We broke into the houses and went upstairs to look ahead for Germans, but none were visible.

I was so scared I could hardly talk. Crouching low, I ran through the backyards and the empty rooms in search of the enemy. A movement caught my eye, and glancing across the street, I saw a middle-aged man and his wife watching us from a second-story window.

"Wo sind die deutsche Soldaten?" I shouted. "Where are the German soldiers?"

"Weg," the man replied. "Away." They shut the window and disappeared.

The bazooka man still had not arrived. Wiseman, Pace, Janovek and I kept close together, then separated. I found myself alone in a backyard. An old man watched me from a homemade air-raid shelter.

"Wo sind die deutsche Soldaten?" I inquired.

"Nah," he whispered, "sehr nah." He shook his head at me, as if to say, Get out while you can. The Germans are very near.

I bent over with my rifle pointing forward and ran to the next house. Burrrrrrrrrrrrrrrrp! A German machine gun fired a long burst. The bullets popped very close overhead.

"Kraut tank!" Marsh yelled. "Machine gun, Sloan. Get over here!" Still in the ditch beside the road, Marsh and McCreary kept shouting at Sloan, who was their machine gunner, to climb the hedge that separated them from him, but he said he couldn't. They cursed him and told him to throw the gun over with some ammunition.

The enemy machine gun fired another burst. Suddenly a number of German machine guns and rifles opened fire on both sides of the road. A halftrack mounting a 20mm cannon edged out from behind a house. Marsh and McCreary poured a belt of 30 caliber at its front. The halftrack backed off. I fired at the houses ahead.

Now there was a spontaneous movement forward, for the enemy

fire was still high and apparently unaimed. We crossed a small park cut with air-raid dugouts and stopped among the houses on the other side. Three or four of us were together in what was now the front. The British tanks were nowhere near, and there were no officers to tell us what to do. Wiseman, Janovek, and I went upstairs and shot in all the windows, ditches, and hedges ahead. Wiseman left, and I went out in the backyard.

A baldheaded young Dutchman in a black suit ran up. "Give me a hand grenade," he pleaded. "I know where the Germans are. Let me kill them."

"OK," I said. "Here you are. Good luck."

He thanked me and ran crouching down a ditch that led out into the fields on our left. I watched him crawl up another ditch that paralleled the road. The German fire continued to build up.

"Shoot, shoot!" I yelled, fanning the area ahead.

"I can't see 'em," Janovek said.

"You *never* see 'em. Shoot where you think they are!"

Ka-blam! A mortar shell landed in the next yard.

"Mortars!" I yelled. "Let's get out of here."

Firing back as we went, we left. Another shell landed across the street. Then one came into the yard we had just left. I lingered a moment on the edge of the park and suddenly found myself alone. I got up and ran through the park. A mortar shell burst in a tree behind me, and I dived for the narrow opening in a thick hedge that formed the south border of the park. A man's body was blocking the opening. It was Josephson, the cook. He was moaning and clutching his right hand, which was wet with blood and looked as if it had been shot off at the wrist.

"Help me," he moaned. "Somebody help me." I knelt beside him. A burst of German bullets crackled in the hedge above us.

"What's wrong?" I asked. "Are you hit anywhere else?"

"No. It hurts."

"Get up and run! For Chrissake, get out of here! The Krauts are coming."

"No, no, I can't move."

"You've got a ticket back to England. Get up and run to the rear."

He shook his head and moaned. I gritted my teeth. To me, a wound was a blessing, a chance to get out of action. I would have been back with the medics by now. Josephson, however, was not a man who had been in action before, and so he looked on things differently. A wound to him was apparently a terrible shock, not a golden opportunity.

"Medic, medic!" I yelled. The Germans answered with a rattling, popping salvo.

Impatient to be on my way, I loosened his collar and bandaged his wrist, which was bleeding badly.

"Get up!" I said again. "I'm leaving. Come with me."

"No," he moaned. "I can't move. I'm staying here."

Another mortar shell landed in the park. I sprang up and ran all the way to the last houses, where the other men had collected and where the tanks were sitting in the middle of the road, still waiting for orders. Covered with sweat and panting from his long crawl up the ditch from the armored-car outpost, a bazooka man arrived on the scene, ready for action, but he was too late. Another bazooka man had made it earlier across the road and been killed. Marsh arrived with his face covered with blood from a bullet that had cut his forehead. He was furious at Sloan and madder still at the British tankers.

As we watched from behind the house, two shells came in almost simultaneously and knocked out the first two tanks. The lead one began to smoke. It turned right, ground forward slowly into the ditch, and stopped. Its cannon went off with the jolt, and the shell screamed into Nunen and exploded against a house. Nobody got out of the tank alive. The hatch of the second popped open, however, and three Englishmen jumped out and ran away.

"Pulling out," someone cried. "Let's go."

One by one, we crawled down the ditch under machine-gun fire to the armored car, where we stopped. Little Johnny Martin, leader of the first squad, tried to soothe Sloan, who appeared to be quite upset. "That's all right, Sloan," he said gently. "Take it easy. We're not going back in there."

With a thrumming roar, three Spitfires came out of the north at treetop height. Their cannons blazed at us, and we threw ourselves on the ground.

"Anybody got a smoke grenade?" Martin yelled. "For Chrissake, throw it!"

I pulled an orange smoke grenade for identification of friendly forces out of my pocket and threw it a few yards away. The British quickly unrolled luminescent orange cloth panels and spread them on the armored car. The Spitfires never came back.

We settled down to wait for the stragglers. Several men were still missing, including Josephson, Wiseman, and Miller from our squad. Nobody knew what had happened to Wiseman and Miller. The Germans continued to mortar the west end of Nunen.

Martin went up to a British tank that had pulled back with us. "Put a shell in that church steeple," he suggested. "The Krauts are using it as an observation post."

The tank commander shook his head. "I'm sorry, we can't do it," he replied crisply. "We have orders not to destroy too much property. Friendly country, you know."

And so we mounted the tanks and pulled out without leveling Nunen, as a good American armored unit would have done, for that is how wars are won—not by fighting 50 percent or 30 percent or even 85 percent, but by fighting 100 percent with every weapon at your command.

We we got back to our old position near Eindhoven and were cleaning our weapons for a rifle inspection, we learned that Sergeant Guarnere of the second platoon, consistently the bravest man in E Company, had led a band of volunteers all the way back to the park and rescued Josephson. They also found Miller—dead in a back-yard. A German had seen him lying bewildered behind a log and had thrown a hand grenade on his back. Five or six other men had been killed. Two were still missing—Wiseman and Bull Randle-man, a massive farm boy who was the leader of the second squad.

Considerably chastened, we spent a very quiet day in our holes, cleaning our weapons. But we were not through with Nunen yet, for at twilight we mounted the tanks again (hating the British for their slowness and their stupidity, their "waiting for orders" and "can't destroy too much property") and went back to the armored car. D Company was in the lead, with E second and Headquarters in the rear. F Company planned to come in from the left flank.

I shook and sweated every inch of the way. When we dismounted near the armored car and moved up, I took good care to go quickly from cover to cover and lie low at the halts. My enthusiasm for the venture was limited.

The Germans opened fire on D Company as soon as it started

down the open road. From the shooting, we could tell that they had moved their outposts to the edge of town, evidently planning to make a battle of it. We hid behind trees and let them shoot.

F Company was late in arriving. The sun went down while we waited. Soon the word came to withdraw. The battalion attack had been called off on account of darkness. With cries of joy, we mounted the tanks and went back to Eindhoven.

Thus ended our rides to Nunen. The communiqués (if they mentioned it at all) probably called it "a reconnaissance in strength." As far as I was concerned, it was a mess. And for my platoon leader, I had only four-letter words.

It was a beautiful day for a drive in the country. The sun was warm, the sky was clear, the air was soft and balmy and yet had the smoky crispness of fall. In the mood for a drive, we piled into a GI truck. Everybody was in good spirits, for we had rested a day or two after Nunen in a field near a hospitable farmhouse where there was lots of fresh fruit and milk. Wiseman and Randleman had both returned to the platoon. Cut off from the rest of us, they had hidden in the village overnight and listened to the Germans search for them. Randleman, who had bayoneted one of the searchers, left for a rest, but Wiseman was as hale and hearty as ever. Josephson had been evacuated, and Miller was dead. Our squad now numbered ten.

Thinking themselves completely safe, for we had no armored escort and the British were still talking as if the war were almost over, most of the men unbuckled their harnesses, took off their helmets, and threw their weapons on the floor.

Each truck in the 2nd Battalion convoy towed a small open trailer that held half a squad of men. Men from F Company began to get into ours. I smiled when I saw their noncom, Mather, my first squad leader in the army. One of the bravest men in F Company, Mather, the skinny, fiery redhead, had helped rally the company when the SS counterattacked outside Carentan and his captain had cowered in his hole and refused to fight. The captain, who was always going back to battalion "to check up" whenever his men went into the attack, was later transferred in grade to regimental special services officer and thus assured of living through the war, while Mather, who was outspoken and fiercely independent, remained a squad leader. As I watched his men get into the trailer, I looked for a familiar face, because this was my old squad, the one in which I had spent my first eighteen months in the army. All the familiar faces were gone.

"How's it going?" I asked Mather.

"Can't complain," he said. "A goddamn ball so far."

"How's Vogel?"

"Fine." Mather jumped into the trailer, and the convoy moved off. Our destination was said to be a village far to the north, near the Neder Rhine, where we were supposed to set up a holding position. The convoy turned onto the main road from Eindhoven, and we settled down to enjoy the scenery in comfort.

"This is a wonderful country, isn't it?" I remarked to Wiseman. "Look at those windmills! Just like in the geography books, aren't they?"

"Sure are."

"The villages are just the way I thought they'd be, and so are the canals and roads and meadows. I love Holland."

"Everybody wears wooden shoes," Pace added.

"Certainly is different from Normandy," Hoobler said, joining the conversation. He hallooed to a couple of civilians who were waving at the convoy. "Those people had no use for us, did they Web?"

"They seemed to hate us. Nobody in Normandy ever volunteered to help us or fight with us. These Dutch are different. They're fine, intelligent people. I understand a couple of Dutchmen have joined the company as volunteers."

"That's what I hear," Rader said.

The talk died out as we passed through another village. The villages are pure Vermeer, I thought. We passed several roadside inns with Oranje Bier signs out front and graveled play gardens for the children alongside and overtook mile after mile of British artillery units. At one place where we stopped for a short break, we met the 1st Airborne Division's rear echelon.

"Where are you headed for?" I inquired.

"Arnhem, mate."

"How's it going up there?" We had had no news since our landing.

"Sticky. The lads are having a rough go of it."

Hogwash, I said to myself. Now they're talking like Americans.

Every GI you meet says his company's been wiped out, it's had the heaviest casualties in the division, there are only three old men left, etc.

We wished the 1st Airborne luck and climbed back onto our truck. The British were brewing tea in the ditch beside their high, boxy trucks. Everything seemed so peaceful and bucolic that it was hard to believe that there was a war on and that anybody was having it rough.

Back on the highway that we had marched down almost a week before, we crossed the Wilhelmina Canal at Zon on a Bailey bridge guarded by British 40mm ackack, went through the village, which had become a headquarters of some sort, and into the pine forest to the north. A few gliders lay scattered about the jump field on the other side like relics of days long dead, but all the parachutes had been picked up. Several hundred prisoners stood in long overcoats in a barbed-wire enclosure on the field. We shouted and cursed at them.

The convoy turned right at the tiny crossroads village of St. Odenrode, bounced over a railroad track, and proceeded six or seven miles to a place called Veghel. We slowed down on a curving road in the center of town and stopped bumper-to-bumper. A few men got up and stretched their arms and legs.

Bzzyoo . . . Bam! A high-velocity shell whipped over our heads like an angry giant bee and exploded against a house at the end of the street.

"88s!" an officer cried. "Everybody off!"

Abandoning weapons, gear, and all self-control, the passengers leaped from the trucks in a wild panic. I knew that we were in for trouble, so I took good care to leave with my rifle in one hand and a box of machine-gun ammunition in the other. I lay down in the gutter. The truck drivers and most of the other men disappeared among the houses.

Only Mather acted like a soldier. Standing livid in his trailer and shaking his rifle at his running men, he shouted for them to come back.

"Goddamn you guys!" he bellowed. "You call yourselves soldiers! Get your goddamn ammo! Get your goddamn guns, you sons of bitches!" His men turned and came back sheepishly. Others followed them to other trucks and trailers. Mather threw gear at his squad with a steady stream of curses.

I smiled at him from the cover of the gutter, where I lay full-length, between the high curb and the thick truck wheels. Mather was the finest squad leader I had ever had.

"Soldiers!" he exclaimed, clearing the last cartridge belt from the trailer and looking down at me. "Jesus Christ."

I laughed. "Looks like we're in for it now," I remarked.

"You said it."

He gathered his men and marched them back to where his platoon was forming. An excited soldier with the white diamond of the 501 on the side of his helmet trotted down the sidewalk.

"What's going on?" I asked, standing up.

"Kraut tanks," he said. He pointed to the head of our convoy. "They're coming in, right on the road there. Jesus, we only got one battalion in town. Our flanks are wide open. Where's your battalion commander?"

"In the rear." I jerked my head. "Name's Colonel Strayer."

He ran away.

Another shell passed overhead and burst out of sight. Officers appeared and began organizing their men. Our company having been cut in half, with Company Headquarters missing somewhere north of town, we were in reserve. D Company went south toward a canal at the edge of the village, while F Company started north, where the tanks were. The British set up 40mm antiaircraft to fire down the side streets.

We drifted off the main road, which had become the center of enemy attention, and stopped in an alley beside a British truck parked near a wall. Squatted on the sidewalk, the driver was calmly brewing tea in a German mess cup as the shells zipped by.

"Hello, mates," he said cheerfully. "Teatime. Getting rather warm here, don't you think?" He stirred his brew.

While Pace and Wiseman distracted him with idle chatter, Hoobler and I moved to the rear of the truck, where we had noticed some loose rations lying handy. We lifted several cans of plums and stew and stuffed them into our musette bags.

"Wonder what's going on?" I said, returning to the tea party.

"Does anybody know?" Wiseman replied.

"If they do, it'll be the first time," Hoobler added.

"Boost me on top of that wall," I said. "Maybe I can see something from there."

Wiseman and Hoobler lifted me up. All I could see was alleys and backyards, with nobody in sight. I wondered where the Germans were.

"See anything up there, Webster?" a new voice inquired. I turned and saw Lieutenant McFadden, my former platoon leader and now commander of F Company. A small, genial, sensible person, he appeared to be as baffled as we were by our truckride's startling end.

"No, sir," I said. "I can't see a goddamn thing."

He went away, and Lieutenant Brownlow came and shifted us deeper in town. After passing a row of dismantled 155s on trailers and a Piat antitank gun crew hidden in a small round, roofed bandstand in the middle of the village square, where several roads came together, we stopped in front of the village hall. Pace and I went inside for a personal tour, but since there was no food or drink, we sat down in a hallway and dozed. I woke up with Rader shouting at me.

"Where the goddamn hell have you been?" he asked. "We're moving out. Been looking all over for you."

"I've been right here all the time."

"This is no place to be. The squad's been outside."

We went back up the street and stopped behind some houses near our trucks, which were still parked bumper to bumper. Nothing happened, so Wiseman and I inspected the kitchens of the nearest houses. Finding them bare, we rejoined the squad, where Hoobler was needling Rice, who, as always, had begun to dig in.

"Digging to China, Rice?" Hoobler inquired, laughing.

"You go to hell, boy."

Rice turned his back, and Hoobler whistled like an incoming shell. Rice threw himself flat.

"Ha, ha, ha! Sure sucked you in on that one."

"Goddamn you, Hoobler, that's hard on a man. It's nothing to laugh at."

"Ha, ha, ha!"

Bzzyoo! A real 88 came in. We dived at the ground. Hoobler stopped laughing. The 88 burst on the main street.

Going to an arched brick passageway that led from the backyard to the road to see what was going on, I found D Company halted on the sidewalks. Sanders, an Aldbourne acquaintance, asked if I had any spare M-1 ammunition.

"I'm fresh out," he explained. "We just caught a bunch of Krauts milling around near the canal and shot hell out of them."

"Wait a minute," I said. "I gave a bandolier to another guy who has enough already. I'll get it off him. Be back in a jiffy."

I ran through the brick tunnel toward a large air-raid shelter in a field behind the next house where Matthews, who had my bandolier, and the rest of the first squad had taken cover, along with thirty or forty weeping civilians. I recovered the bandolier and started back.

An 88 shell came in so close I didn't hear it until it was right alongside. I threw myself flat. Blang! The shell hit a wall fifteen feet away, showering me with fragments of brick and mortar. Choking on the smoke and dust, I got up with my ears ringing and returned to the air-raid shelter. Another shell passed by, and then a barrage landed on the main road, where D Company had stopped. I did not return there with the bandolier.

The first squad had crowded so fully into the little space left by the civilians in the shelter that I was forced to wait out the barrage half in the entrance, not fully protected. The civilians were unnerving. Clutching their children as the shells bammed into their neat homes, they wept and wailed, shrieked and moaned, and sang dismal old Dutch hymns. Some of them knelt and prayed aloud, as if the world were coming to an end.

As far as we were concerned, they had no perspective. This was the safest place in town. Four or five feet deep and with a roof of logs and sod almost as thick, it could have withstood a direct hit from an 88—which was more than we could say for most of the houses. I found the atmosphere so depressing, however, and felt so guilty about bringing this on the little children that I left in the first lull.

Lieutenant Brownlow was trying to restore order in the backyards. No one had been hit so far, and we were all in excellent spirits except Whitesill, who had turned apathetic. Pace thought it was a lark, and Hoobler made a joke out of every shell that went by.

Morning passed into afternoon, with the road cut at both ends of town and no relief in sight. At one or two o'clock, almost a dozen RAF Typhoon fighter-bombers appeared overhead. We waved and shouted as they circled above the Germans through puffs of light flak. One by one, they peeled off and screamed down. They released the rockets under their wings at a target a thousand yards north of us. There was a wonderful sound of continuous booming. Several fires started to burn, and we hoped, when the Typhoons had gone away, that they had put an end to the shelling. But it soon came back as strong as ever.

We moved to an orchard by a crossroads on the northern outskirts of town and started to dig in as fast as possible. This was the front-line reserve position. The orchard was bounded by dirt roads on the west and north, the main highway on the east, and a cobblestone road on the south, where several houses were occupied by Battalion Headquarters and the aid station.

The soil was light and sandy, though occasionally laced with roots, and digging together, one at each end, Wiseman and I went down to water level in about ten minutes. Our slit trench—for we never dug one-man foxholes—was two feet wide, six feet long, and four and a half feet deep.

And none too soon.

Bzzyoo . . . Bzzyoo . . . Bzzyoo . . . Bam-bam-bam!

"Jesus Christ!" I exclaimed, jumping into the hole. "They've seen us." The shells had landed on the cobblestone road.

"Sons of bitches," Wiseman muttered.

We looked up and grinned at each other.

"Here they come again!"

Sitting in an inch of water, I closed my eyes, gritted my teeth, held my breath, and clutched my elbows with my arms around my knees. Three more shells came in, low and angry, and burst in the orchard.

"They're walking 'em towards us," I whispered. I felt as if a giant with exploding iron fingers were looking for me, tearing up the ground as he came. I wanted to strike at him, to kill him, to stop him before he ripped into me, but I could do nothing. Sit and take it, sit and take it. The giant raked the orchard and tore up the roads and stumbled toward us in a terrible blind wrath as we sat in our hole with our heads between our legs and curses on our lips.

"I never felt so helpless before," I confided to Wiseman in a dry whisper an hour after the shelling started. "I'd give a foot to get out of here."

Bzzyoo . . . Bzzyoo . . . Bzzyoo . . . Bam-bam-bam!

Three pounds of TNT. A muzzle velocity higher than a rifle bullet. Hundreds of pieces of jagged, red-hot metal. Black clouds of smoke. 88s. Death.

Three more came in. The Germans were firing in battery, probably from tanks or SPs. The last shell was so close that it clanged when it exploded. Three more arrived. The ground quaked, and a rancid black thundercloud curled down into our hole, making us cough and choke. An ugly chunk of hot steel an inch square plunked into Wiseman's lap. He grinned.

"Close," I whispered. "They're traversing the orchard." I felt as if the giant were near enough to hear me, and I was afraid to raise my voice for fear it would draw him to us.

Three and then three and then three.

No wonder men went crazy in a shelling. It was the worst experience on earth. You could fight a tank and shoot back at an airplane and meet a man on equal terms, but there was nothing you could do about artillery. The Germans called it the whispering death.

A man moaned in the southeast corner of the orchard. "Medic," he called plaintively. "Somebody get a medic. Somebody help me. God, oh God, I can't stand it."

The next three shells came in so fast that their zipping sound was intermingled with the explosions. The giant grabbed our hole and shook it back and forth. I dissolved and waited to die. Each salvo had come closer. This was the closest of all. One of the shells had hit a tin shed ten feet away. The next three would bracket us.

"They got the 3rd Bat," someone shouted. "They killed those 3rd Bat sergeants."

"Now it's us," I whispered.

Wiseman shook his head.

The next three passed overhead and hit the crossroads fifty yards behind us.

"Whew," I said, smiling. "Thank God that's over. Now it's Strayer's turn."

"He can have it," Wiseman grinned. We stood up and looked out. The trees around us were chopped by shell fragments, and the ground was littered with torn branches and frayed leaves. Black craters dotted the earth. Other men rose from their holes and greeted one another.

While we watched amazed, two Sherman tanks waddled out of town on the main road and stopped beside the orchard. We cursed them, because we were afraid they would attract more artillery fire, but not a shell came in.

Toward the end of the afternoon, in another lull, Rader announced that our British rations, which were not designed for an individual but for a group of men, were available for supper.

"Come and get 'em!" Hoobler cried, standing near Rader.

"The hell I will," I answered. "Throw mine to me here."

Lyall, Massaconi, and several others sauntered over to eat above ground with the noncoms. Wiseman joined them. I stayed in my hole.

"It's all over, Web," Hoobler chortled. "Come on out! You're safe." The others laughed.

"Goddamn Webster's got hole-itis," Rader remarked.

Three 88s came in from the north and burst in the orchard. Six men tumbled into Rader's hole. Wiseman landed on my feet in a high dive. I glanced over the crumbling, sandy parapet. Not a person was in sight.

"What did you say, Hoobler?" I called.

"Fuck you."

"Ha, ha, ha!"

The shelling commenced as heavy as before. Wiseman shared his can of beef with me.

At twilight, Talbert, our platoon sergeant, began shouting in alarm. "Out of your holes, men!" he cried as the shells died down again. "We have to go help F Company. Krauts have broken through, outposts driven in. Bring all your ammo. Let's go!"

Well, I thought, climbing slowly out of the slit trench, the shells will catch us above ground now. But if you have to go, you have to go. F Company's in trouble, and we have to help them. We're in reserve, so we have to go. And if we're shelled, we're shelled. There is absolutely nothing we can do about it.

I followed the other men to the north end of the orchard, where we gathered around Talbert and Lieutenant Brownlow and waited. Lyall and some of the other replacements who had never seen a fresh dead man before drifted off to the left to inspect the shredded remains of two sergeants from G Company who had just begun to dig in when a shell landed between them. One of the officers did not consider the sight of positive value, and so he drove them away and forbade anyone else to go there. Finally we got moving.

The dusk was ominously silent. Tensed for the first shells, we edged down a dirt road to the left into a thick forest where F Company was standing in a deep, grassy ditch lined with tall poplar trees. Many of the tree trunks had been chopped by shell fragments. A 57mm antitank cannon was emplaced between two small, half-timbered houses. The men at the gun and in the ditch had a hard, sweating, detached look in their eyes and no words for anybody. All of them stared straight ahead at a narrow field of high, light-green grass and a lush forest fifty yards beyond where the enemy lay.

We passed along the whole company and their unprotected left flank and learned that the outposts had withdrawn of their own accord and that a number of men had been killed by German tanks, including an old E Company man, Lieutenant Smits, a breezy, popular officer from California. The second platoon's noisy Farley, however, had stopped a medium tank with a bazooka on the main road at a distance of less than a hundred feet.

Winding around to the left, we came out on the cobblestone road behind the orchard. Wiley, the big cook, lay dead beside a shell hole in the road, his body sprinkled with rubble and torn leaves. The body of another man was sprawled facedown nearby. We returned to our holes as darkness set in and the evening's shells began to arrive.

I was glad that we had gone to the MLR. The walk had relieved the tension inside me, and the sight of F Company holding firm had been immensely reassuring.

The air turned cold, and a light rain began to fall. Wiseman and I took our raincoats out of our musette bags and put them on and settled down for the night, each of us sitting in one end of the trench with his head on his knees. Our boots were wet through, and the rain and dirt kept trickling down our necks. We were so cold and miserable that we couldn't sleep, but as I remarked to Wiseman, we could thank God for one thing.

"What's that?" he inquired sleepily.

"We're in reserve."

"Why are you digging so deep?" a Company Headquarters man inquired.

"Because I just came up from Veghel," I replied.

"Oh?"

The stranger went away and began to expand his own hole, which was about six inches deep, while Janovek and I dug down and down and down. When we were almost five feet below ground, we widened the trench so that we could lie side by side on the bottom. We got straw from a haystack on the outskirts of town and put it on the floor as a mattress, then laid logs, branches, brush, and sod on top. The Company Headquarters men, who had gotten through to Uden after the Germans attacked Veghel, couldn't understand why everybody else dug so deep. There had been no shelling in Uden.

When our hole was completed, we lay down for a nap. Crumbling sand dripped on us as the walls gradually dried, and a light rain came in the open end, but we were mightily pleased with our new home.

"Webster," Lieutenant Brownlow called down just as I was falling asleep, "get up and come with me."

"Yessir."

I followed him through the apple orchard where D and E companies had dug in east of Uden and along a lane from the orchard to the Eindhoven-Arnhem highway. A large farmhouse and its outbuildings stood on one side of the lane and a thick hedge on the other. In the holiday spirit of men in reserve, a squad of riflemen passed us with helmets in their hands, on their way to a pump farther down the lane that was our sole source of water. The pump squeaked and hissed and gurgled as a man from D Company worked its long, curved handle.

Lieutenant Brownlow turned left and, with his farmer's stride, swung down the highway past a line of British tanks and armored cars parked at the curb. He went into a three-story house on the village square, led me upstairs, and stopped in the second-floor hall. This was sacred territory—the officers' billets—and feeling rather like a slum child in the Waldorf Astoria, I looked around in envy, for their beds, blankets, sheets, and hot and cold running water were beyond anything I could ever hope to achieve. My hole, which I had thought so splendid, paled by comparison.

Turning to me with the look of a timid, overconscientious man trying to be firm and decisive, the lieutenant pointed to a broom resting against one wall. "Sweep it out," he said.

"Yessir," I replied. Boiling mad at my new role of scullery maid,

I took the broom and flailed it against the floor to work off my anger. Officers! I thought. How I love them.

I will be a scout and go ahead and on flank guard and run across the open fields with no cover, because these things are expected of any soldier. I will salute when I have to and stand at attention and say "Yessir" no matter how wrong the officer may be, because that, too, is the army and we all have to be disciplined, for without discipline, you cannot fight.

But when an officer who is sleeping indoors between sheets gets me out of a hole in the ground to sweep his house—well, that's asking too much. The officers ate on tablecloths and with waiters and a wine list on the troopship when we came overseas, then went below to our tiny, sweaty, steerage mess hall and stood over us, shouting: "Hurry up, men, hurry up! There's another company waiting to get in." I didn't like that either.

Nor did I like their seizing the Blue Boar, the best pub in Aldbourne, and making it off limits to their own enlisted men, while allowing all others to come in. That was a rotten, unfair abuse of their rank and privileges. They got away with it, because who were we? We had no rights and no way to protest. They said they were right and we were wrong, and that was that.

Yes, I will endure all the necessary miseries of a world at war, but why do they have to aggravate them by demeaning a man? Aren't they happy with their jump pay? They get a lot more money than we do simply because they are officers and for no other reason. Their risk is no greater than ours, and many of the sergeants are better jumpmasters.

How could anybody be an enlisted man in the Regular Army and put up with this crap for thirty years? Only a bum, a broken man, could do it. I would sooner starve to death in civilian life than be an enlisted man in the Regular Army. And once I am out, as long as I live, I will never "sir" another man again.

These things I kept to myself, of course, for Brownlow had me, and besides, I was young and cowed by rank and never sufficiently self-confident to be outspoken with officers. A real man like Wiseman or Wilson, the Oregon lumberjack in F Company, or Barnson, the wild and woolly scarfaced Swede who had been transferred from F Company after he threw down his rifle in a company formation at Fort Bragg and told off his platoon leader—these men would have told Brownlow where to put his broom. They would have been thrown out of the company the next day, but at least they would still have their self-respect.

They were men. I was a boy still. Brownlow sensed it and knew that I wouldn't have the courage to rebel against him. Brooding on these things, I grew more and more angry. As he stood over me and picked and nagged while I banged around in fury, I consoled myself by remembering what he was like in action and thinking that I was better. You could forgive almost anything of an officer who was good in action. If he wasn't good there, then he wasn't good anywhere.

I returned to the orchard in a violent sulk, washed my face in the pump's icy water, and filled my helmet for shaving. After proclaiming the great injustices that I had suffered to a grinning group of men cleaning the machine gun, I shaved and went back into Uden to be by myself for a few minutes.

Saluting all the officers that I met (and goddamning every one of them, for I had soured on the lot), I strolled through the streets until I came to a bar. I went in and found a number of British soldiers seated quietly at little round tables, drinking watery wartime beer. The room was as neat and clean and warm as a Vermeer kitchen. It took me away from the army to the Europe I had always wanted to see, the Old Country of peacetime. Glad to be a whole man again, alone and on my own, I ordered a beer and sat down at an empty table. The word had come to us that we could now write home and say where we were, so I took a pencil stub from my pocket and a sheet of V-mail and wrote a letter.

The road south was open again, and the mail was going through. With luck, my letter would arrive home in a week or two. V-mail, which was first censored, then microfilmed and flown to the States, where it was enlarged and put in the mails, was remarkably fast. Next to the pocket-size Armed Forces Editions of a wonderful array of books, V-mail was our greatest blessing.

I lingered in the bar till twilight, then strolled back to the orchard for supper, which the cooks, who had just caught up with us, prepared from British rations, stray cows, and other gleanings of the countryside. Then I decided to take a shower.

The night was clear and frosty, the stars very low and winter-bright. Standing naked by the pump while another man worked the handle, I soaped myself off and rinsed the goose pimples. I had not washed all over for about ten days, and the feeling of cleanliness was like a rebirth.

Murmurs of men in their holes in the orchard and in the farmhouse reached me as I went back up the lane, breathing deeply and relaxed and smiling inside. Looking up at the stars and thinking of the men around me who made up the regiment, I gave thanks that I was young and alive outdoors in a fine country with an outfit that I liked. The Brownlows, actually, were few and far between. For this I was also grateful.

"Hit it, hit it!" Rader cried. "Hubba, hubba. Put on all your gear and fall out on the double! We have to go down to Best and help the Deuce. Krauts have broken through."

Enraged at the sudden awakening, for I had been asleep only two hours, having returned from patrol at about 1 A.M., I decided to express my indignation with tardiness, which I knew was more irritating to Rader and Brownlow than anything else I could do. I dressed slowly and climbed out of my hole to put on my boots.

Everybody else had gone. Jerking the laces tight, I slipped under my harness and ran after the platoon, which had lined up in the lane.

"Always late," Rader commented. "Goddamn it, Webster, when are you going to be on time?"

"When this freaking outfit does something sensible."

"You'll never see the day," Pace said.

I laughed.

"Moving out!" Lieutenant Brownlow yelled. "Let's go."

Nobody was very happy about it. Bleary and disgruntled, the whole company muttered and shuffled through the darkness. Best was, we knew, fifteen or twenty miles to the southwest. We could expect a long hike.

The column stopped and started, waited ten or fifteen minutes, and finally worked into position with the rest of the battalion. A number of men were smoking and lighting cigarettes. Nobody made any effort to put them out. We began our march, then stopped again near the British tank on the outskirts of town. The peculiar throbbing of German airplane motors came in low from the north. The plane's machine guns opened fire as it passed overhead, a strange black shape soon lost in the night.

"Put out those goddamn cigarettes!" an officer cried. The smoking ceased, and the line began to move again like an unfolding accordion, as each man passed the word back to observe a five-yard interval. There were no tanks with us this time, for the British had drawn most of them north in a violent effort to break through to the paratroopers trapped in Arnhem.

A flare burst low in the east a couple of miles away, and an enemy machine gun fired a long string of tracers under it parallel to our course. A drum barrage rolled and thundered miles off in the west. The shells lit the horizon with quick white flashes. Their explosions came to us faintly fifteen or twenty seconds later. A battle was in progress in the direction we were going, and we did not look forward to joining it.

The pace was so fast, however, that we had little energy for forebodings. We kept changing off on the machine gun, each man carrying it twenty minutes on his shoulder, then passing it to the man behind him, and we were so burdened with boxes of ammunition that we were very tired by the time we reached Veghel.

In the bitter, frosty cold of first light, the village looked like a Kerr Eby lithograph of First World War ruins. Many of the houses had been shelled and gutted. Mortars had blown the tiles and lathing off many roofs, and 88s had punched holes in the walls. The trees were torn, the windows smashed, telephone wires dangled from their posts. Now occupied by the 327th Glider Infantry Regiment, which had landed by air the day after we had jumped, Veghel had apparently been considered a key position, with bridges over a creek and a small canal and many roads coming together. The Germans had attacked it three or four times in an effort to keep supplies and reinforcements from reaching the 82nd Airborne Division in Nijmegen and the British 1st at Arnhem. The attacks had been partially successful: Blacker and blacker news reached us of the British 1st being ground to bloody rags by the German panzers.

Five or six miles south of Veghel, when we were down to ten minutes apiece on the machine gun, we passed through the village of St. Odenrode, where the Germans had also once cut the road. Several houses were smashed, and there was a dead British dispatch rider lying by the road in his leather gauntlets, knee-length boots, and round helmet.

The box of ammunition that I was carrying was digging into my hand. Company Headquarters had a car, I noticed, but they were too busy saving their own shoe leather to make room for others' necessities.

"Why don't we get a horse and wagon for this stuff?" I said to Rader. The subject had been mentioned before, but I never wearied of discussing it.

"Brownlow won't allow us to."

"God . . ."

"You know Brownlow."

"Boy, do I know Brownlow." I shifted the box to the other hand.

The head of the column left the road and took off cross-country. In spite of the chill in the air, my underclothing was soaking wet and my feet, swollen and throbbing, were burning hot. Finally the order came to take a break. We fell out on the grass.

"Want some milk, Web?" Wiseman asked, nodding at a cow grazing nearby.

"I sure do."

"Let's go."

Tearing up handfuls of grass to feed her, we went to the cow and patted her and made our offering of food. As soon as she began to eat, Wiseman, who had done this many times before, squatted by her udder while I held my canteen cup below the chosen teats. An expert milkman, he filled the cup quickly. We stopped work and drank it down. The milk was warm and wonderfully rich and creamy. I had never tasted anything like it before I had come to Holland. Wiseman started to drain off another cupful.

"Let's go!" Rader cried. "Moving out."

We left the cow and continued west across slightly rolling land of poor farms, wild heath, and small pine forests. After several hours, we stopped by one of these farms and had lunch. Wiseman and I beat the others through the kitchen door and quickly found a can of milk and a cheese large enough for the whole squad. The house was bare and clean but, like all the other farms we had been in, alive with biting black flies that took the edge off the neatness. A further search outdoors uncovered half a dozen eggs in the dirty hay of an empty chicken coop. Delighted with our success, we built a fire in the backyard and scrambled the eggs in an iron skillet borrowed from the kitchen. We cleaned the skillet with sand and water when we were through and put it back in the kitchen. There was no sign of the owners anywhere.

Well, I thought, as we set off again, in better spirits, if the Deuce was in trouble when they called for help this morning, they'll be wiped out by the time we get there. I frankly did not look forward to Best. Meandering around the countryside was far more pleasant than fighting.

Mounting a small rise, we came upon a British infantry outfit dug into the westward slope. A company of the Queen's Own Guards Regiment, they were the neatest soldiers I had ever seen in action. Crouching in holes as square and precise as the Germans', they were all clean-shaven and in regulation uniform, with their helmets squarely on their heads. We knew that the Guards' units were the best in the British army — every man had to be at least six feet tall and a superior soldier—but we had never realized how well disciplined they were on the field of battle. By comparison we looked like a rabble in arms, with our beards and muddy uniforms and tattered gear. Our helmets were worn with a jaunty individuality, and most of their tops had been blackened by cooking and shaving fires, for the helmet served as an all-purpose iron pot. The Guards, who eyed us with the air of men studying a strange apparition, were, we noticed, on the alert and well down in their holes.

"What's up?" somebody asked them.

"Jerry tanks," an Englishman replied. He pointed west. "In the low ground."

The slightest elevation in a land as flat as Holland gave one command of a huge sweep of countryside. From here, at the crest of a sandy, gentle ridge, we could gaze west at least ten miles. I squinted down the slope at the meadows and patches of woods and saw no German tanks. That did not reassure me, for I knew the English did not lie like American soldiers. Everything was so still, and the Guards, who had been in action since Normandy and who yet looked as if they had just marched out of the sentry box at St. James's Palace, were so tense and ready that I was glad when the order came to get going again.

Heading north on a sandy road that ran along the top of the ridge, we heard the rumble of artillery ahead. The light chatter about the Queen's Own died out. We entered a forest of the tallest pine trees we had seen so far. The slamming of many heavy doors came to us from the other side of the forest, where the 502 was fighting for Best. The artillery accentuated the stillness of the woods: We seemed to be moving through silent sleep to a nightmare.

A parachute was dangling from a tall pine fifty yards beyond the road. Two dead men from the 501 lay nearby. Farther along, brightly colored plastic communications wire led to the scattered trenches of an abandoned German position. The artillery fire increased, and a sound of small arms mingled with the booming.

I unslung my rifle and made sure that it was loaded. We emerged from the forest into lush meadowland. An 88 shell passed over, making us duck low as we filed into a deep ditch lined with huge old trees. The high steeple of a very old church stared down at us a quarter of a mile away. I wondered who was using it for observation. We crowded together and began to dig in. The order came to move to another place. Only Rice dug in there. With the dry rustling of many leaves, our own artillery passed overhead, crashing to earth out of sight. The 88 fired again, lower than before: one, two, three. The shells burst in the battalion area and killed several men in the mortar platoon of Headquarters Company, but nobody in E Company was hurt. The heavy tooming of a 50 caliber machine gun answered a crackle of German fire. A lone sniper began to shoot into the meadow.

After we had lain in fear and ignorance for at least thirty minutes, Sergeant Talbert came down the ditch from Company Headquarters and told us that it was a false alarm. "The Deuce has everything under control," he said. "They don't need us after all."

"Thank God," I murmured.

"On your feet, men!" he shouted. "We're going back to Uden."

We stood up in full view of the steeple and filed slowly out of the ditch to a road through the forest behind us. This led in turn four or five miles to the Eindhoven-Arnhem highway.

By now it was late afternoon. We had been on our feet almost continuously for twelve hours, and our feet hurt. Men who had once gone twenty minutes on the machine gun were down to two or three. Their griping warmed the air. Even Rice, who had tied his bootlaces tightly about his ankles so he wouldn't feel the pain as he carried a machine gun for F Company on the march from Toccoa to Atlanta, complained about the soreness and stiffness in his feet, ankles, and the calves of his legs. Thoroughly irritated, I finally wearied altogether of carrying my box of ammunition about the time we passed back by the dead motorcyclist in St. Odenrode.

"Jesus Christ," I said to Rader, "why don't we give this goddamn ammo to Company Headquarters? They have a car."

"You know why."

"I jumped with this goddamn thing, and I've been stuck with it ever since."

"Tough."

"Let's get a goddamn car somewhere and use that."

"Can't. Brownlow's orders."

"I'm not going to carry this thing much longer."

"Hell, throw it away! We have plenty more."

"Throw away ammunition?"

"Sure, we'll never miss it."

"OK." I swung my arm back in an arc and let the box fly. It landed with a thud on the grass.

Lieutenant Brownlow ran up. Afraid that he was going to make me fetch the ammunition, I tensed inside and gritted my teeth, but he passed me by, for he was interested only in a passing British truck. Part of a convoy that was also going north, it bore on its tailgate several men from the third platoon.

"Off that truck!" Brownlow shouted. "Get back in line, all of you!"

The men jumped down and waited for their platoon to come up, while Brownlow upbraided them. "If men are going to fall out now, what will you do when we go to combat again?"

They shrugged their shoulders and scowled at him without bothering to reply.

Colonel Sink was waiting for us on the edge of Uden. As we limped by, he mounted his jeep with his back to the setting sun and welcomed us home.

"Do your feet hurt, men?" he called when we were even with him. "Do your feet hurt?"

Did my feet hurt! I wanted to throw my rifle at him, for the first time in two years.

Yesterday was quite a day, I mused as I hurried back from the medics: I caught diarrhea and voted for Roosevelt.

Now I was bound for the barn on the west side of Uden where we had moved from an outpost in the north several days after returning from Best. The ballot had gone on its way to the States, but I still had the diarrhea, which made me hurry even more.

The first platoon had taken over a large barn and made itself at home in the hay. Supposed to be on the MLR, we had posted a couple of men on twenty-four-hour guard in the field behind us while we slept on soft hay in thin, one-man sleeping bags that had caught up with us with the last of the regiment's rear echelon. It was our most comfortable position in Holland.

But I couldn't enjoy it, because I had the worst diarrhea I had ever caught in the army. I couldn't lie still for more than twenty minutes. Cramped and irritable, I had spent most of the day and night running back and forth to the slit-trench latrine behind the barn, with time out for a mile walk to the medics and a dose of sulfa pills.

It was all the cooks' fault, I mused as I came in sight of our quarters. The bastards were always dirty. They kill a cow and butcher it and boil it hard in pasty gravy and call it beef stew. It almost broke my teeth, but the stew wasn't to blame—it was the washwater afterward. Vile as the British seamen on the *Samaria,* who had set out cold pans of salt water for us to wash our mess kits in, they gave us a single garbage can of soapy water as a battalion rinse. By the time I got to it, the scum was an inch thick on top. The grease clung to my pan, breeding germs, and gave me diarrhea at the next meal. I had spent last night on the run, unable to enjoy the comforts of my sleeping bag.

Well, anyway I had voted. That made me happy. I had to walk almost two miles to cast my ballot, but I would have walked ten, if necessary, because this was my first vote—I had turned twenty-two in June—and I had always wanted to cast it for Roosevelt, the greatest president we had ever had and the only one who ever gave the working man a break.

"Now where?" I muttered as we marched toward a convoy of GI trucks. The diarrhea was still bothering me.

Incredibly garbled in transit, the word had finally reached us that the British had lost the battle for Arnhem. Montgomery's great gamble to flank the Siegfried Line with the 1st Allied Airborne Army and turn the armor loose in the plains of west Germany had failed. It was not, we were sure, through any lack of courage or determination on the part of the paratroopers, but through the slow ineptness of their countrymen in tanks. A good American armored

unit like the 2nd Armored Division, which had helped us in Normandy without any tender regard for property, ammunition, or
orders from the rear, would have broken through to the 1st Airborne Division. If General Patton had been in charge of the effort,
the whole British 2nd Army would have gone through Arnhem and
far beyond.

But the gamble had failed, and so we were trying to hold what
little had been gained by the 82nd and 101st. While the British infantry took over our old area and widened the scattered footholds
into a broad corridor north to the Lower Rhine, the 82nd would
remain on the defensive around Nijmegen and the 101st would dig
in along the river, west of Arnhem. It sounded quite placid, but
skeptical as ever, I took a seat near the tailgate and kept my helmet
on and my rifle in hand. The trucks moved off.

In half an hour we passed a huge field covered with gliders for
the 82nd Airborne Division, and then came to the Maas River. One
of three tributaries of the Rhine that wound through this part of
Holland within twenty miles of one another, the Maas was spanned
by a long steel bridge similar to the one that the German paratroopers had seized at Moerdyk in the movie we had seen before D-Day.
The road curved up to it on a raised approach that paralleled the
river for several hundred yards. Batteries of 20mm and 40mm antiaircraft were dug in along the embankment to protect the bridge
from German air raids, for the Luftwaffe was very much alive in
this area.

The Maas was wide here, and the bridge was almost half a mile
long, but it had been taken intact by a unit from the 504. It was a
daring task for lightly equipped troops. The 504, however, was
equal to it. For my money, the best regiment in the 82nd, they were
old-timers who had fought in Sicily and Salerno. One battalion had
won a Distinguished Unit Citation on the Anzio beachhead, where
the regiment had spent several months as line infantry. Known to
the press as the Anzio Roughnecks, they looked down on the 506th
as upstarts and referred to us as the Walkie Talkie Regiment. It made
no difference now, when we were together in action, and after they
had missed Normandy, the greatest jump of the war. The 504 preferred not to discuss Normandy.

Polish paratroopers in gray berets were on guard at the Maas-
Waal Canal bridge six or seven miles farther along when we drove

by. Dug in deep on both sides of the small suspension bridge, the Poles, who were great people and splendid soldiers, were protecting the crossing from a raid by German paratroopers. They waved cheerfully as we passed them with shouts of greeting. Most of their unit, we knew, had been dropped near Arnhem on the south side of the Lower Rhine in an effort to reinforce the 1st Airborne. The Poles had been severely mauled on the jump field by waiting Germans.

We went another mile or so and then stopped for a ten-minute break under a row of big trees with thick, spreading branches. To our left, several Typhoons and Spitfires circled and landed at an airport some two thousand yards away.

Bam! A shell burst three hundred feet from us in a field between our convoy and the airport. I leaped off the truck and ran for a farmhouse equidistant in the opposite direction.

Another shell burst fifty yards closer. What a country this is! I thought, hoping to find cover behind the house. British planes take off with Kraut tanks firing right under their nose. I thought the 82nd had settled everything up here. Nobody's safe anymore. The only thing to do is to get hit and be sent back to the hospital in England.

I darted around the corner of the farmhouse and almost stumbled on Johnny Martin, who was relaxing in the sun, with his back to the explosions. "What the hell?" I gaped, thinking I had just broken all records for the hundred-yard dash.

"Been here for hours," he grinned.

The rest of the platoon arrived on the run. A third shell exploded near the trucks.

"All clear!" Hoobler shouted from the road. "Come on back!"

We edged across the field to the convoy and returned to our slatted wooden seats. As the trucks started off, Hoobler explained what had happened.

"Spitfire caught an ME-109," he said. "The Kraut dropped a load of butterfly bombs to try to escape, but the Spitfire got him. One of the bombs wounded a driver. Skinny Sisk tried to talk him into dying." Hoobler laughed.

More at ease, we proceeded north. I continued to sit by the tailgate, however, because you just never knew what was going to happen next.

We halted again in the midst of some plowed fields a mile or two from Nijmegen to allow a long train of refugees to pass by. Several hundred in number, they streamed silently out of the city on foot and in horse-drawn carts piled high with bedding and cooking utensils. Women and children predominated. Nobody waved to us or acted as if they were glad to see us. They passed by in silence instead, with crying children and a dazed, defeated look in their eyes.

Once they had trudged beyond us, we began to move again. We made a sharp right at the edge of the city and drove southeast toward a high, forested ridge. More refugees passed us. We could hear very heavy artillery falling in Nijmegen. After continuing five miles, we turned up the face of the ridge, which rose at least three hundred feet above the polder. A key terrain feature originally assigned to the 82nd, this was the highest ground in all Holland.

We drove into the pine trees and stopped. The trucks took off with a rush as soon as we had dismounted, and our own shells whispered overhead and landed far to the east.

"This is the Reichswald," Lieutenant Brownlow announced. "Germany is only a few hundred yards away." That's nice, I thought, quite content to stay where I was. The hell with Germany.

We spread out in the woods and took over a network of German trenches. An enemy strongpoint seized by the 505 or 508, all the trenches were fresh and intact. There were no bodies lying about, and there was little evidence, other than some chopped trees, of a violent struggle. Wiseman, Janovek, and I staked claim on a comfortable, zigzag trench, five feet deep and eighteen inches wide, that had two zigs and a zag, one for each of us. A thick roof of logs and dirt covered most of the excavation.

"Chow call!" Hoobler cried as we began to prepare our gear for the night. We had been told that we would be in reserve here for about twenty-four hours before going north of Nijmegen to an area between the Waal and the Rhine that was known as "the island."

"Come and get it, goddamn it!" Hoobler yelled.

We scrambled out of the hole and ran to him like a pack of dogs. Every meal was a competition, and we wanted to be in at the start, for they were community affairs, a little of this and a little of that, and God help the hindmost. This was due to the nature of our British rations. We had been living on them all but the first three days, when we ate K rations, and then subsisted on apples, pears, and peaches, civilian handouts, and German rations from an Eindhoven warehouse. These were mostly stone-hard biscuits, tasty canned meat, and little tubes of Limburger cheese.

The British rations were better, but that did not decrease the ill will generated at each meal. Somewhat on the heavy side, the food consisted of cans of sausage meat, beef stew, meat and vegetable stew, beefsteak and kidney stew (my favorite), and a rich fruit pudding. Biscuits and dehydrated tea rounded out the menu. Popular with both British and Americans (who would never admit liking anything English), the tea was an ingenious mixture of dried leaves, concentrated sugar, and powdered milk. A heaping spoonful in half a canteen of boiling water made a sweet, hearty beverage unrivaled in our own larder, which had separate packets of sugar for the coffee and no milk.

Unfortunately, a squad of twelve men had to share the contents of these cans equally. It was never done. After they had been heated in the fire, there was no sitting down with one's own complete meal, as with a K or C ration, but rather a hasty sampling of transient cans, with a taste of this and a dip of that, while eleven other people watched to make sure you didn't take more than your share (which they of course expected to be less than they had taken). I hated these meals in Holland.

I sat down near Hoobler and entered the fray. The talk was combative.

"Pass the stew, Massaconi."

"Come on, Lyall, I haven't had any beef yet."

"Jesus, Pace, are you going to hold on to that can all night?"

"Let's go, Webster, give somebody else a chance."

"Keep that pudding moving, Hoobler. You've had it at least ten minutes."

"Goddamn it, Janovek, you're not going to hog *all* of that, are you?"

Swiftly dipping into whatever I could grab, I kept one eye on the other cans to make sure that I wasn't missing anything. Eternal vigilance was necessary, I had learned one day, after becoming deeply involved in a can of stew only to look up and see Hoobler scraping out the last of the fruit pudding.

The only fair solution, we had discovered, was to find a large can, fill it with a quart or two of water, break all our crackers into it, dump in all the cans of meat, and make a stew for the whole squad. We tried to do this whenever possible, because it gave each man a cupful of stew to enjoy by himself.

After supper, we rinsed our spoons in the tea, wiped our hands on our pants, and strolled twenty yards west to a clearing that afforded a beautiful view of the evening's double feature: German airplanes and Allied ackack.

The Luftwaffe flew in at dusk every day to bomb the Rhine bridges at Nijmegen, and the British and American antiaircraft guns greeted them with cascades of tracer. Viewed from a safe distance, the fireworks display was almost as good as the one I had watched from the swamp behind Utah Beach the night before D-Day.

"Beautiful, isn't it?" Hoobler sighed. He thoroughly enjoyed war.

I nodded. The spectacle surpassed any Fourth of July show I had ever seen on the grounds of the Bronxville High School.

A lone high-velocity shell whipped out of the woods just as darkness fell. Passing close to our heads, it sent us diving for the ground. The shell burst in the 3rd Battalion's bivouac.

"Time for bed," I said, jumping up and trotting to my hole. Everyone but Hoobler ran to his trench. He stayed awake another half hour, drinking in the fireworks and chortling aloud at our sudden sleepiness.

The ride was hurried. At full speed, we hurtled downhill and north to Nijmegen, which was under bombardment from enemy siege guns. Extensively damaged by air raids as well as the 82nd's battle for possession, the city was a deserted mass of rubbly streets and battered buildings. There were no civilians anywhere. The tremendous boom of incoming shells spurred our drivers to faster speeds. In a few minutes, we mounted a rise and came to a giant new high-span steel bridge over the Waal River. The bridge was famous already, the story of its capture having reached us several days before.

We raced across the span at full throttle. A sign at the north end told us that Arnhem was ten miles away.

The light faded from the sky. The air turned cold and thick, with a low, wet mist. Our trucks jogged left, followed the high river bank for a mile or so, and descended into flat orchard country. We were on the island between the Waal and the Lower Rhine, with Germans to the north, east, and west, and the bridge we had crossed was our only link to friendly territory. The island was at war. As we passed through the rich orchards, we saw battery after battery of British field artillery camouflaged with burlap-dotted netting. The slamming of the guns made the wet dusk even more depressing. In a chastened mood, we passed a barbed-wire corral of bedraggled German prisoners without the usual curses and fist-shaking. Janovek complained of stomach cramps. My belly turned cold. The diarrhea stirred again. All of a sudden, the trucks jammed together and stopped.

"Everybody off!" an officer cried. "This is it." I jumped down and stepped over to the shoulder. It was almost dark.

"Third squad over here!" Rader shouted. "Third squad over here!"

I picked up my new box of machine-gun ammunition—throwing away the old one had solved nothing—shivered convulsively with cold and apprehension, and fell in line with the rest of the men. The country was so low that it seemed to be below the level of both rivers. The lowness increased the weight and penetration of the damp cold. I shivered again. Something told me that we were headed for trouble.

Rader spread us out five yards apart, and we started off in silence, the only noise coming from our squishing boot soles and the soft clatter of moving thighs against hanging gear. The night was very dark and oppressive. All the artillery had ceased firing.

We marched north on a narrow blacktop road shining with moisture. A ditch filled with stagnant water stood beside the road with 105 craters in it every few yards. Looking beyond these evil black marks, I saw dimly many wet orchards bearing big ripe apples.

Janovek, who had been muttering somewhere behind me, suddenly cried that he could not go another step. "These damn cramps," he said, falling out of the column. "Medic, medic!" He fell down in a tight, writhing bundle. Someone else yelled for the medic. The column kept moving.

Two British soldiers in fleece-lined leather jerkins met us at the next crossroads to guide us to our new position, which was at the front.

"What's it like up here?" Rader asked.

"It's a bloody rest position, mate."

I winced. He was too cheerful.

On and on we went, thinking that we would march all night, until finally we were the only company left in the 2nd Battalion, the others having disappeared en route. D Company and E Company would be on line, we were informed, while Headquarters and F would be in reserve. After about five miles, we stopped in the cobblestone streets of a village of twenty or thirty small houses strung out in the lee of an immense dike that towered over their roofs.

"This is it, mates," one of the guides announced "The village of Randwijk." A column of British soldiers who had evidently been awaiting our arrival marched past us, picking up our guides as they went by.

"Spooky, isn't it?" Wiseman remarked.

"A ghost town," I nodded, feeling the weight of the dike hanging over on us. "I don't like this place."

"Let's go, you guys. Patrol leaving in ten minutes."

"What!"

"Goddamn it, there's nothing to it. Just walk along the dike and contact the Limeys. Be back."

Rader left the barn where we were billeted, and Wiseman and I rose from our bed of hay beside the stinking pigsty and put on our helmets and boots. We were quite unhappy, for it seemed as if we had marched in and fallen asleep only half an hour before.

I slid a bullet into the chamber of my .45, eased the hammer forward, and dropped the pistol into the right-hand pocket of my combat jacket. After feeling for them in the dark, I crossed a bandolier over my chest and tightened the sling on my M-1.

"Ready?" Wiseman whispered. "Here comes Rader."

Accompanied by Pace, he led us out to the street and explained that E Company had to run a contact patrol every two hours from our village almost a mile east to a British position. "It's a snap," he commented.

"Do you mean to say," I whispered, "that almost a mile of that dike is unprotected?"

"Division's really spread out thin."

"Man, it must be."

"Antiaircraft's got an outpost in a farmhouse halfway. Between them and our patrols, we ought to know pretty quick if any Krauts come through."

"Sure. But I don't want to be the one to find out."

We passed a guard at the end of the village, left the road, and cut through an orchard to our left until we came to the dike.

Immense from the village, it seemed even larger close up. As we hurried along its base, looking for infiltrating Germans in slit trenches that the British had dug into the slope every ten yards, I wondered if anyone were lying on top watching us and waiting to shoot us in the back.

Rader rushed along in such careless, confident haste that I thought he would surely draw fire from a thousand yards away, so still was the night and so loud his footsteps. I kept squinting at the meadows on our right for signs of moving men and up the grassy slope of the dike, which was about thirty feet high, for a German's silhouette.

Lucky Janovek, I thought. He's out of this. I wondered where to escape if we suddenly stumbled upon the enemy. The fields offered no cover, and anybody who ran up the face of the dike was asking for death. Rader hurried on. A cluster of farm buildings loomed dark ahead.

"Halt!"

We stopped. The voice was American. It came from the shadows of the first small outbuilding and bade us advance and be recognized, after Rader gave the password.

We gathered around the guard. A small and rather fearful man who seemed very glad to be able to talk with somebody, he told us that a squad of the 81st Airborne Antiaircraft Battalion was on outpost here. Almost half a mile from the nearest friendly forces, he did not care for the isolated position at all. The reason for the outpost was obvious: It was the most logical place for the enemy to cross the dike and regroup in concealment. We did not envy the men who had to hold the place.

Then we came to another ideal entryway. Dominated by a windmill atop the dike about five hundred yards farther east, it featured a long orchard on the north that led straight to the windmill and another, even larger orchard on the south—and no friendly forces to protect them. All the enemy had to do was cross the flat land from the Lower Rhine, sneak through the trees to the dike, dart over it to the other orchard, and set up an attack at leisure. The windmill would afford observation for miles in all directions. If it was true that the German artillery pounding the island was as strong as we had heard, then they would have no trouble at all building up a strong bridgehead here.

We approached a small barn and farmhouse at the foot of the dike with our rifles ready and tiptoed among the buildings, stopping every few feet to listen for a cough or shuffle or clink of metal, but there were no Germans.

"This is a hell of a setup," I commented to Wiseman after we had left the place behind and had begun to relax. "A mile gap in our line and nobody watching a position like this. If I were the Krauts, I'd come right over here."

"This outfit's crazy," Wiseman agreed.

We strolled a few hundred yards farther to a little village built along a raised road that sloped up to the crest of the dike, and went among the houses without being challenged. A guard finally stopped us near the top of the dike. We asked what was new, and he told us in a Cockney accent that it was bloody restful here. Leaving him, we went up for a look at the no-man's-land that lay between us and the Lower Rhine, almost a mile to the north. Nothing appeared to be stirring. Scattered outposts were supposed to warn of enemy movement from villages across the river, but these outposts had limited vision and were not always reliable.

"Let's take a look around," Wiseman suggested, leading the way to a nearby door. "Isn't this a beer joint?" We entered a small tavern on our left. Carefully blacked out, its taps were dry, its shelves empty.

"Limeys beat us to it," Rader said. "Let's go home."

We went south along the sloping road for a mile or so, bore right on a broad highway, and turned right again after another mile. A four-engine Stirling bomber lay on its belly in a pasture near the last intersection.

"Let's take a look at it," I suggested. "Maybe we can find some souvenirs." What I had in mind was warm gloves or a fleece-lined flying jacket. We walked over to the plane and looked inside, but there was nothing portable.

"Goddamn Limeys beat us to it again," Wiseman muttered. "They sure picked this country clean."

We left the bomber in disgust and went down a side road to our pigsty.

Wiseman and I woke up hungry. In fact, we were always hungry, for neither British nor American combat rations were enough to fill a man. You could subsist on them, to be sure, but you were never full. That's why we were always on the lookout for food. We picked ripe fruit from the trees, milked the cows, and filched whatever victuals the civilians had abandoned in their houses. And now came our greatest opportunity to feast on livestock: The village of Randwijk was fluttering and squealing with homeless ducks, chickens, and suckling pigs, all begging to be roasted, fried, baked, or broiled. We planned a royal feast.

But alas, Rader told us that we couldn't even light a fire, for fear of attracting heavy artillery. Dug in along a chain of wooded hills over a mile away, on the other side of the Rhine, the Germans had the whole island under observation, and although our village was hidden by the dike, the least sign of smoke would have brought a barrage down upon us. So we decided to let the animals live.

Our only alternative was to search the houses. Accordingly, Wiseman and I set off after breakfast with an empty pillowcase and, going from door to door, carefully examined the kitchens, attics, and cellars of places not occupied by soldiers. Nobody interfered with our hunt, for the British, who were administering the area, had moved all the civilians several thousand yards to the rear. A lone young man met us at an intersection, chatted with us briefly in German that sounded more German than Dutch, and strolled off toward the Lower Rhine, leaving us to wonder whether we had been talking to a spy. We didn't let this distraction interfere with our main pursuit, however.

By the time the morning was over, we had filled the pillowcase with a couple of pounds of sugar, some ersatz coffee, and a dozen Mason jars of jam, meat, and preserved fruit. At one house we found a bottle labeled SPIRITS that smelled like pure alcohol to me. I

tried a drink and couldn't talk for five minutes; the liquor burned—
and tasted—like smoke from a tar fire. Wiseman, who was more
durable than I was in many ways, claimed that it was merely a Dutch
version of white lightning and offered to split the jug with me so
that we could both get drunk, but I declined. I wanted to get drunk,
but not that badly.

We returned to the squad when we had run out of kitchens. Then
we moved from the barn to a clean little house nearby, where we
spread our sleeping bags on the tile floor of a half basement and ate
lunch. Keeping the liquor to himself, Wiseman provided milk for
us from a passing cow.

The owner of the house made an appearance. A pale, fragile,
coughing man in his middle thirties, he had gotten permission to
return for some medicine that he kept in a cabinet in his bedroom.
One of our varlets had already broken into the cabinet and scattered
its contents about the floor, like some destructive child in malicious
mischief, but the civilian shrugged it off with a quiet smile, got
what he wanted, and left with our promise to take better care of his
property.

Just when we were lying down for a nap, Rader announced that
his squad had been detailed to bury a horse and a calf whose rotting
carcasses were stinking up the neighborhood. Killed by shellfire,
the bloated animals lay on the grass behind one of the houses. While
we worked all afternoon on this melancholy task, the first squad,
which was ahead of us even on details, quickly buried two or three
goats and a pig and then reclined indoors. Since our orders did not
cover people, no one bothered with the dead civilian lying facedown in his black suit in a puddle beside the road.

Both the village and its surrounding meadows had been the scene
of rather brisk fighting. Other dead animals littered the streets and
yards. Several of the houses, hit by mortars and artillery, had
burned to the ground. There were shellholes and empty ammo
boxes and machine-gun belts everywhere. Having found scattered
German gear in the houses we had visited, we surmised that the
Germans had first held the village and then been driven out by British infantry with tanks, whose tracks twisted through the yards like
sunken roads.

The sun faded into thick mist by the time our burial detail was
over. Offered the choice of guard duty or another contact patrol,

Wiseman and I chose the latter, since neither of us could stand the rigid monotony of guard duty. Rader told us he would wake us at 4 A.M.

The Germans started to bombard a position several miles east of us at sundown. Dusk and dawn were their favorite times of attack, and the steady detonations, which came in at about ten-second intervals, set us on edge, making sleep difficult.

Rader woke us at midnight. "Changed the orders," he said, explaining that the first squad would go out at four. We cursed and grumbled, then left the village. The cannonading had increased in both volume and intensity while we had slept. Now a shell came in every five seconds or so. I remarked to Wiseman that trouble was brewing.

"Those Kraut sons of bitches are up to no good," he agreed.

We hurried through the patrol and found that the 501 had relieved the British in the little village that sloped up to the crest of the dike. They, too, were nervous about the bombardment.

Cold with fear and diarrhea, I returned to our house and fell asleep on the hard tile floor. The German artillery was coming in very fast now—a 105 or 155 shell every second. Evil was afoot.

"The Krauts have broken through! Get up, everybody up!"

I blinked and sat bolt upright.

"Quick! Get ready for a dawn attack!"

I unzipped my sleeping bag, ripped out of it, yanked on my boots, and, grabbing my helmet, rifle, and harness, ran outside with my bootlaces clicking behind me. Men were pouring from all the other houses. A thick fog lay over the land, and the air was damp and cold. The enemy artillery had ceased firing. An ominous silence filled the void.

We assembled behind the house that held the first platoon CP and waited. The initial excitement wore off quickly, and after fifteen minutes, I was thinking that this was just another of Brownlow's false alarms. Always cautious, he loved to prepare us for dawn attacks that never materialized.

The only thing we ever had in common, I thought, watching him move about with a tense, worried look on his face, was diarrhea. We both have that now. I went into the garden, and, like a cat, scraped out a little hole, and squatted over it in pain and aggravation.

The platoon took advantage of Brownlow's diarrhea by drifting silently back into the houses while he was absent on missions of relief. I watched them disappear one by one and then scurried back to my own cellar when he went into the garden again. I had just lain down with some other men when we heard a great commotion in the yard. Brownlow appeared at the head of our basement stairs.

"Get out!" he shrieked. "Goddamn you people, the Krauts have broken through! Everybody outside on the double!"

"Oh, shit," I muttered as I passed him.

"Leave your musette bags here," he said. "We're only going to be gone a couple of hours."

We formed quickly on the road, where we learned that the Germans had come over the dike in the dark and that we were going to cross over to their side and cut them off in the rear while F Company attacked from the south and the second and third platoons held our village. Captain Winters ran up with a group that included Carson, a radioman named Hale, and two volunteers—the second platoon's calm and fearless Sergeant Guarnere, decorated with the Silver Star in Normandy, and the third platoon's medic, Roe, who had a pitted face, dirty hands, and a brave heart.

"Let's go!" the captain shouted. We trotted down the road and into an orchard on our left. The fog was so thick that we could see only fifty yards.

When will it come? I wondered. We're going to run right into it in the fog. My fingers, clenching my M-1, were stiff with cold, but I was sweating freely. My heart pounded like a machine gun. Strung out Indian file, we ran along the base of the dike to the first group of buildings, where half a dozen antiaircraft men joined us with a stretcher and a 30 caliber light machine gun. Still running, we suddenly came on McCreary, Matthews, Sawosko, and another man from the first squad moving slowly back toward the village. On the 4 A.M. patrol originally scheduled for us, they had run into a company of Germans digging into the orchard behind the windmill. McCreary was shot in the neck, Sawosko through the leg, but nobody had been killed. Matthews appeared stunned, and Sawosko, who was limping and whose pants leg was covered with blood, had a glazed look in his eyes. Our platoon medic, Longo, dropped out to take care of them.

"Go left!" Captain Winters shouted. "Over the dike, over the dike!"

One by one, we ran up the slope, across a two-lane road on top, and down the other side to a wide drainage ditch about a yard deep. We were in no-man's-land. A flat stretch in full view of the enemy hills across the Rhine, it ran about a thousand yards from this point to the river and, though cut by ditches, offered no cover or concealment. There were no houses nearby, no woods, no walls. I dreaded the time when the fog would lift, as lift it would.

We lay in the ditch and waited for the rest of the platoon to come over. Rice began to dig in, while the rest of us, figuring we had enough protection and not much time, lay flat and hoped for the best.

The fog was lifting, revealing the windmill only a few hundred yards away. Its great arms silent, it seemed to be staring right down at us. I wanted to burn it to the ground.

"Let's go!" Rader said. "Third squad, follow me."

Ducking low, we ran up the ditch toward the windmill, then cut left and stopped in another ditch. Rice began a second hole.

Ku-Rack! A shell whistled above us and burst right above the men we had left behind.

"Dukeman's dead," someone cried. "They got Duke." While we watched, Christenson crawled up and took Dukeman's cigarettes and Carson threw an overcoat over him.

"Poor Duke," Hoobler murmured, shaking his head.

The fog continued to thin. I wanted to return to my own side of the dike very badly. Higher and higher the mist rose as the sun warmed its top. Soon we could see patches of blue sky. The houses, high brick factory chimneys, and round kilns of the enemy villages of Renkum and Wageningen looked down at us from across the Rhine. The hills behind them seemed very high. We could distinctly see the pine trees that covered their slopes.

Captain Winters brought up the rest of the platoon and then shifted us forward to a ditch that paralleled the raised road leading to the windmill. There was a large factory building by the river at the opposite end of the road.

"Krauts!" someone yelled. "Kill 'em! Kill the sons of bitches!"

Their chests and heads in sharp silhouette, almost a dozen Germans ran along a ditch on the other side of the road like clinking targets in a shooting gallery. We drew down on them with cries of joy and began firing. The range was only a hundred yards.

Farther down our ditch, Muck and Penkala, who had spotted an enemy machine-gun crew setting up to fire at us from the corner where the road joined the dike, put their 60mm mortar into action. With a loud pop, the first projectile soared into the air, arched high, and then tumbled to earth. The explosion blew both gunners off the ground, killing them instantly. Muck and Penkala walked the next shells down the ditch toward Wageningen.

"Beautiful, isn't it, Web?" Hoobler smiled.

I laughed. The shooting had relieved my tension and tightened my bowels. My shoulder hurt from the slamming rifle, but I was glad to be fighting at last.

Captain Winters stood up. "Fix bayonets and prepare to charge!" he yelled.

Nobody cheered the order. Apprehensive about crossing a hundred yards of open ground without cover and in full view of the windmill, we rammed the bayonets on our rifles and rose to a crouching position.

Captain Winters jumped out of the ditch. "Let's go! Let's hear a little noise! Kill 'em! Kill 'em all!"

Screaming like Comanches, we ran out into the field, firing from the hip. I began to sidle toward a ditch on the left when I was half-way across. Christenson, who was just ahead of me, wheeled about and goddamned me for shooting so close to him.

"Relax," I said. "I was nowhere near you."

I jumped into the ditch and ran down it. Three or four other men followed suit. Our charge ended at the raised road. It was an anti-climax. Expecting to rush the Germans, we had stopped short with an obstacle still between us.

"That's OK," somebody said who had climbed a hedge and peeked across the road. "All the Krauts are dead. Mortar got most of 'em."

We sat down and waited. The mist was almost gone.

"I don't like this," I commented to Christenson, who was sitting beside me. "We're too exposed. Look!" A barrage of airbursts crumped over a field three hundred yards behind us.

"They're feeling for us, those sons of bitches," Christenson said in a low voice. "And when they get the range, God help us."

"This is a hell of a place to take a break," I added. "Why don't they do something?"

"Anybody up here speak German?" a voice inquired.

"Yeah, I do!" I answered.

"Come here quick! Bunch of Krauts in a garden."

Glad to be on the move again, I got up and ran north beside the road a hundred yards or so to a four-foot embankment that paralleled the dike. Several riflemen and Riley, a big, quiet Headquarters Company machine gunner attached to E Company, were lying on the mound, covering a patch of high green vegetables about seventy-five feet square. "Krauts," Riley said. "A couple have already surrendered."

Pointing my rifle down at the greenery, I stood on the mound and shouted. "Heraus, heraus!" I yelled. "Schnell! Hände hoch. Mach schnell!" I told them to surrender or be killed. They were surrounded and had just one minute to lay down their weapons and come out with their hands high. "You'll go to America," I promised. "Good food, no more war! Heraus!"

One by one, half a dozen burly Germans in spotted ponchos rose like sprouting flowers with their hands in the air. We frisked them as they came over the mound and sent them to the rear. Hard-eyed and almost middle-aged, they bore the double lightning insignia of the SS on their collar tabs. "Polski," they cried, "wir sind Polski." But their German sounded remarkably good to me. We waved them on.

I shouted once more at the garden and then told Riley to spray it with his machine gun to make sure we eliminated any stragglers. He grinned and swung his gun back and forth with a steady tooming.

A shell came in from the south with a loud swishing and burst among the vegetables fifteen yards away.

"Our own artillery!" I yelled. "Let's get out of here!"

Another shell burst about thirty yards behind us. Liebgott, the platoon interpreter, screamed with pain and clutched his elbow.

"One short and one long," I said. "Now they'll fire for effect." I took off running away from the mound. The others ran with me.

"Tell the artillery to cease fire!" we screamed. "They're hitting our own men. Tell 'em to cease fire! Cease fire, cease fire, cease fire!" We could see Captain Winters talking on the radio a couple of hundred yards south.

Brownlow, who was much closer, ignored the cry and ran at us with a boiling face.

"Get back up there!" he screamed. "Goddamn it, you can't run back to the rear!"

I gaped at him. "They'll kill us," I said. "Those shells will kill us all. Tell the artillery to cease fire."

"Go back, go back, goddamn it, go back all you men!"

"Jesus," I said. "Oh, God." I did not want to be killed by our own barrage.

Calling us deserters and waving his carbine at us, Brownlow continued to shout for us to go back. Never having once come to the mound to help or direct us, he now drove us back there with frantic curses, then stopped well in the rear without bothering to send a runner back to Captain Winters.

Furious with helpless anger, we lay down on the embankment and waited for the barrage to fall on us. It was all we could do. We were obeying orders. For the first and only time, I felt like killing an officer. Talk of shooting this lieutenant or that captain was usually just so much talk, I knew, for you were glad to have anybody along in action regardless of how rotten he was in garrison, but for once I truly understood the sentiment and sympathized with it. I would have shot him if I had had the chance. I had more against Brownlow than I ever had against the Germans, who, after all, were just soldiers doing what they had to do.

Several minutes passed. We started to relax. Soon the fear passed and with it most of the hate. I no longer wanted to kill the lieutenant, just to pound his face with a rifle butt.

Rader came up and told me to move back a few yards to a gap in the hedge, cross the road, and keep a watch on the fields to our east. I took a stand by a wooden gate and stared toward Arnhem, which was about eight miles distant. A salvo of enemy airbursts cracked in the air three fields away, leaving a cluster of black smoke puffs behind them. They were getting closer. It was only a matter of time before they found our range. Pace and Hoobler came up to chat.

A German soldier sprang from a ditch two hundred yards to our direct front and ran across an open meadow toward the river. Amazed that a lone man would have the nerve to expose himself on a day like this, I jerked my rifle to my shoulder and trailed him.

When the muzzle was pointed at the leading edge of his chest, I squeezed the trigger. The German dropped as if he had been flattened by a pile driver.

"Yippee!" Pace cried. "You got him." He fired a tracer at the body.

Hoobler chuckled with delight and opened fire with his M-1. The shots made the German's body twitch and jump. I fired twice more to make sure, for I had a feeling that he was a runner, streaking back for reinforcements, and I wanted to make sure he stayed put.

With a kettledrum booming, a cluster of mortar shells walked toward us from the direction of the dike. I wondered why nobody bothered to shoot up the windmill. It was the only logical point of observation. If we lingered too long in one place, sooner or later the observer would be able to adjust fire right on top of us. He was coming closer and closer as it was. I wanted desperately to leave this open tableland for the comfort of Randwijk's cellars.

"We're going to attack the factory," Hoobler remarked, staring toward the Rhine. "Captain Winters thinks that's where the Krauts are coming from."

"Oh?" I said, feeling sick at the prospect of going a thousand yards deeper into enemy territory to storm a huge building with a handful of twenty or thirty men. "I don't want to do that. We'll be wiped out in the process."

Hoobler shrugged his shoulders.

Captain Winters brought the rest of the men across the road and moved us through the gate into a ditch that paralleled the dike. We lay down and waited.

We were beyond the windmill now. There was no front and no rear. From the windmill and the hills beyond the Rhine, the Germans had the observation on us. They laid down strings of mortar and artillery shells in the fields and ditches around us, coming closer and closer and closer. I wanted to get up and run all the way back to our village.

A squad of Germans rose from the ground about three hundred yards east and ran toward the dike. They had only gone a few feet when the British artillery caught them with a remarkably accurate barrage that knocked them flat in two seconds.

We cheered. The British were master artillerymen, and as long as

Captain Winters' radio worked and we had contact with them, we would be assured of some measure of protection.

A cluster of mortar shells landed in the meadow beyond our ditch. We threw ourselves flat and lay still until the order came to get going again, then rose to our hands and knees and crawled forward. Captain Winters was still talking about attacking the factory.

Thirty men attack a factory? I wondered, trembling with fear as another barrage landed nearby. We crawled over a big, freshly killed German whose face and chest were dotted with little red bullet holes and then lay down again. The cracking, banging, crumping death seemed to be all around us. I wanted to dig my way into the earth a thousand feet deep and pull all the dirt in after me.

Our ditch ended at a hedge some thirty feet ahead that cut off our forward vision. Curious about what lay beyond, Hoobler mounted a yard-high mound to our right and looked over.

"Krauts!" he yelled. "Jesus Christ, Krauts!"

He fired a shot at a point just beyond the hedge.

"I got one, I got one! Yahoo!"

Martin, another man, and I ran toward the hedge to open fire. We had only gone a few feet when a German machine gun fired a short burst at us.

A two-hundred-pound man swung a baseball bat and drove a spike clean through my leg. The force of the blow spun me around and knocked me down.

"They got me!" I cried.

What a cliché, I thought as I lay on the ground. "They got me!" I've been seeing too many movies. Ashamed at my lack of originality, I watched the other men run back a few yards and turn around. Hoobler remained where he was. I got to my hands and knees, stood up, and limped to Roe, who was crouching in the ditch some thirty feet away. Shot through the right calf, I could feel blood flowing down my leg into my boot. There was no pain, however—only a stiff, pulling sensation every time I took a step.

I had gotten my wish—a million-dollar wound. My sole concern now was to get back to Randwijk. Over the dike, I said to myself, I have to get over that goddamn dike. I stopped beside Roe.

"Lie down," he said. "I'll fix it." He rolled up my pants leg and inspected the damage. It was a very clean wound, enough to get me out of combat for a couple of weeks but not permanently disabling. The bullet, fired upward, had gone in one side and come out three inches higher on the other without mushing or tearing the muscle.

"Not bad," Roe commented. He sprinkled both punctures with sulfanilamide and wrapped a shell dressing around my calf, then told me to go to the rear.

I grinned. Free at last—from Brownlow, from the army, and above all from attacking the factory. "Thanks," I said. "This is what I've been hoping for."

"Good luck, buddy. Think you can make it?"

"Hell, yes! I'll run all the way!"

Seeing Guarnere close at hand and lightly armed without elaborate webbing or extra ammunition, I offered him my bandoliers. "I won't need them anymore," I explained.

Completely at ease on his elbow in the ditch, he held out his hand and took the bandoliers. I gave my hand grenades to a couple of other men and limped west as fast as I could go. Everybody wished me luck.

The antiaircraft medics were the last men in line. Some shells came in close as I approached them, so I lay flat until the firing had ceased, then got up again. My leg was growing stiffer, but there was still no pain, only a pulling. The medics tried to stop me as I went by.

"Stay here, buddy," one of them urged. "We'll take you out on the stretcher as soon as things quiet down."

"No, thanks," I replied. "I'm not going to hang around this goddamn place one more minute."

"Can you make it?"

"Damn right I can. I'm not going to stop till I reach the regimental aid station." They smiled, and I laughed and told them that I didn't intend to lie here and let the artillery zero in on me. They couldn't understand why I refused their help.

Taking a deep breath, I jumped out of the ditch, crossed a field, and went as fast as I could limp to the raised road where we had killed the Germans. I was on my own now, several hundred yards from the platoon and even farther from Randwijk, and I kept my eyes wide open, constantly searching, and my rifle ready, because I had no idea where the Germans were or whether we still held this area. At last I was across the road, with the windmill behind me.

I had two choices: to wriggle through two ditches in a long L to the dike or to cut across a couple of meadows at a forty-five-degree angle from here and hope that nobody would knock me down in the process. Impatient to reach safety, I decided to run for it. I forced my way through the hedge, dropped into a ditch, picked myself up, and ran into the field where we had made the bayonet charge. A loud whishing came in after several seconds, and an artillery shell blew up behind me. My speed increased.

Another shell came in, much closer. They're shooting at me, I thought, feeling the iron fingers of the giant clutch at my heels. The dirty bastards are firing artillery at a lone man and a wounded one at that. Don't they know I'm through with all this crap?

Whish . . . Blang!

I did not think it possible to move faster, but the last shell showed how wrong I was. It gave me wings.

A German poncho caught my fancy as I approached a grassy embankment two feet high. Make a good souvenir for my sister's boy, I thought, so I copped it up and ran on.

A barbed-wire fence prevented me from sailing over the mound to safety. I threw one leg over in such a hurry that my pants got caught on the wire. Four or five artillery shells of about 75mm caliber exploded in the field beyond the mound.

Christ, I thought, they'll kill me yet. I ripped free of the wire and flopped down behind the low embankment, which barely concealed me. Panting and utterly exhausted, I contemplated another decision—whether to get up and run across the field to the dike or crawl beside the mound a hundred yards west, then follow another ditch south to the foot of the dike. The choice was obvious: I crawled.

Flat on the ground, digging the sides of my boots into the turf and dragging my rifle beside me, I moved with painful slowness through sticky old mud and fresh piles of cow dung. This was a heavily traveled cowpath, but I was no longer particular. In fact, I would have crawled up the longest sewer in the world under the same circumstances. It was a terrible feeling to know that someone was watching for me and would drop another barrage around me the moment I came into the open again.

Pausing for a rest after twenty or thirty yards, I glanced up at the dike and saw two 506th machine-gun crews setting up their guns on the crest. They're insane, I thought. Don't they know what a perfect target they make?

The knowledge gave me selfish comfort, however, for I knew

that no artilleryman would waste shells on a lone man when he could drop them on two machine guns. I got out my identification scarf and waved it and shouted at the men on the dike to make sure they didn't shoot me.

"Don't shoot!" I yelled, standing up and running toward the dike. "Don't shoot! Don't shoot!"

The gunners ignored me as they lay down and began to adjust their elevating and traversing mechanisms.

Stopping for breath at the first ditch we had entered when we had come over the dike, I knelt beside Dukeman's body and patted his shoulder and said good-bye. He was a long way from Colorado and its high, clean mountains.

The machine gunners fired rapidly at a target near the raised road to the windmill. I charged up the face of the dike, across the road between the gunners and the village, and down the south slope. Safety lay in the rear, I knew, and not in Randwijk, which was about 150 yards to my right, for the Germans might be there now. This was no time to find out. I went into a ditch on the border of the first pasture beyond the dike and stopped for another break.

Three shells landed with a great roar on top of the dike where the machine gunners had been. I winced.

Artillery began to fall on Randwijk like heavy rain. Roofs shot into the air with tremendous booms and clouds of smoke and shards from the red tile. It was the end of our rest position.

There's nothing for me here, I thought. I have to go back, far back, back where the civilians are. More determined than ever to stay alive, I crouched low and waded through a stinking, stagnant watery ditch to a line of poplars. They won't get me now, I kept telling myself. They won't get me now. Nobody's going to keep me from that hospital.

My leg was knotting badly, and movement had at last become painful, but I knew that I had to keep going. No medics would pick me up here, and there were no ambulances. Actually, I was quite happy to be on my own. Looking out for myself was something I always liked to do. It was the one thing I could do better than anybody else.

When I had trudged a weary two miles from the dike and was beyond the sound of firing, I came across a large farmhouse standing by a dirt road and a narrow drainage canal that ran from east to west. The hike through plowed fields, over fences, in and out of mucky ditches, and through hedges had exhausted me so much that I decided to stop here until some GIs found me.

A middle-aged Dutchman saw me come into the barnyard, leaning on my rifle, and ran out to help me. He took my arm and led me gently indoors to a wonderful big kitchen where a number of other civilians, evacuated from the villages along the front, had gathered together. The center of attention, I went to a chair and sat down while a dozen people stared at me and murmured with pity in a language so thickly Dutch that I could barely understand one word in ten.

It was not surprising to be stared at, for, dung- and mud-smeared as I was, I would hardly have been presentable even in a pigsty. I hadn't shaved for almost a week, my boots were filthy, and one leg of my pants was covered with dry blood. I told them that I was a wounded American paratrooper and asked them to send somebody for help. A boy was dispatched while the farmer's wife went to the stove and prepared some refreshment. I swallowed eight sulfathiazole pills to prevent infection and sat back and enjoyed the warmth and the attention. German pancakes almost a foot in diameter were set before me with strawberry jam and cups of hot coffee and warm milk. Several children clopped into the room on wooden shoes to stand at a safe distance and stare and whisper.

"Danke, danke," I said, finishing a second pancake. "Wunderbar." The civilians nodded and smiled and murmured together. I didn't care if I ever got to England. This was a better show by far. Two men from F Company came in the door as I downed my third pancake. One, Haney, was familiar to me, but the other was a replacement who had joined the company after I had been thrown out.

Haney sighed in disgust. "Oh Christ, Webster, it's you," he said. "The civilians told us a Limey soldier was dying up here."

I laughed. "All for nothing, isn't it? Well, give me a hand. I suppose I have to get out of here." Hating to leave the farmhouse, I stood up and thanked the civilians for their hospitality. Haney and the other man helped me outside to a bicycle that they had brought with them and put me on it. My leg was so stiff that I could hardly walk. With one man on each side, we started down the dirt road beside the small canal.

"I thought F Company was attacking the windmill," I said to Haney. "How come you're still back here?"

"Only one platoon went out. The others are still in reserve. How is it up there?"

"It's a mess, just a goddamn mess."

"Isn't it always?"

They left me at a little road junction with an earnest young civilian with some sort of armband on and a bazooka team that had dug in beside the canal, and told me to lie down and wait for the battalion medical jeep, which was making periodic trips through here from the front.

Free at last to relax, I gave my rifle and webbing to one of the bazookamen and took off my helmet and rubbed my scalp, which always itched under long confinement. I rolled up my .45 in my identification scarf and hid it in a jacket pocket, to keep it from being stolen by the rear-echelon medics. The jeep arrived a few minutes later.

Driven by an old sick-call acquaintance, it bore on a rear stretcher Sergeant Boyle of E Company, who had been hit in the shelling of our village. A fragment had lain open the back of his thigh from knee to buttock.

"Hold tight," the medics said, putting me on a stretcher over the hood. "We're in a hurry. Have to get Boyle back as fast as possible."

After driving about a mile and a half at top speed, we pulled into the village of Zetten-Andelst and stopped at the schoolhouse, a low building of dark red brick that served as the regimental aid station. I got off the stretcher, went indoors, and sat in the dusty sunlight of a back window. Covered with GI blankets, the bodies of four dead paratroopers lay beyond the window in a narrow alley.

God, I thought, looking out at them, how long does this have to go on?

A dead-white civilian in a black suit lay moaning on a large table in the center of the room while Major Kent, the regimental surgeon, and Doc Feiler, our wrenching little dentist from Greenwich Village, worked over him. Several enlisted men from Regimental Headquarters Company moved about in the background.

This was the first place in the evacuation chain where a wounded man could get really adequate first-aid treatment, and there was a saying that if a man could live till he got here, then he would probably live all the way to the general hospital. Morphine injections and plasma transfusions could be given by almost any aid man at the front, but the really vital attention started here. Whenever possible, the regimental aid station was set up indoors in the sturdiest building available, whether a store, factory, office, church, or railroad station.

Other men, more seriously wounded than I, were brought in moaning, cared for briefly, and taken away in ambulances, while I and the other walking wounded sat in silence against the wall with our backs to the dead men and waited for our turn. It was a strange waiting room, with its little desks and chairs and schoolroom pictures on the walls, the dying civilian on the table—they were giving him plasma now—and the dead men on stretchers outside. Everyone talked low. The only sound was the moaning of the civilian.

Worn out by my day over the dike and so many sleepless nights before, I felt an overwhelming urge to cry, a hate and disgust that I could not stifle. Enough, enough of this! I saw Dukeman dead, the shells falling on the dike, our little village blown to pieces, Sergeant Boyle in agony on the rear stretcher. Oh God, get me out of this now and forever more.

3

Our Home Was Secure

I came back to the outfit when the snow was melting on the 7th Army front in Alsace. It was February, 1945, eight months after D-Day, and it seemed to me as if the war would never end.

Europe, I thought, spitting over the tailgate of the truck that was taking me from the last replacement depot to E Company, God, how I hate Europe. I glared at the cold, wet countryside. Gray snow still lay in the north hollows, but the rest of the low, bare hills were slimy brown with rain.

We were moving up to the front. The rumble of artillery fire got louder, hushing the chatter of the other men in the truck, and I looked away from a Europe that I hated and watched my companions to see if they were as depressed as I was. We had all been wounded in Holland or Bastogne and had been weeks or months away from the outfit.

Only four men are left now, I noticed with a start. An hour ago we had a truckload, and it was noisy and cheerful. But that was before the artillery got so loud. Now the men are quiet, lonely, preoccupied. They're probably thinking the same thoughts that I am—thoughts of home.

It's a lousy world, I thought, staring at the rainy farmland. All those sullen, silent half-timbered houses; the rutted roads, dug deeper by an army of trucks and tanks; the shelled fields and chopped trees and piles of manure in the front yards. This is Europe, poor damned, drained, and beaten Europe. Why can't we fight at home? Think of all the liquor you'd get in a place like Greenwich.

I moved the helmet back and forth on my head to stop the itching and wiped the mud off my face. I felt confused and depressed, because I wanted to come back to the outfit and yet I didn't want to come back—I wanted to go all the way home to America. I've done my bit, I mused. I've jumped in Normandy and Holland. I've been hit twice. Why come back for thirds? Let some other idiot do it. Why come back? All I would have had to do was tell the officer in that hospital that I couldn't take it anymore, and he would have sent me to the quartermaster. Instead of that, I said, "Yes, sir, I'm ready to go back now." I must be crazy.

A GI who had stopped on the shoulder to let our truck pass caught my eye as he stood and watched us. His green jump suit with its big canvas side pockets was black with smoke and rain and dirt and mud, and he was so dead and passive that he didn't even curse our driver as he splashed him. His helmet bore a white spade with a short white bar below—the markings of the 2nd Battalion, 506th—and the sight of him made my heart leap. My outfit, I thought, looking forward to seeing my friends again, that's my outfit.

The truck passed a straggling column of men with mess kits in their hands, slowed down, and stopped at a large white stucco farmhouse. "2nd Battalion!" the driver yelled back at us. "Anybody for the 2nd Battalion?"

"Ho, ho!" I replied, very excited. I wondered who would be left and what kind of stories they would tell and where we would go next. I stood up, shifting my .45 to my right side, slung my rifle over my right shoulder, and jumped off the tailgate. One of the other men, who were from the 3rd Battalion, handed me my duffel bag. "All clear!" he shouted to the driver. "Let's get the hell outa here!" The truck lurched forward, leaving me alone in the road.

I sighed and stared at my surroundings. It was a muddy little village of old houses with steep German roofs. Everything looked tired and cold and wet and shut down. Where do I go now? I wondered, and who will be left when I get there? I started toward the house.

Morganti, the tattooed man with the pirate mustache, the great wit, and the warm heart, came around the corner with a dark green bottle in his hand with a white-enamel snap-on cork. "Webster," he said, "where the hell have you been?"

I was so glad to see him still alive that I could hardly talk. Noticing my eyes drop to the bottle, he smiled and said, "Schnapps." I nodded. "The local Krauts make it out of potato peels. Good schnapps is made from cherries. This stuff is made out of potato peels."

He weaved a little, and I asked where E Company was located.

"CP's in the next house," he replied. "We just came off the line. We're moving out tonight, but the bastards made F Company pull a patrol anyway. No sense at all, but they had to keep the men busy. Killed a couple of good men. This freaking outfit."

Morganti walked off, and I wondered again whether I should have come back after all.

I turned right and walked across a cobblestone courtyard thick with slippery mud and manure to the CP building, where I knocked on the door.

"Come in!" a voice cried.

I entered a narrow hallway piled with army radios and musette bags and bazooka ammunition. The air was warm and close and rich with the homey fragrance of coffee and cigarettes and sweaty clothes.

This is a good deal, I thought, looking around, but it can't be too good or too permanent, because they're not taking care of it. They don't even bother to wipe their feet or scrape the mud off the floor. I guess they're just passing through. If they were settling down, they'd clean it up and keep it neat. I went through an open door on the left to a room where I heard conversation.

It was a large whitewashed parlor with a low, beamed ceiling. A tall, square, blue-and-white porcelain German stove stood in one corner, filling the room with a fierce, wonderful heat. I looked from the stove, which fascinated me because it was the kind I had read about in fairy tales but had never seen before, and saw two men watching me from behind a bare wooden table. I was surprised to see them because they had not been in E Company when I had left.

One was a thin young man with a rather plump, almost babylike face and large brown eyes. His hands were white and clean, his face smooth, and his jump suit looked as if it had just been laundered. He was the first sergeant, age twenty-two.

I glanced from him to the company commander and frowned. What had happened to our old company commander? I knew what had happened to the old first sergeant, Boyle—his thigh had been ripped open by a shell fragment in Holland—but our old Captain Winters, the medal-winner, who was big and hard and aggressive, seemed like the kind of man who would stay around forever. Now he was gone.

Still frowning and puzzled, I took off my helmet and stood before the two men, scratching my head and reluctant to salute. "Is this E Company's CP?" I asked.

"Sure is," First Sergeant Mann replied with a warm enthusiasm that made me think he might not be so bad after all.

"Hello, Mann," I said. "When did you transfer from F Company?" I smiled at the captain. "I thought you were in D Company, sir." I had heard of his reputation as a reckless, savage man, and I was glad to have him for a company commander.

"We came in at Bastogne," the captain said. His name was Speirs. He was from Boston. His voice was hard and harsh, his eyes cold and narrow, his teeth stained with tobacco, but his smile was honest and sincere. "Captain Winters is a major now, up at battalion. Glad to have you back, Webster." He smiled again, and I knew that we would get along well. "We need men like you. Better get some chow. We're moving out in a few minutes. Going south to Haguenau."

"Yeah," Sergeant Mann butted in. "Half the town is ours, and half is Kraut. The rumor is that we're going to take the other half. Guy in S-2 says they're using railroad guns and the Maginot Line on the doggies. Shells are coming in at the rate of eight hundred a day. It looks rough as a cob."

"I hope it isn't *too* rough," I said. "I want to break in easy." I nodded to them and left the house in search of the chow line.

A soldier with an empty mess kit in his hand came out of the second house down and started toward me. Something in his gait and bearing caught my eye. The posture was familiar—straight as a ruler, shoulders back, head high and challenging—and I recognized the helmet cocked flat against the left side of his head, the long, hard, finely chiseled face, the German black leather belt with its GOTT MIT UNS buckle and the Luger slung on the right hip.

"Marsh!" I yelled. "For Chrissake."

His eyes lit up, and he hurried over. "Webster! Keed, it's been a long time."

We shook hands. I was so happy to find him alive and strong as ever that I felt warm all over. I had never been sure that he had liked me before.

Suddenly a battery of artillery from somewhere behind the village fired a barrage. Bop-bop-bop! Bop-bop-bop! Bop-bop-bop! I ducked for the ground. Marsh smiled and pulled me up.

"That's hokay, keed," he said. "It's our own artillery. You'll get used to it again. Better hit the chow line. There ain't much left." He went down the street to a barn, and I started for the mess hall.

Two men from the 2nd Battalion walked out the front door as I went in. They glared at me with the assurance of old soldiers mentally spitting on a green replacement. Irritated by their air, I glared back. Who the hell are you? I wondered, you sons of bitches. Old men! Probably came in after Holland. I started with this outfit at Toccoa. Who the hell are you?

Then I shrugged my shoulders fatalistically, knowing that it wasn't important anymore, remembering that it was always like this when you returned to the outfit: Strangers everywhere, the old-timers thinning out. The Toccoa men are the strangers now, I thought. The replacements have taken over. We're outdated. We don't belong here anymore.

I went through the door into air that held suspended a rich promise of hot coffee and burned stew and walked back to a large, medieval kitchen, where two 7th Army cooks were wrestling a thirty-gallon aluminum pot to a dumping position at the back door. They paused when they saw me.

"Just in time, buddy," one of them said, wiping the sweat from his face. "You almost missed the boat. We thought you guys were through. Here!" He plopped two pieces of toast on my mess kit and ladled a dipper of brown goo over them that looked like Grape Nuts in gravy. "Shit on a shingle."

I laughed, and he piled apricots and hard biscuits and jam on my other pan. I filled my cup with coffee and left.

When I was halfway through the stew, I heard shouting outside.

My stomach tightened and grew cold, and I began to eat as fast as I could. The shouting was followed by a rattling of weapons, the cursing of noncoms, the subdued griping of soldiers moving out. Someone opened the front door. "Hit it, hit it!" he yelled. "On the road! We're moving out."

The door slammed, and I shook my head sadly. The army never changed. You could never get anything accomplished. Go to the latrine, drop your pants, and—bam!—another formation. Start to read a magazine on your bunk and "Everybody outside!" Write a letter, and after the first paragraph: "Let's go! Chow call." Fall asleep in the field, and it was always: "On your feet, soldier! Break's over." Goddamn army. Goddamn the goddamn army.

I dumped my leftovers into the stove in the center of the room, put the biscuits in my pocket, slung my rifle, and went outdoors.

The regiment was moving out, and the artillery was giving them a covering barrage in farewell. Bop-bop-bop! Bop-bop-bop! went the muzzle blasts. Whish-whish-whish, whish-whish-whish! the shells whispered overhead. The salvo crashed a few seconds later in the enemy lines on the snowy side of the bare hills: Bam-bam-bam-bam-bam-bam!

I trembled. The sound was ominous. No good would come of it.

The guns rested a minute or two, then fired again. And again. And again. The guns reared back and belched black smoke, and the shells whispered high above and slammed down like heavy doors, and soon a dull thick rain started to fall, as if in answer. The 506th was going to Haguenau.

"Easy Company, over here!" Sergeant Mann shouted. He moved about briskly, clean and young and still quite eager, and lined the men up three abreast, but it took some time, for the men could no longer be hurried.

I stopped at the first platoon, which was at the head of the column, behind Company Headquarters, and stared at them dumbfounded. Where is everybody? I wondered, counting them with my eyes. There are only eleven men. A platoon should have forty. I counted them again to make sure, but there were still only eleven. I felt like crying.

Suddenly McCreary threw back his head and laughed. "Well, well, how do you do?" he said. "Where the hell have you been?" He and I had wound up in the same hospital ward in England after evacuation from Holland, but he had rushed back to the outfit when he learned that they had returned to base camp, because he wanted to set up a pressing shop with Matthews.

"Where have I been?" I said. "Replacement depots. And rough it was, too," I grinned. "How's the tailoring racket, McCreary? Press a lot of pants in the Bulge?"

"Bite me, buddy, bite me. You're in the first squad now, Webster, the better half of the first platoon. Six men. We're loaded— we've got eleven men in the platoon now." He shook the water off his Thompson and patted its barrel. I fell in beside him, because he was always good company and cool in action.

The parachute artillery's pack howitzers were thundering in the background. Cold, heavy winter rain fell on our helmets and bedrolls and ran down our rifle barrels and dripped off the bottoms of our raincoats onto shins that were already soaking wet. The cannons blasted, the shells whispered and landed with faroff, doorslamming crashes, and I bit my lip and thought how old and familiar it all was and how depressing. And yet it was bearable, because I was back with friends.

In the light of the artillery flashes and what was left of the day, the trucks seemed as tired and dirty and battered as the men now gathering around them. Their windshields were cracked and punctured by bullets. Bullet holes and the rusty gashes of shell fragments marked their bodies and fenders. Some of the doors and tailgates were sprung, and shrapnel had slashed long, thin slits in a few of the canvas tops.

This outfit's taken a beating, I thought. Our trucks never looked so bad before. More than two months they've been going now— from the middle of December to the middle of February—and there appears to be no end.

Sergeant Mann, who had been conferring with Captain Speirs at the head of the column, turned around and yelled for the first platoon and Company Headquarters to get in the first truck and the second and third platoons in the next one. "Load 'em up!" he cried.

I boosted McCreary over the tailgate and handed him our weapons, then climbed in with the others and tried to settle myself comfortably in the tiny space left. After unbuckling my cartridge belt and setting my rifle butt down on the steel floor between my knees, I inhaled and pushed my shoulders back to force the people apart who were crowding me in on both sides. When I was finally at ease, I pushed my helmet on the back of my head and studied the men across from me, searching for a familiar face.

Well, I thought, smiling, if it isn't Sholty—"Moldy" Sholty, as Matthews called him, "the Jet." Sholty was a green replacement just before Holland. Now he's an old man. I wonder what happened to the others. All that's left are Sholty, Wiseman, Marsh, McCreary, Martin, Lyall, Rader, Liebgott, Cobb, and an ex-second platoon man, J.D.

"Hi, Sholty," I said. "Where'd you get the BAR?"

"Hi, Web, long time no see. They gave me this up in the Bulge. All the platoons have 'em now. Supposed to be one in every squad. An 88 got our machine gun."

"Won any crap games lately?" For an amateur with an air of slow amiability, Sholty was one of the luckiest crapshooters in the regiment. He was buying a farm in Indiana with his winnings.

"Haven't hit a game since Mourmelon," he replied. "We haven't been paid for two months."

The driver raced his motor, and I turned to Marsh and asked what had happened to the other men. "Where's Sawosko?"

"Got it at Foy."

"Oh? And what about Muck and Penkala?"

"They got it at Noville. Shell came right into their hole."

"God. Where's Julian?"

"He's dead too, Web. Got it on patrol."

I wondered about the third squad. Where was everybody?

"Pace and Janovek got trench foot. They'll be back. Rice—you remember Rice, always digging in? Lost a leg in a barrage that hurt nobody else. Whitesill's been transferred to a diesel-repair outfit, and Massaconi is back in rear echelon."

"And Hoobler. Where's Hoobler?"

"Dead."

Marsh looked away, and McCreary told me how Hoobler had died while the medic was off looting the dead. They wanted to shoot the medic when they caught him, but it was all talk, and so he was never even punished.

"A lot of guys who were never hit before died in that goddamn Bulge," McCreary said. "I'm telling you, buddy, it was a rough son of a bitch."

I nodded. But there was one person missing who would not be

missed. "Say," I said, smiling, "where's Lieutenant Brownlow?"

"Home on rotation."

The cold iron truck bounced stiffly up and down, slamming us from side to side, and the rain fell on the canvas with a drumming patter. Sawosko was dead. Where was his guitar? He and Hoobler had stayed up half the night in the barn at Uden, just singing songs. Now they were both gone. But Brownlow was alive and home on leave.

A gust of anger blew through me. Then I sighed and closed my eyes, because I knew that anger was useless. I could not change war or the army.

The truck jolted to a halt, as if it had hit a wall, and I woke up in violent fear, terrified by the night and the airless silence that had suddenly replaced the noise and motion of travel. I hope it's only a dream, I thought, seeing nothing. I hope I wake up in the English Speaking Union. Or maybe I'll be in the hospital—that would be even better.

Then my eyes adjusted to the darkness, and seeing the men around me, I knew, with a sodden feeling of despair, that it was no dream. There were Marsh, McCreary, Wiseman, Sholty, and the others. The rain was still falling, the night was even blacker, the front was close.

Sergeant Mann raised the backflap and told us to get out. I stood up and watched the scene that was unveiled as Marsh and McCreary rolled up the flap.

We had stopped in the middle of a wide street that had been heavily shelled. Gutted white houses, grinning with black shell holes, stood like skulls squeezed flat behind the sidewalks. The rubble that had fallen into the street in the shelling had been bulldozed back against them in a mound five feet high. Concrete telephone poles with black wires that dangled like broken gut leaders ran up into the sky at regular intervals from the rubble. The cobblestone road was pocked with shining, water-filled shell craters.

Sergeant Mann returned a few minutes later. "Lock and load," he said. "We're going on outpost."

Outpost! I said to myself, visualizing two men in a slit trench three hundred yards ahead of the Main Line of Resistance. I certainly picked a fine time to come back.

We stumbled after the first sergeant for several blocks and then bumped to a halt beside a high wall topped with concertina barbed wire. Always the cautious soldier, I looked carefully for cover from shellfire and saw none. My stomach felt cold and tight, and I breathed as lightly as possible, afraid that the least noise would call down a barrage. The only sounds were a few whispers and the far-off rumble of the idling trucks' motors. The rain felt very cold. I waited stiffly for the first rustling of the shells that had been promised in such large quantities.

The trucks left with the dry grating peculiar to their kind and slam-banged out of sight. A single cannon fired in the distance. I held my breath as the shell whispered overhead and landed with a faraway bam in the other end of town. The explosion echoed up and down the empty streets. I exhaled in relief. The other platoons moved out.

Now Marsh, who was our acting squad leader, conferred with Mann. The latter went off with the rest of the company, leaving us alone on the sidewalk. Marsh told us to wait till a guide came who would lead us to our positions.

"Let's get off this sidewalk and find a little cover," I suggested.

McCreary feigned surprise. "What's the matter with you?" he asked sarcastically. "Nervous?" He shook his head and clucked his tongue. "You always were too careful."

I stared at the empty street, looking for cover. The house across the way had possibilities. It had only been hit once. Well, I can always run for it and hope a door or window is open. I heard a man's footsteps approach and glanced away in fright.

It was an infantryman with the Cross of Lorraine patch of the 79th Division on his shoulder. Perfectly unconcerned, he kicked and scuffed his way toward us with his rifle slung. "You guys going to relieve us?" he asked.

"OP 2?" Marsh replied.

"Yes."

"That's us, buddy. We always get the shaft." He raised his voice at the men huddled around him in the rain and said: "Let's go. Moving out. Five-yard interval."

I took my M-1 off my shoulder, tightened the sling, and checked the chamber to make sure the gun was loaded, then ran to catch up with the others. The infantryman had already moved off at a fast, careless pace, with Marsh and McCreary beside him, and I did not want to lose them any more than a dog likes to lose its master in a thick crowd. We went through the silent city, stumbling over rubble, falling off high curbs, tripping on chunks of brick, and wading in flooded shellholes, until McCreary broke the silence by asking about the position.

"Watch the wire!" the guide said, holding down a strand of barbed wire that curled across our path. "Here's the deal: outpost in houses."

"Houses!" McCreary exclaimed. "I'll be goddamned. Who ever heard of outpost in houses?"

"Sure, it's a snap. The Krauts sit in their houses, and we sit in ours, and the reserve battalion makes the patrols. We get a little artillery and a few mortars. Haven't had a direct hit yet."

"Sounds like the peacetime army," Marsh grinned. The guide nodded.

Two smiling infantrymen passed us on their way to the rear. Their hands were filled with bandoliers that clacked together and swung back and forth like pendulums. I hurried after them and asked if they could give me some ammunition.

"Sure, buddy. Here, take a couple. We don't need 'em anymore. We're pulling out. Going back to rest camp. Hot damn!"

After winding in and out of streets and alleys and across backyards and vacant lots until we seemed to be hopelessly lost, we came to a big open parade ground, about two hundred yards square, that was surfaced with stone paving blocks shining in the rain. Long, dark Victorian brick barracks three stories high, with very steep slate roofs, bordered three sides of the parade ground. The fourth, or south, side ended at a low stable. All the buildings had been heavily shelled, and there were craters scattered irregularly about the open space.

The guide raised his hand and halted us. "Spread out," he whispered. "They got this place zeroed in." He unslung his rifle and holding it ready, trotted onto the drillfield. He went along the front of the west barracks, darted across a narrow road, and hurried close to the north building. A safety catch snapped off a rifle in the darkness of a big doorway with a pointed arch in the center of the barracks. "Halt!" someone hissed. The guide gave the password, and we moved into the doorway.

We walked up a flight of stone steps ten feet wide and six feet high and halted in a level entryway where a guard stood watch in the shadows. This was the platoon CP, he told Marsh. Martin, who was acting platoon sergeant, took Wiseman, Lyall, Liebgott, J.D., Rader, and a new man, Crist, in with him.

"I guess you guys are on outpost," the guide said to us. "Let's go."

We walked close to the CP building, dashed across an open gap, and went into the stable. Picking our way over fallen beams and piles of rotten hay and old manure, we came to a hole in the back wall about a yard wide and four feet high. One by one, we crouched and, passing through the hole, dropped down four feet to a bare, cratered field fifty yards square.

Diagonally across from us on the left, on the other side of a narrow road, was a ghostly white house as tall and square as a Gordon's gin bottle. Its roof was a patchy mass of loose shingles and uneven mortar holes. Shells of a large caliber had punched other holes in its front and blown out all the windows. From the lines of bullet holes that crossed and recrossed the walls, it appeared to have once been a strongpoint that had been taken by direct assault.

The house had probably been the neat, placid home of a middle-class family before the war, but it was an outpost now, our guide told us. He had no idea what had happened to its owners. The mother and little children had probably been taken off to slave labor camps by the Germans and the father gassed or shot or worked to death in a Lager.

We crossed the cratered field on a slippery mud path and scurried over the road to an eight-foot iron fence that enclosed the front yard. The road ran north on our left a hundred yards to the bank of a creek, where it curved and went between it and the east barracks. A small house stood alone on the other side of the creek, 150 yards away. To our right, the road went straight for fifty yards to a wooden army bridge over a slough that emptied into the stream. Beyond the bridge was a triangular grove of beech trees so stripped and withered by shellbursts that they were more like bare poles than living trees. The grove was about a hundred yards wide at its base. A line of houses, dark and dim in the falling rain, lay beyond the trees.

When everyone was across the road, we followed the iron fence south to a sloping driveway converted by the artillery into a rock garden of jagged masonry. We went down the driveway to a two-car garage in a half-basement. There was three inches of water underfoot, and the air smelled strongly of urine ammonia and the chocolate of ordure.

Almost a dozen infantrymen were crowded together at the far end of the garage, impatiently awaiting our arrival. They were loaded with gear and moving about like restless horses. One of them shined a pencil flashlight at McCreary. "101st Airborne, huh?" he said. "The Battered Bastards. We read about you guys at Bastogne. You done a hell of a job."

McCreary smiled complacently and was about to agree with him and tell him all about it, when the guide, who was apparently a noncom, told the men to leave. They trotted out without another word.

I watched them with gritted teeth. "Rest position, my ass," I said to McCreary. "I never saw guys so anxious to pull out of a rest position. No good's going to come of this place, no good at all."

We hesitated briefly in the garage, as if unwilling to face the fact that we were once again on line, and then Marsh snapped us forward with "Well, goddamn it, let's get out of this swamp!" and led us through a door in the right wall.

We crossed a concrete hallway that evidently served as the community garbage dump. It had everything—ashes, ordure, urine, empty ration cans, wet cardboard boxes, old bandoliers, broken china, a torn blanket, and a mound of potato peels—but most of all it had a smell, the smell of a French railroad station where troop trains stopped and thousands of men had relieved themselves.

From here we entered another, more promising room. About fifteen feet by twenty, it was lit by an open kerosene lamp that gurgled and flickered and flared sideways with the drafts. A steel double bunk with dirty, stained mattresses stood against one wall. At the north end beside the lamp a sandbagged 50 caliber air-cooled machine gun stood ready on a sturdy wooden table, its muzzle pointed at a piece of fiberboard covered with rags that served as a blackout for the only window. A field phone lay next to the gun. To one side of the table was a square, flat-topped tile stove. It threw off a terribly dry heat. The stove had an oven and was evidently stoked from a pile of coal briquettes at its foot. A rough board bed stood opposite the double bunk. Its mattress was spotted and stained and smelled very moldy. Two other mattresses, covered with dirty civilian blankets, lay on the floor in one corner. Near them were three boxes of C rations and a box of D ration chocolate bars.

The occupants, who had been hastily donning their gear, paused and surveyed us with interest. We clustered around the stove, holding our hands out to its heat, and one of the of the infantrymen frowned at us and asked where the rest of our men were.

"We're all here," McCreary said. "Six men and a BAR."

The infantryman shook his head. "We have eighteen men and two machine guns, and we'd still have a hell of a time holding this place if the Krauts ever came over."

McCreary snorted. He had little use for the infantry, who did everything with tanks and heavy artillery and were not inclined to be wild or reckless or high-spirited. "We can handle it, buddy," he said complacently. "We've been in worse places than this."

"You can have it," our guide smiled. "Are you the squad leader?"

"No. Marsh here is."

"Maybe you both better come with me while I show you the setup. It's a pushover. All you have to do is stand guard at night and scrounge all day. Officers never bother you, and the artillery isn't much." He paused and looked down at McCreary, who seemed awfully small.

"Did you notice that little house across the stream about 150 yards north of here?" McCreary nodded, and I listened closely. "We think it's a Kraut listening post, but we're not sure, because we've never seen them. That creek is the front. It's called the Moder River."

The sergeant led McCreary and Marsh through the hall to another basement room, which was less comfortably furnished than the first one. I followed them, because I wanted to learn all I could about the position. We went through a squeaky wooden door in the east wall and climbed a wooden staircase powdered with rubble. Now we were on the first floor, about six feet above ground on the road side and ten feet above the river, which was some fifteen yards wide. We turned left and scuffed through a narrow hall that was ankle-deep in plaster and bits of brick and lath and halted at two French doors at the south end. The doors framed a small outside balcony with a waist-high iron railing, and through them we had a commanding view of the woods and the stream below.

A rifleman stood watch at one of the doors. He turned when he heard us and looked at the sergeant, who told him to go below and prepare to move out. The sergeant beckoned us alongside with a jerk of his head. "Watch those woods!" he whispered. "If the Krauts ever come over, they'll probably land at the edge of the woods and sneak through 'em to take you in the rear. Another company's got a machine gun dug in near the road at the other side of the woods, but you'd better keep your eyes on them all the time anyway. And stay away from the water! The engineers have mined all the bushes on the banks."

"What about the big field out there?" I inquired. I could barely make out a wide plain stretching away from the opposite river bank.

"Nothing there for a mile but a big farmhouse five hundred yards southeast of here. There must be Krauts in it, because the artillery is always shelling the place, but we've never seen any. The Haguenau Forest is a mile away, on some low hills, and it's lousy with Krauts. You can see 'em moving around like ants in the daytime, but they won't bother you." He led us back into the hall and through a door on the left into a small room, saying over his shoulder that this was where they kept their heavy 30.

Two men lounging by a 30 caliber water-cooled machine gun sandbagged on a marble-topped table with thick claw legs twisted their heads at our approach. The sergeant nodded to them and patted the gun barrel, which was aimed at the woods below. "This is a good place for your BAR," he said. He told the others to bring their gun down to the cellar and get ready to leave. The gunners smiled and started flinging sandbags to the floor.

"Our living room," the sergeant said as we entered a high white room that faced west and south. In worse condition than any other room, it had apparently been the center of resistance when the house had been taken. We went through it and then across the hall to another balcony, which faced east and directly overlooked the creek. "A good guard post," the sergeant commented. "Who knows? The Krauts may get the notion to come straight over some night."

Before we returned to the basement, he paused in the hall and jerked his head up at the ceiling. "There's nothing much above here," he said. "Just two empty floors and an attic. We burned all the woodwork, the banisters, shutters, and doors, before we found coal for our stove. There's a toilet in the attic, but no running water. We use it when there's no artillery coming in."

The two machine gunners crowded past us and hurried downstairs, kicking the debris ahead of them. We followed.

By now, all the infantrymen but our guide and the gun crew had gone away. We watched these last men gather their gear and ammunition. When they were ready to leave, McCreary, who was very friendly and well-mannered, escorted them to the garage door and bade them farewell. They wished us luck and disappeared into the night.

Overwhelmed by the sybaritic luxury of good beds, a warm room, a hot stove, and lots of food and rations, McCreary smiled at us when he came back. "Boys," he said, picking out a can of Meat and Beans and setting it on the stove, "we got it made."

"Looks good to me," Cobb said, sitting up on the top bunk and swinging his legs back and forth. "Where's the nearest Krauts?"

"Hundred and fifty yards north." McCreary pointed at the blackout board with his left hand while he turned the ration can with his right.

"That's nice, but isn't it just a little close?"

"Aw, hell, it's only a listening post."

"Who are they listening to—us?"

"The hell with the Krauts," said Winn, a new man. "I've had enough of 'em. Where's the booze?"

"Any gals in the neighborhood?" Cobb inquired.

"When do we eat?" Sholty asked. "I haven't eaten since supper."

"You fellows shut up and let me sleep," McCreary grumbled. He lay on a floor mattress with his face to the wall.

"Let's not be antisocial, Mick," Marsh snapped. "Just for that, you'll be the first man on guard. We still have a war to fight. Sholty, get your BAR and come with Mick and me." He blew the ash off his cigarette and continued: "We'll stand guard an hour apiece at the French doors upstairs and then put in another hour on the phone down here. The phone man will wake up the next guy to go upstairs. OK? Now, Mick, for Chrissake, wake up!" He yanked off his covers and rolled him away from the wall.

"Jesus Christ, Marsh, why pick on me?" McCreary muttered. "You're the goddamnedest would-be squad leader I ever saw." He got up, stretched sleepily, put on his helmet, slung his rifle, and trudged after Marsh.

A mortar coughed while they were gone. We stopped talking and held our breath, but there was no explosion. "Must have been a flare," Cobb said. "Maybe they heard us." We started to talk again, more quietly than before. A high-velocity shell whipped past the garage door, sucking wind, and crashed near the stable with a report that was muffled by the rain.

"Eighty-eight," Winn said.

"Awful close," I added, shivering. "Well, hell." I started to unlace my boots.

Marsh and Sholty came back, and a flickering, smoky peace descended on the phone room. I loaded my .45 and put it beside my head on the mattress and closed my eyes. Cobb was already snoring on the top bunk, and Winn was dozing in a chair beside the telephone table. Soon the only sound was snoring. We were on outpost.

Next morning the rain had cleared and the sun had come up strong and bright, making the fears and forebodings of the night before seem asinine. Everybody was in a good mood. McCreary and I were squatting like fakirs over three cartons of C rations bequeathed us by the former tenants and were passing judgment on the contents as we sorted them out. The undesirable brands were goddamned and flung angrily into an empty box, where they would be held in reserve for use only in an emergency.

"Think we'll ever get any of those new C rations?" I asked. I knew perfectly well what the answer would be, but I wanted to stir McCreary up a little.

"When the war is over," he replied, sucking on a cigarette stub, "they'll hand 'em to us as a bonus when we come down the gangplank in New York. The quartermaster and the Air Corps are getting 'em now—like the good cigarettes. We have to settle for Chelseas and Raleighs and corned beef hash."

"And LEMON JUICE POWDER, SYNTHETIC," I said. I threw the glassine envelope at the box with all the force I could muster.

"What are we having for breakfast?" Marsh asked, poking at the fire in the stove.

"Meat and Beans, buddy," McCreary replied. "Any water left for coffee?"

"Just a little."

"I seen a well in them woods," Cobb said. "Any volunteers?"

"I'll go," I said, putting on my helmet. I fetched a white enamel pail near the stove and went out to the well. An 88 zipped close overhead when I was crossing the bridge on the way back, and I told the others to move fast outdoors, adding that I thought the 88 was watching this place. McCreary put a frying pan on top of the stove and started heating a mess of Meat and Beans.

"If only I had some garlic," he murmured, "even this might taste good." Cobb began to heat the coffee water.

"Let's go scrounging today," Marsh suggested. He peeked over the chef's shoulder and noticed that the meat was sticking to the frying pan. "Better stir it some more, Mick."

"Bite me."

"We need skid," Cobb said.

"And lush."

"And spuds."

"And coal."

"And garlic."

"And women. Jesus, I could screw a sheep."

Wheet, wheet! Someone whistled for attention on the phone. I picked it up. "OP 2. Webster speaking." I listened with a scowl, then slammed the phone down. "Dirty bastards are planning a patrol for E Company. Everybody stand by. Shit!"

Cobb's hand paused en route to the frying pan. McCreary stopped in front of Marsh with a biscuit can extended. Sholty, who was brushing his teeth, stared dully ahead, seeing nothing, his toothbrush firm on his upper gums. Marsh's hands stiffened on the bootlaces he was tightening.

The noise, which we had all heard, grew louder. A freight train puffing and chuffing in the sky. It came in from the east: Choo-choo-choo-choo-choo! As it passed overhead, everybody involuntarily ducked toward the floor.

The train went on. A couple of seconds later there was a tremendous explosion a quarter of a mile to our rear. The house rocked back and forth.

"Hit him again!" McCreary shouted, shaking his fist at the sound. "He's Irish."

Everybody relaxed and started talking fast.

"Heavy stuff," I said excitedly. "A railroad gun or the Maginot Line."

We discussed the railroad gun for a while and how we hoped that it was true that large-caliber artillery was usually saved for rear echelon, and then started eating. When we were through, the phone tweeted again. McCreary answered it. He listened for a while and then set it down with a sigh: "Portugee's giving us a new phone," he said. "The 79th Division wants this one back. Rader says Captain Speirs and Major Winters are coming down here to study the situation and terrain for the patrol, so nobody leaves till they're gone. Better clean your weapons. They just might hold an inspection."

Soon there was a scuffling in the rubble outside, followed by splashing footsteps as someone came in the garage. A thin dark boy with a long, animated face and pop eyes darted in. "Hi ya, fellows."

"What ya say, Portugee?" McCreary replied.

"Can't say it here, ha, ha, ha. How are the Krauts treating you?"

"We've been welcomed," Sholty said. "An 88, a 270, and a mortar."

"I still say it's the best goddamn setup we ever had," McCreary said. He looked around challengingly. "Tell us about Company Headquarters, Luz."

"Say, if you think you got it made, you ought to see those bastards! Fucking blue-star commandoes." Luz was in Company Headquarters as a radioman, but his loyalty remained with the first platoon, where he had started. He bent over the table and detached the old phone from its cord and put a German one in its place. He had unrolled the German wire on the way from the platoon CP in the north barracks, and now he would roll up the 79th Division's American Signal Corps wire on his return.

But Company Headquarters, a political scene not admired by riflemen, was still on his mind. "Them rear-echelon bastards are sleeping on *sheets!*" We couldn't have been more astounded if he had said they were walking on water. "They have running water, electric lights, and two cooks. *Two* cooks! One ain't enough for twelve men. Better start cleaning your gats, men. Some of you are going on patrol."

"Is that official?" Marsh inquired.

"From the Company Headquarters' latrine. Know any better source, Marsh?"

Two men were talking in the yard outside.

"Must be the captain," Luz said. "Him and Winters left the CP right after yours truly. Let's go watch 'em draw fire." He led the way out to the garage.

The officers stood in the middle of the yard, below the French doors, on a slight mound, like Napoleonic marshals at Austerlitz, and swept the scene with their arms, now pointing at the woods, now at the Moder River, now at the farmhouse strongpoint and the distant forest, where enemy soldiers were crawling about like upright ants among the pine trees. It was a clear blue day with unlimited visibility, but they showed no concern.

We watched them awhile, muttering low about their attracting the attention of the 88 to our home, and then went indoors. Luz fetched the GI phone and started back, rolling up its wire on a hand reel as he went.

McCreary alone remained outside. When the officers saw him, they joined him on the threshold of the garage. "Hello, Major," he said pleasantly, as one equal to another. "Hello, Captain. Patrol going out soon?" He leaned against the wall with a cigarette dangling limply from a corner of his mouth.

"Yes, McCreary," Captain Speirs replied. "In just a few days, Platoon leaders will pick the men. S-2 wants some prisoners."

"They always do. Why don't they get 'em themselves, sir?"

The officers laughed and said good-bye, and McCreary returned to the basement in a thoughtful mood. "OK, men," he said quietly, "the coast is clear for scrounging. Sholty, do you want to stay by the phone while we look around?"

"May as well. I have to clean the BAR anyway. Hurry back."

"Remember," McCreary said to the men getting ready to leave, "everybody home before dark." He turned to me. "Let's go together. There ought to be a lot of stuff in these houses."

The flat, bare, brown land beyond the river was silent and peaceful, as if catching its breath after the rain, and there seemed to be a touch of spring in the air. Three P-47 fighter planes were circling lazily amid tiny black puffs of flak far to our right rear (for we were actually on the very tip of a long, thin finger thrust deep into enemy territory by the 7th Army on the Rhine plain of Alsace), but there was no sound of war on the ground. The sky was a clear blue that seemed even clearer after days of storm and overcast, and the air smelled fresh and wet and countrylike, with the fragrance of moist earth and decayed leaves. The snow had disappeared from the north hollows. Hard little green buds were already pushing out on the tree branches.

I smiled. It's going to be an early spring, I thought, feeling a great relief. Maybe things will be better now; things are always better in the spring. I breathed deeply, grateful to be alive to enjoy the simple pleasures of earth and sky, and listened for shells. There were none. "Great day, isn't it?" I murmured.

"It sure is. Spring, Goddamn!" McCreary inhaled. Everything was running in our favor, even the weather. "They say it was the worst winter in fifty years," he remarked, blinking at the sky and smiling. "Thank God it's over. Let's go."

He scurried up the driveway to the road, turned left, and ran across the bridge over the slough and past the base of the woods to the first house. "Damn it," he muttered. "We're too late." He pointed through the open door.

Two soldiers were leisurely pulling out wardrobe drawers and flinging their contents behind them with both hands to the floor of what appeared to be the parlor. One of them, a square, squat man with wide shoulders, a long trunk, and very short legs, held up a tablecloth, examined it critically, and remarked in a wonderfully rich Brooklyn accent, "This'd make a choice scarf."

"Yeah," his assistant replied sarcastically, without looking up, for he thought he felt a camera hidden in the corner of the drawer. "If you got a neck like Gargantua, it'd make a hell of a scarf, a hell of a scarf, Eddie. It's OK for you, but it ain't for me, it just ain't my style. Goddamn! No camera."

I nudged McCreary, and we both walked in. When he heard us come, Eddie quickly shoved the tablecloth into a big pants pocket and stared at us belligerently until he recognized us. Then a huge grin spread across his lined, brown face, and he said: "A couple of boys from E Company. What are you guys doing here? This is protected territory. D Company's got the franchise."

"We're just looking around, Eddie," I said. "Any houses left for us?"

"Sure, sure—across the bridge. Help yourself. Where are you guys located?"

We told him and invited him to pay a visit, adding that we were always home.

We ran back across the bridge and over the cratered field to the shelter of the stable wall, where McCreary stopped and lit a cigarette. Even outside, the stable gave off a disturbing order of burnt powder, moldy hay, old manure, and horse piss. After lingering here a minute or two, we decided to follow the course of the slough back to a group of houses several hundred yards west, instead of going through the hole in the wall to the barracks area, where we knew some machine gunners and the men from the platoon CP were at large.

We turned onto a narrow street and walked along a sidewalk for a ways. Then we picked a house at random and went in, wrinkling our noses at the musty smell and stale air. We could tell immediately what had happened here, for everything was more or less intact, though somewhat rearranged.

Apparently soldiers had come to the door one day and told the civilians to leave immediately, without taking anything with them. The soldiers had then taken over. One of them had ripped off a heavy lace curtain, while another had broken some of the dark Victorian furniture. A German or American bravo (but more likely the latter, for the Germans usually took better care of their billets) had flung a large Mason jar of preserved peaches at a four-foot wall mirror, breaking them both. The broken glass and the garbage lay where they had fallen. Smashed cut-glass decanters were strewn about the floor. The bureau drawers had all been pulled open, for this was the first act of any invader, drawers often being hiding places for jewelry, watches, cameras, sweaters, and wool socks. Some of the men also liked to fondle women's underwear.

The second story was in worse shape than the first, for the house had been hit by mortars. Chunks of lath and plaster lay white and chalky on the floor, and the bedclothes in one room had been ripped by shrapnel. From the bloodstains on the sheets, it was apparent that someone had died here when the shelling had started. I stared at it and wondered who he had been, whether a soldier or civilian. How would you like to come home to this? I asked myself.

A wrecked house and a bloody bed, smashed mirrors and torn furniture.

The basement was flooded with black water that appeared to be rather deep. "Spuds!" McCreary exclaimed, pausing on the last step. "Looks like coal, too." He eased his foot into the water. It was only four inches deep.

Lighting matches as he went, he swished to an empty gunnysack near the stairs, lifted it, and carried it to a pile of potatoes in the far corner. "Wonder how the infantry missed these?" he speculated. He threw them into the bag as if he feared that someone would catch him in the act and make him give them up.

I went to a mound of coal in another corner, picked up a gunnysack, and slipped the briquettes into it one by one. About six inches long by two thick and three wide, they were an excellent fuel.

When our bags were so full that we could barely lift them, we felt our way in the dark back to the kitchen. McCreary set his load down in the front hall, straightened up, and suggested that we take a break. We stood erect, inhaling and throwing back our shoulders and working them around and around, and stared dully out the front door, which he had left open. A bird twittered far away, but there was no other sound.

With a great, ringing roar, a shell landed on the sidewalk five yards to our left. We threw ourselves flat and cursed. The day had seemed so perfect.

"Mortar," I hissed. Where had it come from? Who had been watching us? We were at least three hundred yards behind the front, hidden from enemy view by many buildings, and yet someone had seen us and called down fire. "They've seen us, they've seen us," I said in a panic.

McCreary made no reply. Instead, he lifted his head quickly, like a dog that hears someone approach, and squinted outside. He appeared to be concentrating on something far away.

A few seconds later, another shell exploded, only a yard or two from the front door. The bitter black smoke puffed into the room. McCreary snapped to his feet, grabbed his sack of potatoes, and darted off.

Coughing and gasping and almost paralyzed with fright, I lay flat and shook my head to stop the ringing caused by the detonation. I felt lonely, abandoned, hopeless. We're hidden from the Germans, I thought, and yet somebody has seen us and told them to shell us. And it's not area fire, because it's too accurate. I couldn't understand it.

They'll get me if I stay here, I thought, and if I go out, I'm likely to run smack into one of those damn things. What should I do? Hide in the cellar? Mick would laugh me to death. I'd sooner meet the mortar. He's probably laughing at me now. Oh well, the hell with it.

I jumped out the door, ran down the steps, and took off on the path. "McCreary!" I yelled. "McCreary, where are you?"

Shouting his name, I ran a short block that seemed very long, turned sharply, and bumped into McCreary, who was leaning against a brick wall, smoking a cigarette, waiting for me.

"What's the matter?" he inquired innocently, his eyes twinkling. "Scared?" He blew the ash off his cigarette and gazed up into the sky.

Still trembling and so excited I could barely talk, I wiped the sweat off my face and took a deep breath and told him I was afraid I'd lost him.

"You have to listen for those shells, buddy," he said in a rather professional tone. "You have to time 'em. Walk slow and listen for 'em, and when you hear 'em coming, hit the dirt." He blew a smoke ring. "You ought to know that by now, Webster."

I looked down at him, so calm and cocky, and smiled, for he did not fit the popular conception of a paratrooper as a big, lean man. No artist would have asked him to pose for a recruiting poster. Short and fairly plump, his general appearance was genial. He never exercised if it could be avoided, religiously dodged all details, and concentrated his energy on the pursuit of food, liquor, cigarettes, and women. Nevertheless, he was always calm and cool and forward in action.

But still I disagreed with his artillery thesis. "I don't listen for shells when I'm out in the open," I said. "Not me. I run like hell from cover to cover. The slower you move, the more time they have to hit you. You can't hear a mortar most of the time anyway."

"I can hear 'em, buddy, and that's good enough for me. Let's go." He blew the ash off his cigarette, swung his potato sack on his back, and started off.

Supper that night was a gala affair. Each of us had returned with food or fuel or household knicknacks, and Cobb regaled us with tales of his explorations of the battalion front with his buddy Morganti, who had wind of a liquor cache lying close to a German position. Morganti, he said, was in OP 3, the first barracks near us, where two squads of Headquarters Company machine gunners were stationed.

Marsh was standing at the stove, stirring a pan of diced potatoes. For the time being, he had been appointed head of the household by our platoon leader, but he still deferred to McCreary in matters concerning the finer things of life. "Think they're done yet, Mick?" he said.

Sholty, who had been dozing on the top bunk, woke up and blinked down at them. "Aw, you guys don't know how to fix spuds," he said with disdain. "You have to slice 'em real thin and leave 'em in water awhile. Them's not thin enough."

"Nobody's asking you to eat 'em," Marsh said. "There's plenty of C rations left—help yourself." He looked at McCreary, who was poking around in the potatoes with a trench knife, and sought his approval before lifting the meal from the stove. McCreary went on poking, so Marsh speared a slice that looked especially appetizing and handed it to him on a fork. "Try this one," Marsh urged.

His buddy took the fork daintily, popped the offering into his mouth, chewed it lightly, rolled his eyes toward the ceiling, and nodded approvingly. Marsh removed the pan from the fire. "Come and get it, men!" he yelled.

We hit the pan with a wild, scraping clatter. Sholty played a very active role in the assault.

"Well, well, how do you do, Sholty," McCreary exclaimed. "I thought they weren't good enough for you. Come on, now, leave a little for the rest of us."

When the potatoes were finished, we relaxed on the beds to wait for darkness and guard duty upstairs. Still hungry, I decided to make a pudding. While the other men, who had somehow never acquired a taste for them, watched in horrified fascination, I took four fruit bars that I had been hoarding from my pocket and laid them beside me. Duty-bound to be generous, I inquired dully whether anybody else would like one.

"I'd sooner eat Chopped Pork and Egg Yolk," Winn responded.

"You can say that again," Sholty added.

Cobb held his nose, Marsh frowned, and McCreary shook his head in benign tolerance.

"In that case," I said, brightening, "I think I'll make a fruit pudding."

"God."

I laughed and fetched my canteen cup. After unwrapping the fruit bars, which were composed of mixed dried fruit and were quite dark and heavy and sweet, I crumbled two dry crackers into the cup, added chunks of fruit, stirred in a little water for pliability and a little grease from the frying pan to give it a plum-pudding richness, carefully tamped the dark mass into the cup with my fingertips, and then set it on top of the stove.

The others watched in silence. Finally, Winn stood up and stared down into the cup.

"Wiseman's sending up three dozen more bars from the CP," I told him. "Want some?"

He shook his head. Eating fruit bars was something that was just not done in the army.

Soon the phone whistled. McCreary humphed and lifted it up. "OP 2," he said. He listened thoughtfully and nodded his head from time to time. "They won't like it and neither will I . . . OK, buddy, I'll tell 'em."

He hung up the phone and sighed. "That goddamn patrol. The lieutenant's picked the men."

Everybody stopped eating and looked at him.

"He picked 'em, not me, so don't cry in my beer. We're so damn shorthanded down here that we can't spare anybody, but they're taking half of us anyway. It's the same in all the other platoons. That's right, Cobb, you're one of 'em. I'm another. And Winn, you'll carry the BAR. Sholty's just got a pass to Paris."

Another day passed, with further expeditions to the nearby houses, some close shells, and a 105 that bracketed the house, driving Cobb down from the upstairs toilet with his pants around his ankles. We swept the refuse in the hall into a far corner, cleaned off the stairs, and hauled water from the well in the woods.

Now it was night again. McCreary and I went to Company Headquarters to fetch the rations.

Company Headquarters was located five or six blocks west of the barracks square in an undamaged three-story house on a wide intersection and was by far the best of the company's billets. Directly across the street in a small vacant lot, the company's three

60mm mortars were set up for battery fire in separate holes five feet square by four deep. They were laying down a barrage as we approached.

The muzzle blasts lit the scene with quick flashes, and the noise was deafening. They would fire three or six or nine, and then there would be a lull that in its way was as deafening as the coughing thunder that had gone before. A noncom shouted, and the men rose out of the earth like black geysers and slid shells down the tubes and ducked back into the earth as the shells went off. It was like some hideous, noisy nightmare.

Rader led us though the front door of the CP and held it open for us. When we were all in, he closed it, so that no light would show outdoors, and opened a door to the left. We entered single file.

"My God!" McCreary exclaimed, overcome by the contrast with the violent scene outdoors. "Civilians."

We had entered the living room. Clean rugs, overstuffed furniture, framed pictures on the wall, electric lights burning—everything was in order. There was even a player piano.

Sergeant Mann was playing gin rummy on a blanket-covered table in the center with one of the louder, more objectionable cooks, while Luz, sprawled comfortably on a fringed couch, cleaned a P-38 pistol. A couple of runners and radiomen were chatting in the far corner.

Luz brightened when he saw us. "You guys hungry again?" he asked, throwing a D ration at McCreary. "Think fast!"

"We're always hungry," I said, inspecting the room with obvious envy. "We're hungry because you guys get the rations first."

McCreary, who had caught the D ration, dropped it on the floor with loathing. "Boy, have you got it made," he remarked. "How do you get a deal like this?"

"We're 4F, buddy," Luz replied. "Company Headquarters. Kraut generator runs the lights. We swiped it in the Bulge." He commenced cleaning his P-38 again. Nobody else greeted us.

The mortars stopped coughing, and just when the silence was growing unbearable, a group of men came in from each of the other platoons. They nodded to us and stood against the wall, muttering at the luxury. Absorbed in his card game, Sergeant Mann ignored them just as he had ignored us. When he had finished his hand, he looked up and asked if everybody was here. "Tonight we get PX rations and 10-in-1s," he announced.

"It's about time," someone remarked.

"At ease! I'll do the talking here."

The men glared at him.

"We've broken them down as fairly as possible, so don't feel gypped if you get Chelseas and razor blades instead of Camels and Hershey bars. OK, Luz, pass 'em out. Each platoon take one of these empty boxes for its PX rations."

McCreary, who was constantly improving himself and who suspected everybody else of doing the same, had no faith in these ration breakdowns. He had a nose for fraud and did not intend to have his men shorted by liars, politicians, dog robbers, cooks, and company clerks. He watched with narrow eyes and a projecting lower lip as the rations were distributed. Two cartons of Luckies went to the third platoon, two Chesterfields to the second, and Raleighs to the first. McCreary exploded.

"Wait a minute, Portugee!" he hissed, low enough so that Mann wouldn't hear him. "Give me those Camels down in the box! Yeah, them. You're not gypping the first platoon, buddy." He frowned.

Luz jerked his head at Mann, who was absorbed in other trivia, muttered something about "goddamn orders," and quickly switched brands. He liked the first platoon. There was nothing, he claimed, that he wouldn't do for us—"after I've done it for myself." He left McCreary and dropped equal shares of gum, toothpaste, soap, razor blades, V-mail, and Tropical Chocolate in the three platoon boxes.

McCreary's eyes had been dancing all over the room, seeking other treasures, especially those shortstopped by Company Headquarters. He nudged Rader and pointed to a carton of Hershey bars on the table at Mann's elbow. "What's the deal, buddy?" he hissed. "Ask him, ask him who gets the Hershey bars!"

Rader was reluctant. Not inclined to argue with those above him, he usually took all rations and details without question or complaint. He cleared his throat, coughed, and asked, "Uh, Sergeant Mann, who are them Hershey bars for?"

"Company Headquarters," Mann snapped, plainly showing that he regretted not having hidden them. He sighed, for the ration breakdown was always contentious. The platoons came in like hungry wolves and circled and snapped and howled whenever they saw a decent cigarette or a good piece of candy go to someone else. He sighed again and repeated that they were for Company Headquarters. "We didn't have enough for everybody," he explained, "so I thought it'd save a lot of bitching if we held on to 'em and equalized it next time."

"Next time, my ass," McCreary grunted. "You guys . . . Time you get through with the rations, we're lucky to eat Chopped Pork and Egg Yolk. We ought to be glad that rear echelon even lets us eat."

He shouldered a case of 10-in-1s (a day's ration for ten men in one box) and slammed the door behind him.

"Time to take down the blackout," Marsh said, for morning had come again. I removed the stick that propped shut our window covering at night and gently lowered the board, with its padded edges of ripped blanket that kept the light from shining out through the cracks.

The little German house across the river caught my eye and made me frown. Something was wrong over there, something had changed. "Jesus," I whispered, "Krauts."

"Uh oh," Cobb murmured.

"We have company," McCreary said.

"I noticed the shutters were closed last night," I said. "Now they're all open. If we don't get them, they'll get us." I ran for my rifle.

"Nah, hold it up!" McCreary snapped. "I have a better idea. That place is too close for mortars or artillery, and shooting an M-1 will only let 'em know for sure that we are here. I have it. We'll bazooka the joint." Keeping his eyes on the house, he picked up the phone and whistled for the CP.

"OP 2, McCreary speaking. We spotted a houseful of Krauts. Think you can get us a bazooka, quick? It's the first place north of here, right across from OP 3. Step on it, buddy! They've probably seen us, too."

He set the phone down, and Marsh began to organize protection for the bazookaman. I was to cover him outside, while the rest of the men watched from upstairs windows and McCreary stayed by the phone.

Someone whistled in the mouthpiece a few minutes later and told him that Luz had just passed the platoon CP on the run. He was carrying a bazooka. Marsh suggested that the CP tell the machine gunners in OP 3, who had been getting rather close fire from the 88 around their top-floor lookout, to cover the house, in case any Germans tried to escape from its rear. "This is going to be good," Marsh remarked.

Someone pounded and clattered across the road and into the garage and then burst into the phone room. It was Luz, with a bazooka in one hand and a bag of ammunition in the other.

He stepped to the window and slapped McCreary on the shoulder. "Hiya, Mick, what's new? Look at Sholty, all dressed up like a soldier."

Sholty grinned. "How's it feel to be up front, Luz? Different?"

"It's a change. A man gets tired of easy living."

Marsh nodded at the house while Sholty, who was due to leave today on his pass to Paris, took the BAR and went upstairs to cover the house from a window there. "We saw 'em airing it out a little while ago," Marsh said. "Better put a couple of rounds in the basement. We'll cover you. Webster'll go out with you."

Luz turned to me. "Hiya, Dan'l. How's the dictionary?" He trotted outside. "Let's go up the road to the last fence post," he suggested. "You lie down and cover me, and I'll shoot from behind the post. Got three rounds. May as well use 'em up. Hell, we're not paying for 'em, are we, kid?"

I smiled.

We stopped at the last fence post, which was of fieldstone and about two feet square, and Luz's eyes narrowed as he gauged the distance to the target. He leaned the bazooka against the post, removed three shells from their fiberboard cases, and laid them neatly in a row on the sidewalk.

"Are you ready?" I asked nervously, keeping my eyes on the house. There was no sign of life in the dwelling.

"I'll give 'em a reveille they'll never forget," Luz laughed hoarsely. He slid round into the bazooka's rear, knelt, and tilted the muzzle up, ready to fire. "Lie out in the road there, will you, buddy?" he said to me. "Cover me, kid, cover me."

I walked out into the street ten feet and lay down in full view of the house, with my M-1 pointed at the nearest window. The cobblestones near my nose smelled wet and flinty, reminding me of some rocks that I had found in the Yosemite River when I was ten years old. I felt very homesick and tired of the war and suddenly wondered if I would ever see the States again. Luz hissed, and I nodded. "Give it to 'em."

The rocket shot out of the bazooka and, streaking fire and smoke, burst with a terrific concussion against a basement window, blowing off the shutters. Luz reloaded quickly and fired another round at a second window, with the same result. The third round went upstairs and blew up indoors.

"How's that for shooting?" Luz asked. We both stood up and stared at the house. It appeared to be totally lifeless. There was no sound, no movement. A few wisps of smoke clung to the walls, drifting up toward the sky, and then a bird twittered briefly in a bush near the river, which was still with the stillness of death.

"Let's go back inside," I said, tense and somehow unsatisfied. "I guess they've had it."

"Like shooting fish in a rain barrel," Luz said. He slung the bazooka over his shoulder, and we turned and started back. There was still no noise or movement in the house.

"God!" I exclaimed, ducking low.

A high-velocity shell whipped past us with a terrible, angry buzz and burst against OP 3. We looked up. The shell had hit only a few feet away from the machine gunners' lookout post on the top floor. We ran for the basement.

"Some shooting," I panted. "They're sniping again. That 88'll be the death of us yet."

Marsh met us at the garage door. "Nice going, Portugee," he said, slapping his back. "You sure put 'em in there."

"I gave 'em a reveille they'll never forget," Luz said, laughing. "Anytime you want anybody blasted up here, just give me a ring. Ask the operator for Luz. Demolitions our specialty. Found any safes yet, Marsh?"

"Nope, but we're looking."

McCreary came out and invited Luz in for a cup of coffee, but he said he had to leave right away. "No safes, no Luz," he explained. He said good-bye and walked off.

Marsh watched him go with admiration in his eyes. "That crazy Portugee's got more guts than anybody else in E Company," he remarked. "He's one of the few guys who doesn't change from combat to garrison, he's always the same—crazy."

After we returned to the phone room, we studied the German house. It appeared to be completely dead.

"Well," Sholty said, "I guess those guys will keep their blackouts up from now on."

"And so will we, buddy, so will we," McCreary replied, lifting our board and jamming it tight against the window. "From now on, this thing stays up day and night."

Four days and five nights. We've been here only four days and five nights, and yet everything seems to be coming to a head. The patrol, the 88, and 105, the railroad gun, and the mortars—they're going to come together, but there's nothing we can do about it.

Every time I go outside, I feel self-conscious. All those silent houses across the river, so close together. I bet there's a squad of Germans in every one.

Germans in the next house all the time. How many of them? Did any of them escape that night and tell their buddies about our position?

The way they bracket this house with artillery. And that 88. They level it on anyone who moves too slow. The direct hit on OP 3. Lucky nobody was hurt, but there'll be other times. Maybe we're next. One shell can punch a hole in the wall and kill us all.

Someone is watching us. We can't see them, but we can feel them. The people are too German. The houses are German. The stoves. The furnishings. All the street signs end in "strasse."

They left their mark on this town, as if they intended to reclaim it someday. Maybe the civilians are part of it. They drift by us during the day. How do we know they're not Krauts? They walk slowly and study us carefully, mentally calculating, mentally adjusting fire.

I don't like it a bit.

Winn stood shivering at the French doors and studied the scene outside. Bushes and trees and rocks and houses that were innocent and harmless in the daytime had a way of become quite ominous at night, and the closer the patrol came and the more he thought about it, the more the shadows looked like men, the more the noises sounded like Germans creeping over the rubble. The searchlights were on tonight. Probably a patrol going out. Patrol—he hated the word. Suddenly his mind snapped alert, and he leaned forward and stared southeast, at the Haguenau Forest.

Little blue lights were moving about in the trees, a mile away, blinking on and off as they passed behind the trunks. He ran downstairs to Marsh, who was gossiping on the party line with the CP and a kibitzer from OP 3, and said breathlessly: "I saw lights out in those woods full of Krauts, little blue lights. Maybe they're bringing in tanks. Jesus, Marsh, we couldn't stop 'em. They can cross the big field before the artillery could zero in on 'em."

"Hold it, fellers," Marsh said over the phone. "Winn thinks the Krauts are bringing tanks into those woods on our right front." He told Cobb to stay below, and went upstairs with the rest of us, each with a weapon in his hand. We were all anxious to see this great phenomenon—lights in the forest at night.

As we crowded around the balcony, we saw the lights wink on and off. They were scattered through the woods like fireflies. They have a lot of nerve, I thought, showing lights on the front. Either they're crazy or careless or very strong, or else it's some kind of trick. A sane man wouldn't even light a match at night.

"Looks bad," Marsh murmured. "Might be tanks. Might be supply trucks or troop carriers. I don't like it, keed, I don't like it a bit." He scowled.

"What'll we do?" Winn asked. "They're too far away for mortars."

"Let's get the artillery. They can blast 'em right out of there." He pulled a compass from his pocket, raised its lid, and, sighting through its aperture, took an azimuth reading. "How far do you think it is?"

"About a mile," I volunteered.

"More like a thousand yards," McCreary said.

"I'd say a mile," Winn said. "Looks that far in the daytime."

Marsh shrugged his shoulders. No two men ever agreed on distance, especially at night. He thought it was a thousand yards. "Keep an eye on 'em, Winn," he said, snapping the compass shut, "and let me know if they start moving across the field. Come on, fellers, let's go down and call the artillery."

We trooped below, where he blew in the mouthpiece until he got a response from CP. "Say, Martin," he exclaimed, "we saw half a dozen blue lights moving around in those woods way off to our right. The boys think that maybe the Krauts are bringing tanks up for an attack. It sure is a good artillery target."

A call for artillery had to go through channels, from outpost to platoon to company to battalion to regiment to division to artillery battalion to gun battery, and the thought of it apparently so exhausted Martin that he heaved a sigh that was audible to everybody in our cellar. "OK," he said apathetically, "I'll ask company about it. What's the range and azimuth?"

"A thousand yards at eighty degrees, Johnny."

"Sit tight. We'll let you know when the shells are on the way."

Marsh sat by the phone, smoking nervously, for it was the first time he had ever dealt with the artillery. He hoped that everything would go off well. Men had been killed by amateurs (usually officers) who played with artillery without the knowledge or experience that it required. When the phone hissed, he jumped up and snatched it greedily. "Another five minutes, huh? OK, keed, I'll tell Winn."

We smiled, and he went back upstairs. Winn was very glad to see him, confiding that the cold and the darkness and blue lights were getting on his nerves. Marsh patted him on the back and returned to the phone.

A few minutes later, Martin called again. The shells were on the way, he said.

"On the way," Marsh repeated to us. He leaned back and stretched out his feet. "This is going to be good: Let the artillery do it."

Three howitzers fired a salvo in the hills behind Haguenau. We heard the shells' quick whispers come right at our house. Whish whish whish!

"Hit it!" Marsh cried.

We dove for the floor. Three shells exploded almost simultaneously in the front yard, between our house and the road. The ground rocked and heaved and a rain of rocks hit the wall.

"My God," McCreary gasped, "they're shelling the house!"

Marsh rose from the floor in a fit of violent anger and grabbed the phone just as Winn rushed in.

"Marsh, Marsh!" Winn yelled, "they're shelling us! Stop 'em! Tell 'em to cease fire!"

"Hello," a cool voice replied from the depths of the big brick CP building, "Martin speaking."

"Jesus Christ, tell the artillery to cease fire!" Marsh shouted at him. "They're landing on our doorstep!"

"Ha, ha, ha. You're getting chickenshit. They're nowhere near you."

"Goddamn you, come here and listen to 'em! They're shaking the house."

"You're nervous in the service."

"Goddamn you, you'll get us all killed! Call that goddamn artillery right now or I'll come up there with an M-1 and *make* you call 'em! You hear me?" He slammed the phone down with tears of anger in his eyes and exploded into a rage against Martin.

We waited a long time and finally, when no further shells came in, went up and watched the lights again. All of us were angry at Martin and even madder about the artillery, which had apparently taken the thousand yards from our house to the woods as the total range, instead of adding to it the distance from the cannons to the house.

"Well, hell," I sighed, "maybe it's just trucks on resupply."

An 88 zipped past us and burst several hundred yards away.

"I saw it!" I exclaimed. "I saw the muzzle flash. Give me that compass, Marsh. I'll take a reading on the next one."

There was another flash a few seconds later. I pinpointed it and counted till I heard the thump of the cannon's report. "A thousand yards at fifty degrees," I said, repeating it over and over to fix it in my memory. "We've finally spotted that 88. Must be dug in out there. Let's put the artillery on it."

Marsh looked at me incredulously. "No thanks, keed," he drawled. "We've had enough artillery for one night."

"But if we don't knock it out, it's going to get all of us one of these days."

"Nope. No more artillery. Not tonight."

"Marsh is right," McCreary said, ending the discussion. "Those guys at the CP will only louse it up again if we start messing with the artillery. If they loused up once, they'll do it again. I got no faith in 'em. Just remember one thing, buddy: If the Krauts ever come over here, we'll have to beat 'em off with M-1s and hand grenades. There's nothing else to count on and nobody else to help you."

McCreary, Cobb, and Winn left for the patrol at twilight. But we were not as understrength as we had been the day before, when they had gone back to the Rhine-Marne Canal for the rehearsal, for we had received four replacements to help us hold the house tonight. Fresh from basic training and four weeks' jump school, they had arrived in Europe only a week or two before. It was the first time we had ever received replacements on line, and none of us liked it, because we thought it meant that we would stay in combat much longer than usual.

Products of the eighteen-year-old draft, our newcomers seemed terribly young and green, and we all felt sorry for them, coming so suddenly to an outfit on line. Previously it had been the custom to receive replacements in base camp and work them into the regiment there, so that they could get to know the other men before they went into action. Now they just threw them in and let them take their chances. I did not envy them.

Of the four, Lamb appeared to be the most competent, probably because he was a southerner, and I never met a southerner who wouldn't fight. An Alabama boy, Lamby was stocky and calm and self-assured. Kohler was more talkative. A preacher's son from Baltimore, he appeared to be quite good-natured and friendly, with a great deal of common sense. His swearing was the kind to be expected from a preacher's son—virulent. The third man, Hickman, was a sturdy, smiling, talkative Indiana farm boy who wanted very much to kill a German, while Hudson, the fourth replacement, was so quiet and shy that it seemed he would require the most looking after of anybody.

While they were chatting together in their new quarters, I went to the garage entrance to check the weather. I wore my usual daytime indoor ensemble—a wool undershirt, jump pants with suspenders, and unlaced jump boots—and found the weather quite cool.

I don't feel right in Europe, I mused, listening to the rain on the leaves and the murmuring of the replacements indoors. There's something tentative and embarrassing about the dead land and the drab, defeated people in black that reminds me of a trip to the slums. I want to get away from it, not to know about it. Hit me again, and send me back to England.

I sighed and unrolled a rubber raft. I fetched a bicycle pump and began to inflate the raft, which the patrol would use to cross the Moder River that night.

Things are changing, I thought as I heaved up and down on the wooden pump handle. The replacements have added a new dimension, robbing us of our exclusiveness. And trouble has started already. It was bound to start as soon as Cobb and Morganti found some liquor.

The house where it was hidden was under direct observation of the Germans, but they had darted into it and found several cases of schnapps. Accompanied by Wiseman, they had stacked the cases in a courtyard. Alas, the Germans heard them and put mortars on the area. The cases were smashed, but they managed to salvage two bottles apiece. The Germans shot at them with rifles as they ran off, and Wiseman was nicked in the knee. Several men got drunk that night and ended up fighting among themselves.

Things are always changing, I mused. Just when you have a nice place, something comes along to mess it up. The essence of life is change, not stability, but I can't get used to it. I want everything to stay the way it is.

"Next!" I shouted, straightening my back and panting, for the pumping had been hard work. "Who's next on the pump?"

Marsh came out with the replacements, and they all took turns while we stood around and talked. Since there were two more rafts, we were still at it when night fell.

Once the rafts were ready, Marsh and I lingered briefly and then went to the road to investigate a noise that we had heard there. Its front sandbagged against enemy fire, a heavy tank squeaked and clanked toward us on the pavement. It stopped between our house and the little wooden bridge and, holding one tread stationary, ground around until its 76mm cannon covered the big field. We went up to it.

"Hi," I said to a man lounging in the turret. "Sure is good to see you guys."

He nodded, dimly visible in the thickening darkness. "Say, buddy," he said, leaning over, "where's this big farmhouse we're supposed to cover?"

Marsh told him. The tanker nodded again, and Marsh added that if the Germans sent up a flare, they would see the farmhouse all right. "You can't miss it," he said. "It's the only living thing in that whole goddamn field."

"Watch yourself," I suggested. "There's an 88 zeroed in on this area. If you have to shoot, you'd better get behind our house right afterward or it'll be your ass."

Marsh gave him the azimuth of the farmhouse, and he swung the cannon till it was pointed at it. "OK, buddy," the tanker said. "We're ready."

Marsh lit the lamp. "I can't believe it—Sholty on a pass to Paris," he said. "And Mick—I sure hope nothing happens to Mick."

"He'll be back," I said. But I wasn't so sure, for the night was quiet and ominous.

"Poor Mick. I hate to think of losing that little guy. And Winn can't swim, you know."

"I know." I felt guilty about that. After two months in the hospital and two months in replacement depots, I had come back and was letting a man who had not had any rest for almost seventy days go on a patrol that I should have volunteered for. The patrol had to cross a swift stream, and that man couldn't swim. If he died, I would be guilty. No one else felt this, but I knew it would be on my conscience. Winn, you have to make it, I thought, you have to make it.

In the next room, Kohler and Hickman were talking about the time they had once had on pass together in Baltimore. I could hear subdued laughter. Hudson and Lamb were upstairs, on guard together.

"Well, keed, it's nine o'clock," Marsh sighed. "Let's go." He told Kohler to watch the phone and led the way up to the machine gun, which we moved to the porch that overlooked the river and faced due east. Working as quietly as possible, we set the gun up on the wide stone railing with the muzzle pointing at the basement of the bazookaed house.

"Damn dark," Marsh whispered. "No searchlights tonight." He pulled the bolt handle back and eased it forward. The gun was half-cocked. One more yank on the bolt handle, and it would be loaded and ready to fire. We kept it half-cocked as a safety measure.

A flare burst. We froze.

Facing the enemy, in the most exposed position in the house, we knew that we were asking for trouble if we ever shot from here, for the muzzle blast would be visible to all and especially the 88, which we dreaded above everything else. But this was the only place where we could give the patrol adequate covering fire. If it were ambushed from the nearest house, we would run three belts through the gun if necessary, because the lives of about twenty men would depend on us. I was not brave, but I knew enough about war and fighting to see the value of our position and the necessity of our using it to help the patrol, even if it meant almost certain death for us.

"I'm going down and tell Kohler to let us know when the patrol has left," Marsh said after the flare had died out. Before I could reply, he was gone.

I did not like it there alone. The front was remarkably quiet, as if lying in wait. The 88 seemed to have fallen asleep. Enemy mortars shot one or two flares off to the left, over town, and no high explosive. Our own artillery, warned of the patrol, rested on its guns and waited for the whistle signal for their great barrage. The searchlights were out; we did not want to illuminate our own men. Our side shot no flares. There was no small-arms firing. There was no moon; there were no stars. Silent and tense, the outposts on both sides of the Moder River watched and waited for the first burst of fire.

I heard a scraping sound behind me and turned to see Marsh coming back. The patrol had left the house, he said, adding that we would carry the machine gun down through the woods to the bank of the creek as soon as we heard the men pass below us on the opposite shore.

"Eeeyah!" someone screamed at the crossing point. There was a thrashing in the water and then silence.

"God," I murmured. "Winn." I pictured him dragged underwater to his death by the weight of his BAR belt.

We waited and waited. Marsh sighted along the barrel to make sure the gun was aimed properly and adjusted the elevating and traversing mechanism. "Poor Winn," he said. "Wonder what happened to those other guys? I don't hear anything."

"Maybe they lost the rafts."

Marsh shrugged his shoulders.

I held my breath and listened for footsteps, but there was only the soft hiss of the light rain on the bushes below. A shingle slid off the roof with a terrifying clatter. "Jesus Christ!" I exclaimed, jumping.

"Spooky, isn't it?"

"Man, I'll say. Where is that damned patrol?"

This balcony gives me the creeps, I said to myself. It's too exposed. That 88 will pick us off as soon as it sees our tracers.

Putut . . . pututut . . . pututututut!

"A Thompson! They've surrounded the house already," Marsh said.

The patrol had passed by us so quietly that we hadn't even heard them. Now they were assaulting the first objective, a house far in town. Rifle grenades crashed, fragmentation grenades thumped low, and M-1s joined the Thompson with their heavy bamming.

"Come on, let's go!" Marsh cried. He pulled the bolt back, yanked out the belt of ammunition and pushed it into its box, swung the gun to his shoulder, tripod and all, and hurried for the stairs. I picked up two boxes of ammunition and told Kohler and Hudson, who had come up to us, to take the other two.

We ran recklessly down the stairs, through the cellar, and out the garage. Marsh led the way along a slippery mud path through the woods and threw the machine gun down by the rope across the stream. Wiggling on his belly, he twisted and turned until the gun covered the farmhouse strongpoint. I flopped down beside him and fed the belt into the gun. Kohler and Hudson dropped the other boxes beside us and lay down five yards to the rear, ready to move up in case we were hit. The small-arms firing continued. Then we heard a piercing whistle.

"Get ready, boys," Marsh said. "Here comes our artillery."

The 60s coughed and belched sheets of flame; the 81s lit the night with volcanic flashes; lightning from the 75s and 105s flared behind the western ridges. Salvo after salvo of shells whispered through the sky above us and fell like thunderous rain on the silent city. The barrage had begun.

As the exploding shells flashed red and orange and the night came alive with the coughing and bopping of the mortar and artillery batteries and the door-slamming detonations of the patrol's covering fire, we smiled and shook our heads in wondrous admiration.

"Beautiful," I murmured. "Isn't it beautiful?"

"Them poor Krauts," Marsh smiled.

It was the best barrage we had ever seen, and we lay still and rejoiced in it. As we stared up at the town, we heard a harsh, crashing report near the platoon CP and saw a sheet of flame and a red ball dart across the river into the basement of a German house. Our 57mm antitank gun had commenced firing.

"Look!" Marsh exclaimed, pointing straight ahead. A house had started to burn half a mile away.

"I hope they burn the whole town down," I said, feeling relaxed and safe and strong.

Toom-toom-toom . . . toom-toom-toom . . . toom-toom-toom! The D Company machine gun fired up the river.

Burrp . . . burrrrrrrrrp! an enemy machine gun replied. It was aimed straight at Weeks's position in the woods behind us. We flattened ourselves and watched the two guns duel, their bright-red tracers crossing and recrossing above us with vicious crackles.

There was a frantic shouting on our left, a rattling of weapons, a screaming of orders. The patrol was returning.

"Let's get out of here," I said.

"Hokay, keed," Marsh replied. "We've done what we were supposed to."

He jumped up and started back toward the house with the gun. We followed him indoors, for our job was done. We had covered the closest house while the patrol had gone out and had covered the farmhouse for their return. Now we wanted to get back to the cellar before the enemy reacted with mortars and artillery.

An 88 buzzed over us like a huge angry bee and smashed into the D Company dugout. The 50 caliber ceased firing. German mortars coughed in town while enemy rifle and machine-gun fire welled up among the houses.

"Just in time," I muttered, darting into the phone room. "My God!" I exclaimed, rearing back.

McCreary, Cobb, and Winn were sitting calmly around the table, drinking coffee. They were very happy. They had started across the creek, they said, when their boat had capsized. All of them had lost their weapons. Winn, who had indeed given the shriek we had heard, had drifted downstream a hundred yards, but had wiggled through the mined bushes on the bank and saved himself. The boat drifted away. They had hurried back to the house, borrowed more clothes from the replacements, and tried again, but had not been able to cross the swift-moving stream. So much time had already been lost that Lieutenant Jones, the patrol leader, had ordered them to stay inside while the patrol went on. They were overjoyed. The S-2 officer, who had also been repulsed by the river, had stayed with them.

An 88 shell burst with a ringing crash in the trees thirty yards away, and soon another crashed on the road.

Down at the crossing, exposed by an enemy flare, the patrol scrambled across the creek on the rope or pulled themselves over in the sole remaining boat. We could hear them shouting and arguing. Vest, the company mail clerk, drew his pistol to kill a prisoner wounded so badly he wasn't worth ferrying across, but Mann ordered him not to shoot, so they left the dying German on the other bank.

We heard them running through the woods toward us. They burst into the garage just as the 88 ranged in around the house. I watched the men run in, all black-faced and furious, and saw two shells burst in the yard just beyond the driveway.

Everyone crowded into the phone room as the shells darted around the house in search of stragglers. Their drawn, blackened faces lit by the flickering, black-edged flame of our little lamp, the twenty-odd men of the patrol filled every foot of floor space, crammed together on the bunks and mattresses, and made the small room seem even smaller and more close.

They were wild with hate and the fierce release of men who have just made a successful attack and, having risked being killed, have instead done the killing. They surged viciously around two small, sallow, very calm prisoners in long-visored cloth caps, so eager to kill them that the least wrong word or movement on their part would have meant their death.

But the Germans were older men, without the cruelty and hot blood of the young, and they knew how to act under the circumstances. They stood calmly and stared without expression at their captors. Mortars coughed in the background, shells rang closer and closer to the walls, the machine gun burped over the river, the house rocked with the near-misses, and through it all the prisoners stood coldly unconcerned and perhaps even slightly amused, as if they thought that we were taking the war too seriously. When someone who was particularly exercised elbowed them or shouted at them or yanked them about, they merely shrugged their shoulders and rolled with the punches.

A salvo of shells burst near the road, and a small man from Company Headquarters who had been wounded in the head by a fragment from a German hand grenade screamed in pain and fright: "Kill me, kill me! Somebody kill me! Oh, Christ, I can't stand it!" He began to cry.

The room went quiet, and the Germans stiffened as everyone's eyes shifted from the wounded man to them, for as Germans, they were held responsible. The man was eased to a bunk, and the eyes spoke a single thought: I'll kill you for this. If he dies, you go with him.

Marsh turned to McCreary for a bandage. The little man opened his eyes and saw the Germans in their long-visored caps. He cried out and thrashed with pain.

"Lemme kill 'em, lemme kill 'em!" one man yelled. He pulled out a pistol and rushed at the Germans.

"Get outa here," Mercier, a sergeant in the third platoon, said, holding him off. "They want these bastards back at battalion."

The man put the pistol back in his holster with muttered goddamns.

His face red with blood, the little man kicked and squirmed and sobbed aloud. It was almost more than I could stand to watch him. "Morphine!" I said. "Give him some morphine."

Someone opened a first-aid packet and pushed a morphine Syrette into the wounded man's arm.

McCreary snatched up the phone. "For Chrissake," he hissed to Rader, "call Company and get a stretcher down here quick!" He chewed on a dead cigarette with tears in his eyes.

"Kill me! Somebody kill me! Oh, oh, oh! Mercier! I want Mercier! Where's Mercier?" the wounded man cried like a frightened child calling for its mother.

Mercier stepped over to him and held his hand. "That's OK, buddy," he murmured, "that's OK. You'll be all right." The man subsided, and he patted Mercier's hand and wiped his own eyes with his sleeve.

Three shells came in so fast and close together that the detonations and the sound of their flight intermingled. The house quaked. The wounded man started up with a piercing shriek.

"Take it easy, buddy," Mercier said, easing him back. "Everything's going to be all right."

I watched them with wet eyes. Mercier, one of the top combat men in E Company, was so big and hard and strong, and the wounded man was small and pitiful enough to be his hurt little boy. I knew he was going to die—I could tell by looking at him—and I didn't want to see it. I had had enough. I left the room. One more scene like this, I thought as I went out to the garage, and I am through for good. Why did I come back to this?

"Oh, kill me!"

I gritted my teeth and stared at the night, not caring how close the shells came. The night smelled cold and old and wet. Burnt gunpowder of the 88s gave it a special flavor. In a lull, I heard footsteps pound across the vacant lot and into the garage. Roe and another medic stopped when they saw me. "Where is he?" Roe panted.

"In the back room," I replied, "I'll show you."

Our own artillery was still falling in town. The enemy house burned brighter than ever. Flares popped and glowed all along the river line. German mortar barrages ku-rumped around the house, in the woods, along the banks of the creek. The wounded man was numb to it all. Relaxed at last by the morphine, he lay limp and moaned softly.

Roe quickly unrolled the stretcher, and then he and Mercier and the other medic slid their arms under the wounded man and lowered him onto it.

The movement made him shriek with pain. McCreary sucked hard on his dead cigarette, and my eyes clouded over again.

The Germans watched the wounded man without sympathy and relaxed when he was ready to go. Their crisis had passed, they knew. They were no longer in danger of being killed.

The patrol filed out of the room. When the way was clear, Roe took the front of the stretcher and the other medic the rear. They lifted it gently and started off. Mercier walked beside them, holding his friend's hand and telling him over and over again that everything was going to be all right.

Some more shells came into the yard, so they set the stretcher down in the garage and waited for a lull. When the firing stopped and they judged that it was time, they started off again. I watched them till they disappeared, and then went back indoors.

Our room seemed as empty as a night club after a large, noisy party has left. We could even hear the flickering of the lamp's flame, or imagined that we could: It was that quiet.

The quiet indoors was a remarkable contrast to the night outside. Once so still and ominous, it was now a heaving volcano of fire and flashes and flares, as the enemy reacted to the patrol and the artillery barrage. German mortars walked up and down both banks of the river, across the open field, through the woods, along the road, and around the barracks square. The machine gun died out, but the 88 continued to make us twitch with its angry buzzes and ringing explosions. Alien and strident in a situation where neither side dared to show the tiniest match flame, the burning house stood out in the dark city like an angel in hell.

While we busied ourselves preparing for a restless night that we feared might even bring a counterattack, the upstairs guard became aware of a strange noise down by the crossing. The noise was a gargling, choking, wheezing sound that could have been made only by a man shot through the lungs. The abandoned prisoner was still alive.

"Let him die," McCreary said when he heard the news. "He doesn't have long to go."

"No," I replied. "If we leave him alone, the Krauts are likely to hear him and come back for him. He'll tell 'em about our house, and they'll put the 88 on it."

"Oh, hell."

"I mean it. Look at the way the 88 followed the patrol into the house. Look what it did to D Company's 50 caliber."

Marsh nodded his head. "Pretty risky out there with all those mortars," he said.

"I'll go," I replied. "It's him or us."

"You're crazy."

"No, I'm cautious. I'm going to swim the creek and finish him off with a trench knife. That way they won't hear anything. I don't like that 88."

I changed into a pair of wet fatigues that I had washed in the afternoon, put my trench knife in my pocket, and went outside.

Alone in the darkness, I found my courage less strong than it had been in the company of the other men in the phone room. But the fear of the 88 kept me going until I was well into the woods.

With a tremendous roar, half a dozen mortar shells landed together on the other side of the creek. I went back to the house.

McCreary welcomed me. "We were really sweating you out," he said. "Thought maybe the Krauts would be using that guy as bait for an ambush."

"We'll get him with hand grenades," Marsh suggested. "OK, Web?"

I nodded.

We tiptoed back down the forest path through the bare, black, dripping trees, and stopped behind a two-foot mound that ran along the river's edge. The rope that the patrol had used was still in position. The wounded German lay out of sight on his back near the other end, which was tied to a concrete telephone pole about fifteen yards from us.

He must have heard us coming. For a few moments he held his breath and stopped groaning and gasping and wheezing, evidently hoping that we would not notice him. But he couldn't stay quiet long, and soon the ghastly, sucking wheezes commenced again, loud as ever.

Poor bastard, I thought, listening to him. He's trying to hide from us. He's dying, and he knows we want to kill him. What a fate: to gasp your life out all alone in the mud of a dirty little creek, helpless to hold off the slow death that is inside you and the quicker death that is walking up on you on the other side of the water. A death without love, a death without hope. God, who invented war?

But if he gets back alive, I may be dead.

"OK," Marsh whispered, "let's throw 'em."

We pulled the pins on our hand grenades and arched them across the river at the sound of the wheezing. One of the grenades ex-

ploded, the other was a dud. There was no change in the breathing noises. We went into the house, got two more grenades, and
tried again, without success. The German continued to moan and
wheeze.

"The hell with it," Marsh said. "Let him die. They won't come
after him."

We gave up and went to bed.

Just before sunrise, Cobb, who had also considered swimming—
until he had heard the mortars—strolled down to the creek, threw
one grenade, and killed the helpless, dying German. Our home was
secure for another day.

The author, during the liberation of Eindhoven
Photo by Hans Wesenhagen

Corporal Donald Hoobler

Celebrating the liberation of Eindhoven. The soldier on the right, Webster wrote on the back of the photo, is Wiseman, "who dug most of my foxholes for me. . . . He was a brave, rough and tough miner."

Photo by Hans Wesenhagen

Colonel Robert F. Sink
Courtesy U.S. Signal Corps

Public head-shaving of collaborators, Eindhoven
Photo by Hans Wesenhagen

Private Robert Marsh

The Berghof, Hitler's house for guests in Berchtesgaden, at the end of the war.
The author and his friends joined in raiding the wine cellar.

Captain Ronald Speirs

Private Ralph Trapazano

A drawing of the author by a German woman in Saalfelden, 1945

4

HITLER'S CHAMPAGNE

It was spring again, the early spring of 1945, and we were deep in the enemy's country, on the plains of Bavaria. By this time, many of the mourners who had bowed their heads at Littlecote were in turn themselves mourned, and a squad of twelve counted itself lucky if it had two men left who had jumped in Normandy.

We had been searching for the front for several weeks and hadn't found it yet. From the Rhine River, where we had lived in apartment houses on the west bank and listened to the infantry mop up the Ruhr Pocket on the opposite shore, we had ridden 40-and-8s in a huge semicircle through Germany, Holland, Belgium, Luxembourg, and France, back into Germany again.

Our journey was delightfully noncombatant. The air was warm and sweet, the countryside newly green. Bedded down in hay provided by Colonel Sink, who knew what we wanted, we hung our feet over the side of our little boxcars, munched K rations, shot at passing trees, and admired landscapes that were not crowned with airbursts. We passed as tourists through cities like Aachen, Sarrbrucken, Kaiserslautern, Luxembourg City, and Sarreguimines, and finally stopped at Ludwigshaven, where we switched to DUKWs and set off with the 7th Army, still in search of the front.

All the rumors were encouraging. A GI in the Transportation

Corps said that the front had broken up completely. The Germans were surrendering by the thousands, an MP told us. A Red Cross girl claimed that organized resistance had ceased altogether.

We drove through Ludwigshaven and crossed the Rhine on the long, swaying Ernie Pyle pontoon bridge. From the ruins of Mannheim (dead rotting in the rubble, no civilians on the streets), we turned east and going uphill, entered beautiful country very like the Catskill Mountains. Heidelberg stood undamaged, on the lovely Neckar River, but we continued through it and eventually crossed the Danube at Ulm on another pontoon bridge. On we went, still looking for the front, through the Pfalz, Baden, Wurttemberg, the prettiest part of southern Germany, collecting a battle star for a campaign that involved no shooting.

The once-mighty German army was in a state of utter dissolution. Everywhere we went, enemy soldiers flowed to the roads like rivulets running downhill after a rain. We relieved them of their watches, pistols, and binoculars and sent them on their way to rear echelon, for which we couldn't be bothered with them now. There were just too many of them. They had been a novelty at first—live Germans by the hundreds—but the novelty wore off quickly, and we grew bored with them, so merciless in victory, so fawning in defeat.

We sunbathed on the breaks and spent each night in a village, where we commandeered the dwellings and bade the civilians be on their way till morning. We ate fried eggs and canned beef and drank the liquors of a continent, ranging from French cognac and German schnapps to Russian vodka and Hungarian kirsch. We slept between sheets and took hot baths, and no one traveled without a corkscrew, a frying pan, and a radio. Though it was forbidden by the clean-minded young men at SHAEF (farther in the rear than ever before), some of us even fraternized with the local Mädchen. Kommen Sie here, baby!

We had pulled off the Munich-Salzburg Autobahn at twilight, after the 3rd Battalion, which was in the lead, had been ambushed at a blown bridge. It was the regiment's first action in southern Germany. A pocket of Germans who had apparently not heard the news of their nation's collapse had opened fire on the 3rd Battalion as it was halted at the gap in the great six-lane superhighway. Several men were killed who had been with the regiment since its start. The rest dismounted and spent the night climbing a mountain and flanking the ambush.

We enjoyed a more civilian evening. After backing up and turning around, we went to a Hansel-and-Gretel village, filled with wounded SS men, a couple of miles north of the Autobahn and spent the night frying eggs and drinking new milk and old brandy. We switched on the electric stove in our chalet and fried a few dozen Grade A, we slept between sheets on soft double beds, and we did not envy the 3rd Battalion.

Now another day had come. "Hit it, hit it!" the CQ cried. "Moving out in half an hour."

I wriggled out of my mummy-type, one-man sleeping bag and sat up on the living-room floor, where I had gone to sleep. The CQ had left the door open behind him, and the icy blast of air that came in made me shiver and cringe. It was still dark outside.

Muttering obscenities, I looked at my watch. It was only 4:30, an hour before the normal reveille. I shuddered. We only rose this early for a dawn attack. I did not look forward to fighting again. It was too late in the war to risk being killed. I was an acting noncom, a squad leader, but I still did not want to get killed.

My assistant, J. D., and I were the only men who had been in Normandy. The other ten had come in as replacements afterward. Not one of us had been in this same squad a year ago. In fact, half the men were young boys from the eighteen-year-old draft who had been in the army only long enough to take thirteen weeks' basic and four weeks' jump training before going overseas as replacements. It was a good squad, though, and I was glad to have it while my regular leader, Marsh, was on furlough in the Riviera.

After I had gotten the men up, we gathered in the warm kitchen and ate breakfast. The dawn attack was the main topic of conversation. With the Alps running like jagged sharks' teeth on the southern horizon only ten or fifteen miles away, we were all concerned about the so-called National Redoubt, the mountainous stronghold where Hitler had allegedly ordered the SS to make their last stand. It was one of those fight-to-the-last-man stands he was always ordering (how seldom they were executed!), but its basic idiocy did not make it any less menacing to us. We did not look forward to cleaning out the Alps in a tedious mountain campaign, now that the war was almost over.

We lingered so long in the kitchen that our platoon sergeant had to come in and roust us with an obscene blast for holding up the company. He left, and I went to the living room and put on my musette bag and harness. Still the cautious soldier (made more cautious by experience), I checked my cartridge belt to make sure I had everything. I would never move out unless I had everything.

Yes, it was all there: bayonet, canteen, shovel, compass, wirecutters, first-aid packet, and the .45 I had bought from the Air Corps to keep from getting my throat cut on the jump field in Holland. I took two hand grenades from my pockets and hung them on my suspenders. My rifle was loaded, my stomach full, a fifth of kirsch was in my pocket. I was ready to go into action. I picked up a box of machine-gun ammunition, told J. D. to check the house for misplaced or deliberately forgotten grenades and ammunition, and led the squad outside.

It was bitter cold. The puddles in the roadside ditches had frozen over in the night, and a heavy frost shone like the moonlight of D-Day on the roads and fields. The ground was frozen hard.

We ran down to where the rest of E Company was stamping their feet and milling about in a cloud of frozen curses, fell in place in front of the second squad, our rivals in all scrounging and the avoidance of details, and came to attention under the glare of Captain Speirs. After a count had been taken, he gave us at ease and explained our mission.

"We're going into the Alps," he said, "as soon as the goddamn DUKWs get here. The war's almost over—just a couple of more days now—and I don't want to lose any of you men in an ambush, so keep your weapons handy and be ready to fight the minute you hear the first shot."

A runner pounded up the road and saluted. They talked briefly, and then he left and the captain informed us that we had to meet the DUKWs on the other side of town. He faced us in that direction and gave us route step. D Company was already moving out ahead of us.

The village was asleep. There were no civilians or wounded Germans on the streets. The only sound was the distant crowing of a rooster and the heavy tramp and muffled clatter of the battalion as it marched along.

This was where I belonged. I had come back to it twice, after minor wounds in Normandy and Holland, and I wanted to stay with it to the end. I did not like the army and I would never again "sir" any man as long as I lived, but as long as I had to be in the army, I wanted to be in the 506th.

I looked at the sky and then at my watch. Five-thirty and already getting light. But it was a dull light, with no clear sky and a mass of very dark clouds lowering on the earth as for a thunderstorm.

We passed a grocery store that had just been abandoned by Company Headquarters. A wild mass of slave laborers and ex-prisoners of war was rushing in and out of the doors and windows, scrambling for boxes and cans and shouting and shoving and tearing at each other like hungry tigers. Some were short Mongolians, others big Nordic men, but all were Russians, with homemade red stars in their buttonholes.

"Rooski, Rooski!" we shouted, waving to them.

They grinned at us and commenced scrambling again.

We continued a quarter of a mile beyond the village before we saw a convoy of DUKWs moving slowly toward us. We halted on the road while the DUKWs smashed down a fence, made a half-circle on a frozen meadow to our left, came back on the road, and lined up bumper to bumper, facing south. The maneuver, which took twenty minutes, was accompanied by stamping feet and impatient cursing as the men got colder and colder. The last DUKW made its turn, the lowering sky broke up, and it started to snow. We climbed in.

I took a stand near the front, to see what was going on, while the others, who were less curious, huddled together on the cold metal floor. Finally the convoy moved off with the waddling motion peculiar to these vehicles, which resembled a pontoon on wheels and rode like a sailboat in a gentle swell. The cursing subsided to snores, shivers, and lewd mutters of complaint.

It was snowing so hard that we could only see about fifty yards ahead. The DUKWs went up and down some low hillocks, turned left on the Autobahn, moved tentatively ahead a mile, and halted.

I shook the snow off my helmet and checked my watch: 6:20. It was going to be an awfully late dawn attack. Perhaps it would never come? I could be home frying eggs.

The memory of the kitchen reminded me of other warm things, and suddenly I recalled the kirsch. I snaked the bottle out of my pocket and glanced casually around the DUKW. The coast was clear: Most of the men were sleeping with their arms folded on top of their knees and their heads buried in their arms. Nobody was watching me but J. D., a big replacement named Smith, our lieutenant, our platoon sergeant, and Liebgott, now the first platoon's interpreter–radio man. I unscrewed the cap and took a drink. The warm, sweet liquor made my body glow. I took another drink.

"Dibs," said Liebgott.

I nodded and handed the bottle to Smith, who had priority because he was in my squad. He called it "cough syrup, worse than rum," and drank more than I had. Liebgott was next.

"That stuff'll kill you," McCreary said, blinking up at us. He extended his arm. "Give me a drink."

Liebgott passed the bottle to J. D., who tilted his head back and gargled. The bizarre noise woke the rest of the men, and they studied him with thirsty eyes. I cursed him for drawing attention to the kirsch. "We could have kept it up at this end," I said. "Now we have to pass it around."

The snow stopped, and a cold wind came off the Alps to clear the sky and chill us further. In the light of a sun that glared without warmth, we saw a blown bridge half a mile downhill from us. There were three small houses just this side of the bridge. Men were dismounting from the DUKWs ahead and running up and down on the pavement, shadowboxing and waving their arms and clapping their hands together to warm up. Others started to heat their rations over little cardboard fires lit in cleared spaces on the highway.

Captain Speirs came alongside and told us that we could dismount if we wanted to. "We're in for a long wait," he explained. Three or four men jumped out and started to run up and down, whooping and hollering.

An old man left one of the houses on a bicycle and pedaled slowly toward us. He got off as the road grew steeper and walked beside his bicycle. While the rest of us watched in jeering disgust, two bravos held him up.

He was a very old man, pale and frail and hollow-looking, with a goatee and a black serge suit, and he was panting deeply from his uphill climb. He looked as if he were dressed for church. For all we knew, it might even have been Sunday. Days of the week meant nothing to us in the field.

"Hände hoch!" one of the heroes yelled, covering him with a Luger.

We snickered. "Look at the brave soldiers!" someone shouted. "Combat men!"

The old man dropped his bike so fast its lamp broke. His hands shot in the air. He trembled violently.

One of the bravos frisked him and yanked out a heavy silver pocketwatch. He waved it triumphantly in the air. The whole company hissed him. His buddy fished through the civilian's wallet and displayed a handful of paper money. He, too, was hissed. The old man pleaded with them tearfully, but they sent him on his way.

I looked at them both and shook my head. Tough guys. The biggest looters were seldom the bravest soldiers. In fact, as Captain Speirs, who had been decorated three times for bravery, more than once remarked, there was an inverse ratio between courage and looting. Ashamed of the deed and yet powerless to undo it, since one of the men was in Company Headquarters and the other was a noncom (politically appointed, through court intrigue in our former captain's quarters), I glanced away from the old man's pleading eyes as he shuffled timidly by, and studied the snow on a tree across the road. This was indeed some dawn attack.

We turned right almost at the blown bridge and squeaked and swayed and slipped down a narrow dirt road into a cold, dark valley. The DUKWs that had gone before us had churned the snow to a black slime that offered no footing. Our driver wrestled and cursed to keep from sliding off the crown into a rutted ditch alongside. Tall, overhanging pine trees, brushed in passing, softly dumped their loads of snow on us, and soon the column slowed down to less than a walk as more and more of the ponderous vehicles floundered from their course and struggled to regain it. The temperature in the valley was below freezing, and the air was very still and ominous.

We left the road, nosed up onto a railway roadbed, and jolted along the cavities where the ties had been. In their retreat the Germans had ripped up both ties and rails with one of those wasteful machines that are good only for war. The tracks lay off to one side in strange, twisted shapes. Gradually the roadbed curved to the left. As we crossed a little wooden trestle spanning a rocky brook, we saw, half a mile away, the gap in the Autobahn that we were by-passing. The bridge foundations jutted out into the air fifteen or twenty feet on both sides, and the crumpled black mass of the span lay in a rocky gorge a hundred yards below. It was a neat job of demolition.

Most of the men were sound asleep by now, for it was not a very exciting journey. Only J. D. and I stood erect. We had finished the kirsch between us, and thus fortified, were ready to face whatever perils or adventures lay ahead.

"I don't like it," I said thickly, swaying with the DUKW. "It's too quiet."

We passed a snowy clearing with a cluster of little gingerbread houses right out of *Grimm's Fairy Tales*. J. D. frowned at them.

"Look at that," he said. "All closed up and not a civilian in sight."

"And no white flags. They always put up white flags before."

I shook my head. You could count on trouble when the civilians took off.

"We're due for a fight," I muttered, gripping my M-1. "We've had it too easy: no patrols, no attacks, no combat, no artillery. All we've done in Germany is sleep in houses and eat fresh eggs. It can't last forever."

"I don't like it either. It's just too goddamn quiet."

The wind had died down, the sun had grown warm, and the snow was melting fast. For the first time today, we could see the Alps. They looked much closer in the bright, clear morning air than they had at twilight, when they had appeared to be ten or fifteen miles away.

The surrendering Germans swelled from rivulets into tidal waves. In one meadow we saw several thousand squatting in a docile en-campment guarded by three bored American MPs. When others came to us on breaks and with a strange and almost touching but still typically German mixture of pride, arrogance, and humility, begging to be allowed to surrender to a high-class airborne unit, we waved them off and airily told them we couldn't be bothered. They would have to swallow their pride and surrender to rear echelon.

It was a time of great gaiety. Victory was in the air and the Wehr-macht was melting away before our eyes into a shabby mass of bewildered men wandering sullenly along the same road on which they had marched in triumph five years before, when their chosen leader had launched them on history's darkest wave of barbarism and extermination. Trucks and tanks from other American units came onto the Autobahn at every intersection and passed us with waves and shouts. The drivers all wore bright scarves and old civilian hats. Even the tank commanders, who normally never shifted their eyes from the terrain ahead, called and waved and gave the V-sign.

Wherever a PW enclosure or slave-labor lager was liberated, the ragged, hungry inmates poured onto the highway that a maniac had built to enslave them and their children and their children's children. "Deutschland kaput!" they cried to us happily. No matter how tattered their clothes, the freed men had all taken pains to fashion tiny ornaments of their national colors for their buttonholes. They wore them as proudly as medals for bravery: the red star of Russia, the tricolor of France, red and green for Italy, blue, white, and gold for Yugoslavia. There were Poles, Czechs, Greeks, Belgians, Dutch, Magyars, Slovenes, Lithuanians, and many others, all former slave laborers or prisoners of war.

I was glad, when I saw them, that I had come back to the outfit and gone into Germany. For the trip, with its views of the lagers and prison camps, had finally convinced me of the need to drive the Germans from the face of Europe. How could a civilized nation run concentration camps and murder millions?

Soon we were passing the remnants of Germany's greatest evil, the concentration camps. The sight, after so many years of propaganda, of those striped uniforms, so like pajamas, that signified endless death on the widest and most coldly methodical scale, was very chilling.

A lone man from Dachau wandered out of a field when we were halted by the road and talked in a dazed way of the death that the Germans had planned for the world. He spoke of his years in Dachau and the thousands that he had seen die there. Others came up shortly afterward, and soon we were passing them by the score. It made us feel good to think that our army had set them free.

The DUKWs rolled on, past der Chiemsee, a lovely blue lake with a yacht basin near a resort hotel that had been converted into a Wehrmacht hospital, and then pulled off onto a grassy shoulder for a ten-minute break. We dismounted to relieve ourselves and stretch our legs and frisk the passing Germans.

While we were lolling on the grass, someone motioned for silence. "Do you hear that?" he asked, jerking his head toward the Alps. "Sounds like thunder."

I listened carefully. There were no clouds to make a thunderstorm, but there was thunder.

"Man, Web," J. D. said with a worried look on his face, "it doesn't sound good, does it?"

"No," I agreed, biting my lip, for I recognized the sound, "it doesn't." It was a rolling barrage.

We left the Autobahn at the next side road and plunged down toward the artillery fire. Our mood changed from holiday excitement to silent foreboding as we descended and came upon more evidence of war than we had seen since Ulm.

Knocked out by aircraft, two yellow-brown Wehrmacht halftracks stood at the edge of the first forest trail. There were three fresh graves in the woods nearby, with German helmets on the top of rough, pine-bough crosses. A P-47 fighter plane lay tilted like a huge stiffened silverfish among the tall dark pine trees farther on. We passed foxholes and slit trenches and a burned-out antiaircraft halftrack at a crossroads. Its dead cannon still pointed at the sky.

The sound of firing got louder and louder, and the Alps came nearer and nearer. This was the National Redoubt, and we were going into it.

Nobody slept in the DUKWs anymore. Instead, the men stood ready with their weapons in their hands and stared anxiously at the cold, gloomy woods all around us. The road circled a low, bare hill where the enemy had abandoned four 105mm cannons in the snow on the reverse slope, and then it went through a pass pocked with shell holes and strewn with smashed trees and abandoned GI gear and helmets. We started down to the valley where the shells were falling with the slam of heavy doors.

The valley ahead of us was about three miles wide and four or five miles long. Its floor, patches of green meadow and golden grain land, was composed of low, gently rolling hills. Bigger, steeper, pine-covered hills bounded the valley on three sides. The Alps rose on the fourth, or south, side.

They were dark and ominous, immense, towering over all wars and all humanity. Everything about them was cold and hostile: the gray rocks, the thick grass and heavy moss that ran from tree level to the rocks, and the blue-green pine forests that cloaked their massive bases. A bitter wind blew down at us from the blinding white snow on the fangs that were their summits.

"Get ready for an ambush," I said, trying to appear calm and not quite succeeding. The other men nodded and said nothing. They had been ready ever since we had left the Autobahn.

Our convey rolled onto the valley floor and turned right. A jeep from another unit overtook us with a steady honking. "Off the road, off the road!" yelled a major standing beside the driver. He waved us aside with a violent gesture.

We went to the shoulder with a quick swing and stopped. The artillery fire was very close now. I felt like vomiting.

Their fronts sandbagged against Panzerfausts, a column of heavy tanks clattered past us in the wake of the jeep. Crouching, clinging infantrymen with fixed bayonets and a faraway look in their eyes covered their tops and knelt behind the turrets. They passed us without a word or wave of greeting and were gone as swiftly as they had come. The artillery fell like summer thunder.

Our DUKWs returned to the road and commenced their journey in a silence of their own. They turned left, away from the bombardment, and then right, and came out on a muddy lane running straight toward the Alps. A convoy of trucks and halftracks several hundred yards long was parked on the left shoulder. They bore the Cross of Lorraine insignia of the French 2nd Armored Division, a unit manned by former sailors, now in green combat suits, who still wore black berets with bright-red pompons. The DUKWs slowed down by them and stopped suddenly, jamming up together.

Pop! A sound like the report of a German rifle went off to the right of our DUKW.

"SS! SS!" a Frenchman cried from a halftrack opposite us. He pointed excitedly in the direction of the sound.

"Ambush!" I yelled, clicking the safety catch off my rifle. I started over the side, then looked out and froze in position. "Jesus," I whispered.

A French tankman stood ankle-deep in snow in a young pine forest beside the DUKW with a smoking Belgian automatic in his hand and a cigarette in the corner of his mouth. A young German boy in his early teens dressed in a long Wehrmacht overcoat, lay dead at his feet. Hatless and unarmed, his body bore no gear whatsoever.

Two other boys, similarly clad, knelt behind the body, their mouths and eyes wide open, their faces paralyzed with fright. As they stared helplessly at the Frenchman, he blew the ash off his cigarette, put the pistol against the second boy's forehead, and spattered his brains red and yellow and purple on the snow behind him.

One of our replacements turned fishbelly white and vomited over the side. "God, oh God, oh God," he moaned.

The Frenchman stepped up to his last prisoner. This boy was the youngest of the three. He had never shaved. He had soft brown eyes and a fresh, cheerful pink adolescent face that had never been creased by worry or the awareness of death. All the thoughts that old men have but that he had never had before crowded in an instant into his mind and came out in his eyes and on his forehead. Framed by the dark pines, he put his hands together and prayed and cried softly and waited to die.

The DUKW moved forward, and we heard the shot from the distance.

I turned to a cocky, bubbling young replacement who had been eager to see action. "There's your goddamn war!" I said. "How do you like it?"

He gulped and shook his head.

A narrow pass through a dripping, rocky gorge took us out of the valley and through the foothills into the Alps themselves. The men relaxed and lay down and began to doze off. We wound round and round, up and down, till it seemed to those of us who were still awake that we must be hopelessly lost.

At last our sideroad joined a better one near a dark brook, where a lone enemy soldier stood beside a signpost in a black tanker's uniform, the same kind worn by SS armored troops. One of our men who was Jewish and had no love for the SS studied him with narrowed eyes.

"Sind Sie SS?" he inquired, his rifle at his hip, leaning toward the German.

"Nein. Ich bin Panzergrenadier."

Unconvinced, our man clicked the safety off his M-1.

"Hold your fire!" we shouted, not wishing to witness another murder. "He's harmless."

Our friend ignored us. He was from the Far West, and he had something else in mind.

"Sie sind SS!" he yelled. "Dance, you son of a bitch!" He shot around the German's feet.

The German pranced and cavorted. I didn't know whether to laugh or cry. Captain Speirs yelled back for the man to cease fire. He lifted his rifle with a grin, and we drove off.

Roused by the shots, the rest of the men came to life. They stood up and yawned and stretched their arms and legs and studied the mountains and admired the speed with which we were traveling, for we were going downhill in a great rush, as if the drivers had finally found out where we were going and were in a hurry to get there. Rounding a bend, we popped out of the dark gorge and raced toward a little Alpine village that sloped up prettily from a rocky river ten yards wide.

There was a sign at a bridge we had to cross to get into town. When we read what the sign said, we screamed with joy. It was Berchtesgaden.

White flags hung from the carved wooden balconies of the hotels and inns that lined the steep, narrow streets, and a few of the older civilians came outdoors to watch us drive in. The DUKWs crept slowly into the center of town and stopped.

"This calls for a drink," one of our replacements said. J. D. and I gaped as he pulled a fifth of Gordon's gin out of a big pants pocket. "Found it in the last billet," he explained, passing it around. Four fingers were left when it reached me.

"Bet I can drink it in one minute," I said, hoisting the bottle. "A thousand francs. Any takers?"

"I'll bet you can't," the replacement, Neumann, said. "Another fifth says you can't."

"You got another one? Man, you guys learn fast. Here goes." I upended the bottle and started to drink. Neumann timed me, and the rest of the squad looked on. The gin was gone in forty seconds. I put the new fifth in my musette bag and began to enjoy Berchtesgaden.

A bright clean resort village of about eight thousand inhabitants, Berchtesgaden rested for the most part on the south slope of a hill surrounded by glittering mountains of breathtaking beauty. The houses were built in the traditional Alpine style, with rocks on the roof, carved wooden balconies at each end, and fresco paintings of pastoral or religious scenes on the stucco walls. The village had been a modest German mountain resort long before Hitler made it famous.

Even after six years of war, the shops still catered to tourists. There were camera stores (with no cameras), chocolate shops (without chocolate), and restaurants (without food). The places that had sold resort wear had no clothing—it had all gone for the war— and the ski shops had no skis. Innkeeping was the major occupation, and almost every building bore the sign of a hotel, inn, or Gasthof.

None of the natives could say, as they had in other towns, that they had not liked Hitler, for their absolute loyalty to the Nazi cause had been assured years before by the SS and the SD, who allowed only certified, bonded, 100 percent Nazis to live so close to their leader's chalet.

The gentleman who had so popularized this once-obscure village that its name became known throughout the world had not lived in Berchtesgaden proper. He had taken to himself, instead, a private mountain, der Kehlstein, which rose abruptly from the river we had just crossed, on the town's southern fringe. Der Kehlstein had been fenced off, guarded, and maintained as an SS preserve, with its own heavily patrolled roads and massive, camouflaged barracks. Halfway up to an elevator that ran through solid rock to the Eagle's Nest stood a chalet, der Berghof, which had served as a guesthouse.

It was a neat arrangement, worthy of a knave who gloried in murder and lived in fear, and so the British, in one of the light, personal gestures that they used so well to brighten the war, had bombed the mountainside with blockbusters. The SS had vanished among the craters thirty feet deep, and the tidy estate had been converted in an instant into a landscape resembling the face of the moon. The former owner had died far north in Berlin in the crumbling, rotten ruins of his Thousand Year Reich, and a new day came for Berchtesgaden.

We lingered in town awhile, then moved off to a large house beyond, where I fell asleep under a pine tree. The DUKWs left us without regret, having found us too casual for their taste, and at 2:30 a convoy of GI trucks took us to a settlement of long, white, two-story chalets on a highway about a mile and a half north of Berchtesgaden. The new billets were laid out as precisely as an army camp, and they were separated from the road by a smooth lawn a hundred feet wide.

After a long wait while the civilians decamped and the billeting officer apportioned our quarters, Captain Speirs made a little speech. "We're going to live in these houses," he said. "They were built as apartments for the families of the Gestapo that used to guard Hitler, so we don't care what you do to them or take from them as long as you keep them neat. Not a single civilian will be allowed in the area. The whole town is SS, and if you don't want to lose your jump pay for six months for fraternizing, you won't be talking to any Krauts around here.

"We'll stand guard on the road and around the apartments to keep the civilians out and be ready in case the SS comes back down the mountain to raid us. A lot of 'em haven't been accounted for yet. The Kraut soldiers will be turning themselves in at a big PW enclosure a mile down the road from here. The second platoon will guard this enclosure. Rest of the company stays here."

The company split up at the captain's order. McCreary's squad and mine wound up in the last chalet to the north. J. D. and I staked a claim on the best bedroom by throwing our gear on the floor and then set out to reconnoiter the billet. It was the best we had had in Germany. There were three big bedrooms in the upstairs apartment that we occupied, with a full-sized living room, a separate dining room, a tiled lavatory with a modern tub and toilet, and, best of all, a large kitchen at the south end with three exposures.

The kitchen was painted a warm yellow, with red flowers on the drawers and cupboards. It featured a massive icebox, a six-burner electric stove, and a table long enough to seat half the squad at a time. Pots, pans, chinaware, and condiments were all in place. Nothing had been removed or disturbed. We began to brew a pot of ersatz coffee.

Once it was ready, we sprawled around in the bright warm kitchen and listened to the radio, which had been brought in. The sky had clouded over outside, and a thin, cold drizzle was falling as the sun went down. The kitchen seemed very warm and cozy.

Christenson, who was now our platoon guide, came in with an air of whiskey and a wide grin on his face. He waved a piece of paper in the air. "At ease, goddamn it!" he shouted. "Get a load of this."

We looked up.

"It's from Corps. Just came in. Here's what it says: 'Effective immediately, all troops will stand fast on present positions. German Army Group G in this section has surrendered. No firing on Germans unless fired upon. Notify French units in vicinity. Full details, to be broadcast, will be issued by SHAEF.'"

We let out a great shout of joy.

"Yessir," Christenson said. "Looks like the war is over. And we couldn't end it in a better place."

"What you got there?"

I stood shivering in the drizzle near the front door and frowned at Luz, the company comedian, as raucous and funny in combat as in garrison, and O'Keefe, who was one of our younger and more gentlemanly replacements. They had just pulled up in a boatlike vehicle that resembled a miniature DUKW. A mortarman, Garcia, sat in back.

"A Schwimmwagen," Luz replied. "Took it off a Kraut down the road." He got out, and O'Keefe and Garcia stood up in back and heaved the front end of a large wooden packing case over the side for him to grasp.

I looked in the box. My eyes widened, for it was filled with bottles. "What the hell?"

"Champagne," O'Keefe said. He had gotten down to take the rear of the box. "OK," he grunted, "I got it." Staggering under the load, he, Garcia, and Luz started indoors. I followed them like a hungry dog.

"Where the hell?"

"Hitler's cellar."

"What!"

"Sure. From his hideout, der Berghof, the halfway house."

"Well, here, let me give you a hand. My God, we have to get this upstairs before McCreary sees it. I'll be goddamned."

We strained, stiff-armed and panting, to carry the champagne quickly beyond the reach of the second squad, and unloaded it in my room, where J. D. promised to keep an eye on it. "TO equipment," Luz said. "Every man gets a jug."

While the rest of the squad crowded around, whistling in astonishment, I dropped my voice and asked Luz and his helpers what they were waiting for. "Let's get some more," I suggested, snatching up my helmet and buckling on my pistol belt. We ran down to the Schwimmwagen and swarmed aboard like pirates boarding a galleon. Luz was at the wheel, and he was in his element—noisy recklessness. "I should have been a midget-auto racer," he remarked, zooming into the first curve. He slammed on the brakes. The Schwimmwagen skidded around the corner, and he spun the wheel and straightened her out. My heart beat in my throat. O'Keefe and Garcia clutched the side and said nothing.

"Out of the way, you sons of bitches!" Luz roared at the night. He gunned the motor, pressed on the horn, and blared his way through Berchtesgaden at fifty miles an hour. "Goddamn Nazis!"

We hurtled recklessly through the wet streets to the south end of town and across the narrow bridge there. Soon we passed a concrete blockhouse and the high, barbed-wire fence that bounded Hitler's private mountain and then started uphill. A GI with the 3rd Division patch on his sleeve reeled and retched his way down the middle of the road. Luz honked and yelled at him to get out of the way, but he was too happy to care. He had a bottle of champagne in one hand and a P-38 in the other. "Whoopee!" he shouted, firing the pistol in the air.

"We better hurry," Luz said. "The dogfaces are drinking it dry."

The craters were all around us now, but fortunately none of them blocked the road. There were shattered trees and the grotesque ruins of barracks and other buildings on both sides.

Luz accelerated. It seemed as if the whole world were racing for der Berghof, and he didn't want to come in last. The higher he went, the thicker grew the stream of vehicles, until it became almost a solid mass, bumper to bumper. Recon cars, command cars, jeeps, DUKWs, halftracks, Volkswagens, Schwimmwagens— all were headed for the wine cellar. Luz drove on the left and passed as many of them as he could, but finally the traffic was so thick that he had to fall in line.

The road leveled off at last. We rounded a curve, and I gasped at the sight ahead. It was unforgettable: the nightmare looting of der Berghof, Hitler's secondary chalet. None of the blockbusters that the British had dropped in the vicinity had hit the house, but several smaller bombs had caved in the roof, shattered the windows, and rearranged the lawn. Spoilsport SS men had finished the job by setting the place afire. The front yard was a hideous mass of bomb craters, blackened timbers, broken glass, and jagged chunks of brick and mortar. Scores of paratroopers, Frenchmen, and 3rd Division soldiers lurched around noisily, stumbling in and out of the house.

Der Berghof was built on the side of a hill adjoining the mountain that bore the more famous Adlerhorst, or Eagle's Nest, which stood three thousand feet above us. The road to the elevator to der Adlerhorst was blocked by bomb damage, so for tonight we had to be content with der Berghof.

Luz drove into a parking place opposite the concrete chalet and stopped. A couple of French tankers in GI overcoats and dark-blue berets with bright-red pompons came up and greeted us. Was it true, they asked, that the war was over?

We nodded. O'Keefe, who had studied French, told them of the latest news on the radio. "La guerre est finis!" he said. It was May 5 and peace was still a rumor, but the rumor was strong enough to convert to fact.

The Frenchmen grinned and shook our hands. "La guerre est finis!" they shouted, yanking their pistols from their holsters. "La guerre est finis! La guerre est finis!" They fired wildly into the air.

The shooting stopped all motion. The souvenir hunters froze in their tracks and looked around at the night. There was a scramble for weapons in all the vehicles.

"SS!" someone shouted. "It's an ambush! They've come back!"

"La guerre est finis!" the Frenchmen yelled, louder than before.

"The war's over!" we chorused. "The war's over!"

"The war's over!" everybody shouted. "La guerre est finis!"

Those who had pistols fired them at the night. The shots and shouts echoed happily through the Alps. Men danced and shook hands and slapped backs and drank toasts to peace amid the monster's ruins.

"Come on," I said impatiently. "Let's get going." We stumbled blindly across the muddy rubble to some wide stone stairs at the east end of the building and felt our way down to the first level. It was totally dark here but not quite deserted, for a swirling, livid mob of soldiers banged and cursed and tripped and fell all around us.

We groped forward to the first room, lit a match, and saw several dozen fine radios sitting on the floor and tables. Ordinarily these would have absorbed our energy and attention, but we had not come to Hitler's home to take his radios. We returned to the stairs and felt our way down one more level to the wine cellar. A sound of drinking and carousing, of cursing and bottle-breaking rose from there. We hurried to the bacchanalia as filings to a magnet.

The wine cellar was on the lowest level of the hillside house. A huge room chiseled out of bedrock, it was filled to the ceiling with metal bottle racks on which a few thousand fifths, liters, and magnums still remained. Wild-eyed warriors lit matches, held candles, and worked squeegee German flashlights while their buddies snatched the bottles off the racks and put them in pockets, bags, boxes, and other containers. Everyone appeared to be both drinking and drunk. In their haste, they had broken so many bottles that the floor was flooded with wine. The room smelled like the inside of an old sauterne bottle.

"You hold the matches," I said to O'Keefe. "We'll get the jugs." I was vastly excited by the tumult. "We have to work fast." The mob was pouring downstairs like commuters to the Times Square Shuttle. Garcia and I reached up, snatched trophy after trophy, and laid them carefully in the wooden box. Soon my arms began to tire. Working more slowly, I had the leisure to read the labels.

"That damn cheapskate," I said in a disappointed tone of voice. "Nothing but wine: Rhine wine, red wine, white wine, Liebfraumilch, Chilean Riesling. Where's the hard liquor?"

"He didn't have any. At least, if he did, we couldn't find it."

"I'll be damned. Imagine a man that powerful drinking such cheap booze? If it was me, I'd have filled this place with calvados, cognac, and Johnny Walker's Black Label." I clucked my tongue, quite disappointed in Hitler.

"Better hurry, Web," O'Keefe said. "We're almost out of matches. Stick to the champagne. That other stuff doesn't taste as good."

I nodded and moved off to a dark spot where a row of Piper-

Heidsieck lay undisturbed. Four layers of bottles now rested in our box. Another would fill it. The box was quite large—over a yard long by two feet wide and deep—and it would be very heavy to carry up two flights of slippery stairs.

"That's it," O'Keefe sighed as the match burned down. "Goddamn!" He threw the stub away and shook his hand up and down.

The box was heavy indeed. When we bent to lift it, we found that we could only carry it about a foot off the floor, with frequent breaks. Weakened by the liquor and constantly thrown off balance by the uncertain footing and the newcomers who almost knocked us down as they plunged toward the cellar, we had to stop and rest every few feet, Our trip out took a good twenty minutes.

We stopped at the head of the stairs to straighten our backs and, breathing deeply, watched the spectacle outside. Hitler's last garden party, an insane confusion of lights, drunks, rubble, and rain. Then we carried our swag over to the Schwimmwagen and wrestled it aboard.

"This calls for a drink," I said as we started back to town. I reached behind the seat and pulled a bottle of Mumm's from the packing case. I tore off the seal and the wire fastener, fired the cork at a passing weapons carrier, and gave the bottle to Luz. The four of us killed it quickly, then started another, which we finished at the foot of the mountain.

The drizzle turned to heavy mountain rain so cold that it froze our bare hands and the tops of our knees, but we were numb to it all. We drank a third bottle of Hitler's champagne and smashed its carcass against a German house. Careening through the empty streets of Berchtesgaden, we broke into the chorus of "Roll Me Over."

What a party we had that night! Take a squad of twelve young men who had set out for war and found Berchtesgaden instead, add thirty bottles of Hitler's champagne, mix with the strongest rumors of peace, shake well in the Alps in spring, and you've poured our party.

Popping corks, spilling champagne, breaking bottles. Raucous laughter, ringing shouts, loud choruses of lewd ditties. Have another glash. Here, goddamn it, lemme pop that cork! Ish'n thish wunnerful? Shugalug! Fill 'er up, O'Keefe! It'sh all on Hiller.

V-E Day came three days later, but we didn't wait to celebrate.

We celebrated the night of the fifth. And the sixth. And the seventh. And the eighth, which was V-E Day proper, a glorious blue day that Captain Speirs spent throwing his empty champagne bottles off the balcony of his chalet and shooting at them blearily with a .45.

Somebody found a cognac factory down the road and wheeled in a hogshead for the first platoon. When this had been drained—it was rather green but speedy—we simply fetched another from the same source.

Wine, beer, and all blends and ages of hard liquor were available for the asking and almost every house and Bierstube within short driving range. If a sudden thirst overwhelmed you en route, you stopped the first stray German soldier and took his canteen. None of them ever carried water.

Other things were also free. The regiment, always so short of vehicles that it had to use farm carts and captured trucks the first few days in action and borrow transportation like DUKWs thereafter, suddenly found itself completely motorized, with every man who could drive the proud owner of his own nearly new vehicle. Some rode motorcycles, others preferred a Volkswagen or Schwimmwagen. The cowboys rode SS horses and soon formed the 506th Parachute Cavalry, a marching, racing, and polo society that lasted till the horses were finally worn out. Each squad had two or three Opel Blitz trucks, standard in the German army, for military duties and at least one informal vehicle for scrounging and Fräulein expeditions. Our platoon sergeant went helling down the highways, siren shrieking and bell clanging, in a civilian fire engine. He was the terror of Bavaria.

From a distance the caravan looked pink in the setting sun, but those who passed it on the road saw that it was mostly green and yellow-brown. The green was the uniforms of the passengers, the brown the standard color of their vehicles.

It was an enemy battle group composed of scattered units that had retreated so far into the mountains that they could retreat no farther, and now they had come down from a distant Alpine valley to surrender. There were division headquarters units, Volkssturm companies, antiaircraft platoons, quartermaster supply battalions— left with no supplies and no one to give them to if they had had them, for almost the whole army had disintegrated in the broken terrain and the wild scattering of the last few days of war.

Strung out along the highway north of Berchtesgaden, they looked more like a tribal movement than a military convoy of the nation that had been the scourge of all civilization only a few months before. The cars and trucks and wagons were piled high with tents and bedding and cooking utensils, and they moved without precision or uniformity. Since many of the vehicles were drawn by horses (for the Wehrmacht had relied heavily on animals for its transport), the convoy's speed was geared to the pace of its slowest dray. A rifleman walked twice as fast.

Stretched out on their belongings, the soldiers, who had lost their purpose on V-E Day, rode languidly on this last trickle of a once-mighty flood. None of them carried weapons or wore helmets. The only reminder of an age that had passed was an occasional clanking halftrack or self-propelled gun.

The convoy was more than a mile long, and our men, who stood and watched it pass the compound for almost an hour, all commented on the profusion of women. The American army, which liked women just as well, we noted, had nothing like it. There were German WACs, Luftwaffe Mädchen, young refugees from bombed cities who had attached themselves to the soldiers for bed and board. The German men studied the Americans with a professional interest that was returned in full, but the women, who had no such fraternal curiosity, saw us only as the enemy and looked away when we whistled and shouted, "Kommen Sie here, baby!"

The sun went down behind the jagged wall of western mountains just as the first vehicle in the convoy turned into the auto park beside the PW enclosure a mile north of us on the main road from Berchtesgaden to Munich. This was the concentration point for all surrendering Germans in the region. A guard told the lead vehicle where to park, and the passengers got out and marched with their gear through the main gate to a group of camouflaged green huts in a pine forest just inside the enclosure.

The camp had served a different purpose ten days before, when the Germans had run it and held captive several thousand Allied prisoners. Now under the management of our second platoon, it stood in a thin forest on the sloping base of a mountain. It was almost half a mile square and was surrounded by double barbed-wire fences. Guards stood watch in rough wooden huts on stilts at each corner while others patrolled the wire on foot. The buildings were one-story barracks so adroitly camouflaged with dappled-green paint that they were almost invisible from two hundred yards away.

The auto park beyond the wire, at the south end of the enclosure, was rapidly filling up with every conceivable type of civil and military vehicle. All were available for the taking. News of the give-away spread with the speed of light, and the throngs of paratroopers who came to help themselves gave the place the Sunday air of a giant used-car lot where everything was free and nothing was guaranteed. Men argued over choice staff cars, while others raced motors, tested brakes, or siphoned gas to refuel previously selected autos. Amateur mechanics had a field day.

The camp was also filling up, but nobody came to claim the Germans except for KP and other details. The barracks had long since been occupied and the overflow sent forth beyond to pitch their tents by units in the open. As night came on and the sky turned green in the east and a deep blue overhead and the stars came out very bright and close—for the stars were always close in the Alps—the German soldiers lit hundreds of small campfires on the slope and gathered around them, as soldiers had for thousands of years, to cook and chat and laugh and sing. For them too, the war was over.

Now they would be given discharges and sent home on foot or by whatever vehicles could be spared. The second platoon, assisted by S-2 and counterintelligence officers, had examined their Sold-bucher, or pay books (which gave the Germans' service records), had taken away their weapons and ammunition, and were holding them while their names were checked against a master list of war criminals. Every country in Europe had supplied names for this list, mostly from SS units that had wiped out entire villages and provinces of people behind the lines in Poland and Russia. Nothing would bring back the murdered civilians, but it was hoped that at least a few of the murderers would be punished. The bulk of the captives, of course, were innocent. They would be turned loose in a few days to find their way to what was left of their homes, while the war criminals would be transferred to maximum security prisons for trial.

The second platoon thoroughly enjoyed their work in the camp, for it was not without its rewards—both day and night. They stripped the incoming prisoners of watches, cameras, field glasses, pistols, and liquor, and, when darkness came, invited the choicer camp followers to come into their barracks and bundle.

It was widely believed that the mountains around Berchtesgaden were the hiding place for vast loot that had belonged to Hitler's top henchmen. Strong rumors said that there were art treasures nearby in secret cellars and gold bars stacked high in dripping caves. So one day three of us set off in search of easy money. We mounted J. D.'s German army ambulance, which had already carried him on a series of disappointing searches for loose women.

"Gotta get some fraternizing," J. D. said as he tooted at the gate guard and turned right on the road to town. He jerked his head at the back compartment, where a mattress lay covered with blankets and comforters. "A man's gotta be ready all the time. You can't tell when some little gal is going to jump in and throw it at you."

McCreary, who was with us, laughed. "That goddamn J. D.!"

Colonel Sink flashed by in a massive black Mercedes, with Blacky Wilson, a former mortarman in F Company, at the wheel. We grinned. Everybody liked to see the colonel having a good time.

On the eastern outskirts of Berchtesgaden, J. D. checked the gas gauge, muttered, "Low again, goddamn it," and pulled into a service station. Nobody came out to help us. "Self service," he said, jumping down and going to one of the pumps. "You hold the nozzle, Web, and I'll crank it till she's full."

He heaved the handle round and round, but still no one came out of the station, which was built of rustic wood and adjoined a small Alpine house. When the tank was full, he hung the hose back on its hook and drove off.

"Isn't this the life?" he commented. "Everything on the house. Want a car? Take your pick. Need gas? Help yourself. Deutschland kaput." He honked at a German cavalryman, trying to make his horse shy.

"Let's keep on the sideroads," I suggested. "The GIs have probably checked the main ones pretty thoroughly by now."

J. D. turned off on the first dirt track and followed it to the foot of a big mountain.

"Hold it up!" I exclaimed. "I saw a door in the mountain."

"Oh, hell. Doors in mountains . . ."

"There it is. See?"

J. D. hit the brakes, and the ambulance coasted to a halt in twenty yards. The brakes were rather weak. We backed up until we were alongside a wooden door set into a wall of rock. The door, which was partially hidden by undergrowth, appeared to be very sturdy. We leaped out and ran up to it.

"This is just the kind of place," I said excitedly. "I'll bet they hid the loot right here!" Visions of gold bars and chests of jewels danced through my head.

We smashed the lock with our rifle butts and surged in. A mine shaft, higher than a man, it ran straight back into the mountain. There were a couple of picks and shovels near the door. McCreary lit a match and started walking, then lit another and another. The shaft ended before the third match went out. Cursing, we turned back and hurried into the warm daylight.

"Well, hell," I sighed, "the only thing to do is keep looking. I'll bet there's a pile of dough around here somewhere. It's a logical hiding place. All we have to do is find the right tunnel."

We followed the sandy, rutted little road around the base of one mountain after another, trying this mineshaft and that one, and becoming progressively less enthusiastic. Finally we spotted a heavy wooden door on a footpath more than a hundred yards above the valley floor and decided that this would be our last attempt. It appeared to be the most promising, because it was the most inaccessible and because someone had taken pains to camouflage it with pine boughs. We dismounted and climbed up.

The padlock was four inches long, an inch thick, and so rusted that it refused to yield to several butt strokes. I decided to shoot it off, then thought better of it and just gave it the hardest blow I could. The cover broke and the lock's guts fell out. I was glad that I had not shot when I looked inside, for the cave was filled with boxes of blasting powder.

"Enough of this crap," McCreary said, starting back for the ambulance.

"You can have your goddamn treasure hunt," J. D. echoed. "I'll take women any day. Let's round up a couple of those Luftwaffe Mädchens and go have ourselves a ball."

We drove out to the nearest highway and continued west till we came to a signpost at an intersection. I studied the place names and, since none of them was familiar, suggested that we go straight ahead. "There's a lake four kilometers from here," I said. "It's called der Königsee, the king's lake. Let's take a look at it."

We were not the first arrivals at the lake. Scores of GIs were running in and out of the little resort buildings on the shore while others made off with rowboats and canoes or sunned themselves on a sandy beach that curved around the north end of the lake, which ran about three miles from north to south and varied in width from a quarter to half a mile. Nobody was in swimming.

J. D. sized up the situation and took immediate action. The main body of soldiers was concentrated along the beach, but practically no one was exploring a group of two story boathouses to our left. That was the place to go. He stepped on the gas and darted up to the third boathouse just as two men from the second platoon came outside with a big red-and-black Nazi flag in their hands.

"Where'd you get it?" I asked. Like everyone else, I had always wanted an enemy flag for a souvenir.

"Up in the loft."

We jumped down and ran indoors. The loft was a high-ceilinged attic filled with all kinds of awnings, tarpaulins, oars, and other boat gear. Standing against one wall were three ships' flagpoles. We grabbed them, unrolled the flags and cut them free, and stuffed them into our big pants pockets.

"Let's go," J. D. suggested. "Maybe there's a boat downstairs."

A door in the loft led down a flight of creaking, musty wooden stairs to a covered slip below, where two electric sightseeing launches were tied to narrow wooden docks. About thirty feet long, the boats had rows of padded seats on deck astern, a striped awning overhead with fringed sides, and a wheelhouse close to the bow. J. D. started to tinker with the controls.

"Anybody in there?" someone shouted.

"We're all here," I replied. "Come on! We're going for a ride."

Half a dozen men from the second and third platoons came out on the dock and jumped aboard. Four of them were carrying cases of Lowenbrau beer.

The motor started to purr softly, and J. D. shouted: "All aboard! Let's go, goddamn it! Moving out!"

McCreary and I cast off the hawsers while J. D., who claimed to have manned a craft like this at home, backed her into the stream.

"Port the helm!" he cried. "Avast the rudder! Starboard the bilges! All ashore that are going ashore! You don't 'ave to go 'ome, but you cahn't sty 'ere!"

We slid out into the sunlit lake, and J. D. leaned out and goddamned a couple of GIs who cut across our bow, then swung us around till we were headed for the far end. The others started opening the beer. The label was good—in fact, one of the best in Europe—but the taste was bad, for the beer was weak, watery wartime stuff, not worthy of its name. Nevertheless, it was beer, and we pretended to enjoy it.

As we finished each bottle, we cast it into our wake and opened fire on it with our pistols and rifles. The shots echoed and reechoed among the stone mountain walls that surrounded the Königsee on all but the north side, and GIs in lesser craft ducked and cursed our singing ricochets.

"Did you hear what they found down the road a couple of hundred yards from the bathhouses?" a second-platoon man asked. "Goering's art collection! The fat son of a bitch hid it in a special cellar, then poured cement over the door. Worth millions of dollars. And do you know what the 1st Bat found? Four million dollars in gold."

"No kidding?"

"Hell, yes. They're opening safes with bazookas at Regimental Headquarters."

The boat purred down the lake until we were more than halfway to the far end. J. D. headed for what appeared to be a white church to starboard. It stood on a flat peninsula of about 250 acres of meadowland at the foot of a big split between two mountains. Three or four farmhouses dotted the meadow behind the church, which was close to a stone pier that ran out into the lake. The pier was lined almost solid with canoes and rowboats. Dozens of GIs were sauntering on the quay, going in and out of the church, or sitting by little round tables in a beer garden opposite the front door. J. D. worked the launch into an empty space, and we leaped out and headed for the beer garden.

We shouted at several other E Company men sitting under a tree with steins of beer in hand and then went into the church, which appeared to be a medieval monastery that had been converted to a fine Old World inn. The dining room was cool and whitewashed, with a high, beamed ceiling that made it seem like some castle hall. It was still serving beer and lunch, we noted, but the tourists were all in brown and few of them were paying for their food.

We sat down on rough wooden benches at a big table and greeted the waitress who came to serve us. She rattled off the menu. "Gut, gut," I said, understanding only half of what she had said, "und viel Bier. Wir haben Bier sehr gern."

It was a splendid meal—soup, roast veal, boiled potatoes, cabbage, swiss cheese, and pumpernickel bread—and the price was incredible—about forty cents apiece, including two beers.

"You going to pay her?" one of the other men asked indignantly. "Goddamn Krauts."

"Why not? The money isn't worth anything. Anyway, J. D.'s loaded. Give her some of that money you got in Buchloe, J. D. Military government says it's no good, but she won't know the difference."

He peeled off half a dozen bills from a dirty wad that he always carried in his pocket and threw them on the table. I counted them mentally. They came to ten times the price of the meal. I slipped a couple of cigarettes under my plate as a tip and told the waitress how much we had enjoyed the food. She grinned and said, "Danke, danke."

We walked out slowly into the warm summer day and gazed about us at the blue lake and the great, steep mountains with a thoroughly satisfied feeling.

"Isn't this great?" I commented as we strolled back to the launch. "I'd like to come back here someday as a civilian and spend a weekend."

"We really got to Berchtesgaden at the right time," J. D. agreed. "You can't beat it."

But it was too good to be true. Just when we were comfortably settled and had PWs doing our KP and other household chores and were unofficially organizing the area into regimental territories, the division staff got wind of our homestead and decided to oust us.

A few days later, an advance detail from the 327th Glider Infantry Regiment stalked into our chalet suburb and without so much as a by-your-leave, chalked MAJOR SO AND SO AND CAPTAIN SUCH AND SUCH and 10 OFFICERS and 20 ENLISTED MEN on our doors. When we asked what was going on, they informed us with obvious relish that the 327th was going to take over Berchtesgaden. The 506th, they leered, was being exiled to an obscure valley farther south in Austria.

We moved out at night and after several hours' drive, wound up in the attic of a chalet smack against a mountainside.

5

AFTER THE FIGHTING

"Hey, Web, Christenson wants you at the CP. Shake a leg!"

I jumped off my bed and ran downstairs and up the street to the next house, where Christenson, Hale, and Liebgott lived with our platoon leader and half a dozen men from Company Headquarters. I knocked on Christenson's door.

"Come in."

"You wanted me?"

"Got a deal for you."

"Oh?" A deal was usually a euphemism for something undesirable.

"You've been after me for the next advance detail. Now's your chance."

I smiled. Advance detail meant first crack at the new billets, perhaps two days in advance of the company.

"Liebgott and Neumann have had plenty. Today it's your turn."

"Thanks."

"Pack your gear and report to the CP at nine o'clock."

I lingered a moment to inquire why we were moving out so suddenly. We had been in Kaprun only two nights and a day.

"You know the army, so don't ask me why," Christenson sighed. "Goddamn if I know why we're leaving or where we're going. Do you want to go or don't you?"

"Sure, sure."

"Better get going. It's 8:35 now. And don't tell Liebgott I sent you. Krauts can't understand his Yiddish, but he's jealous as hell of these deals, so just keep your mouth shut."

"OK."

I ran back to my billet and packed. I slipped into my harness, hunched my musette bag into a comfortable position on my back, buckled my cartridge belt, slung my rifle, and went to the CP, where a jeep was waiting with a driver and an interpreter from each of the other platoons.

"Going along?" one of them asked jovially.

I nodded.

"Maybe this time we'll find all the gold that Himmler dug out of the Jew boys' teeth."

I took a seat behind the driver.

The Camera Killer came out the front door and jumped into the front seat. We started off. God, I thought, staring at the back of his head, why does this guy have to come along? Of all the officers who could have been in charge . . . I had first met the lieutenant when, as an S-2 officer, he slept through the patrol in Haguenau. Switching to E Company for the trip through Germany, he had distinguished himself by seizing a camera from a German woman in a Bavarian village, throwing it to the ground, and shooting it with his pistol. For this exploit he had been dubbed the Camera Killer.

"Anybody know where we're going?" I asked.

"Nope," the man next to me replied. "Someplace far away, I hope. I want to line up a shack job before the company pulls in. Nice day, isn't it?"

"Wonderful. This is the prettiest country in the world. I've been all over the States, but I never saw anything as pretty as these Alps. They're even better than the Tetons."

We dipped into the valley's floor and crossed a stream that ran down its center. Now we were passing a clean little white church on a knoll that overlooked the village of Kaprun. Surrounded by rich green meadows, Kaprun was a small settlement of about four hundred people in very old chalets and Gasthofe. It had once been a minor resort, catering to bicycle tourists too poor for the more famous places in the Tyrol. Two inns with carved wooden balconies lined with gay flowerboxes faced a dusty little village square, and there was a scattering of small shops on the tree-lined streets.

We left the village on an uphill road and wound round to the right, passing two children in shirts made from parachute silk evidently sent home by their father from some drop zone overrun by the Germans. I wondered what had become of the parachute's owner. The square gray ruins of a medieval castle next appeared on our left, commanding the approach to the Kaprun Valley. The walls of the castle still stood, but the roof had tumbled in years before. Through the open gate, we would see a wild mass of trees and shrubs growing in the courtyard where other soldiers once had drilled.

From here we had a splendid view of the land ahead in all its rich summer colors. Pink, white, red, and gold flowers dotted the green meadows. Above them on all sides, blue-green pine trees flowed up to gray rocks and clean white snow on the mountaintops. The Kaprun Valley joined a larger one here at right angles that was two or three miles wide and that ran east to west between a snowcapped mountain range on the south and a lesser range on the north. The mountains ran as far as the eye could see. Straight ahead to the north at a distance of about five miles, a bright blue lake sparkled between two wooded mountain ranges. A village dominated by a church with a high Norman spire ran out into the lake on a promontory at midpoint.

"That's Zell am See," the Camera Killer remarked. "Regimental Headquarters and the 3rd Battalion. Beautiful, isn't it?"

Soon we were in the big valley, near a grassy airfield with a small camouflaged hangar where several GI trucks were parked. Paratroopers were climbing in and out of three or four light planes and a big, three-motored JU-87 transport nearby.

The road curved left and then right along the end of the lake, and the Camera Killer pointed at a farmhouse high on the mountain to the west and said: "Third Bat found a big rocket scientist hiding out up there. They're going to ship him back to the States. Isn't that a pistol? We win the war, and they ship the Krauts back to the States."

To our right, a path and the tracks of an electric railway ran side by side along the lake into town. Paratroopers on horseback and afoot moved about with noisy gaiety under trees along the path while civilians by the dozen fished in the lake and other GIs rowed or canoed on the water.

"Summer in the park," our lieutenant noted. "Isn't it great? There's the colonel's hotel. Best in town. You know the colonel." He laughed and pointed down a side street to a lovely old gabled building on a point. Officers sat at little iron tables on a veranda nearby.

"This town used to be a big Kraut resort," the lieutenant continued. "Nothing but hotels and inns. Beats the hell out of Columbus, Georgia, doesn't it?"

"Yessir."

"Lake's three miles long and a mile wide. You men ever get the time and the transportation, you ought to go for a swim. The colonel's going to give the best beach club in town to the regiment. Nothing but the best for the colonel."

"Yessir."

"I heard rumors the Krauts sank a lot of gold bars in the lake to hide 'em for the next war. The colonel's got a detail on it now."

We continued through Zell am See and down the valley in which it lay for another six or seven miles, past some very small villages and a burned-out enemy halftrack at a crossroads, and entered another, smaller valley that ran at ninety-degree angles to this one. A large village rose before us on a low hill in the center of the new valley.

"This is it," the Camera Killer announced. "This is Saalfelden. Last big intersection on the road to Germany. That rocky pass straight ahead in those mountains leads to Berchtesgaden."

We stopped at a house marked with a Headquarters Company guidon, where he chatted briefly with a second lieutenant who appeared to be an old acquaintance. Then we drove farther into town and stopped again.

"Everybody off," the Camera Killer said brusquely. "E Company's got this street for its billets. You men take the first four houses. Run the Krauts out and get enough space for your platoons."

He turned to me. "You—what's your name?—come with me. We'll get the billets for Company Headquarters and the first platoon."

The other interpreters went into the first house without knocking and shouted, "Raus, raus, schnell!" The Camera Killer and I hurried to a clean, whitewashed three-story home and beat on the door. A pale, thin young man with thick glasses and timid, watery blue eyes opened the door and blinked at us in fright.

"Guten Tag," I said.

"I speak English," he replied. "What do you want?"

"Your house," the Camera Killer said. "You have thirty minutes to move. Get along!"

"Better leave the radios and cameras," I added. "Cameras are strengstens verboten."

The young man swallowed hard. His face wrinkled as if for tears, and he shook his head and frowned and whined that he had a very sick father. "He's a dentist," he explained. "He can't move because he's sick and because he has very valuable equipment here. Take that house next door; it has lots of rooms. There are many kitchens. Your soldiers will like it very much. See, it is an apartment house, with three flats. It is much better for you than this."

"You have half an hour," the Camera Killer said with an edge in his voice.

"But my father is sick. He is old. He is a dentist. This is a very uncomfortable house. You will like that one much better. There is not enough room here. We do not have enough beds. My father . . ."

"Shut up!" The Camera Killer took a piece of chalk from his pocket and wrote CO. HQ., E CO. on the door. "Get your goddamn father out of here in thirty minutes or we'll throw him out."

We moved on to the next place. The young man, obviously 4-F and therefore doubly contemptible in our eyes, for he was quite unlikable and without any physical defects, stood in the doorway and wept softly, making no move to obey the order.

"Some companies let the Krauts live in the basement," the Camera Killer noted as we entered the next house and started up the stairs. "They keep 'em around to cook and wash the dishes and sweep the floors and do the laundry, but Captain Speirs doesn't believe in that and neither do I. Krauts only get in your hair if you let 'em stay in their own houses. I say, move 'em the hell out! The bastards moved everybody else out of Europe, made 'em slave laborers, put 'em in concentration camps. You have to be hard on these people."

His voice carried into all the apartments, which were the ones the weak young man had so strongly recommended, and soon every door was open and the whole building, which was three stories high, was filled with whispers of fear as the residents peeked out and saw us climb the stairs.

We reached the third floor and knocked at the apartment there. A German officer about thirty-five years old answered the knock. I greeted him and looked beyond at the living room, which was bright and sunny and gay with pretty yellow wallpaper and Van Gogh prints on the walls. A smell of milk and diapers and powder and soap filled the air. Four small children who had been playing on the carpet scrambled to their feet and ran to their mothers in tears. The crying set off a chain reaction in two wicker bassinets and in a baby at a mother's breast, for the room was a veritable maternity ward of babies and mothers. They gathered their children around them and talked softly and patted their backs and stared at us with frightened eyes. There were four women altogether.

I couldn't do it. Turning to the lieutenant, I said: "Let's try another place, sir. We can't run little children out in the street."

"The hell we can't! They're Krauts, aren't they? Tell 'em to get out in half an hour."

"But sir . . ."

"Goddamn it, tell 'em to get out!"

The infant wailing reached a crescendo.

"God," I muttered. Raising my voice, I explained to the German officer that we were requisitioning the house for our billets. He and the women and children had thirty minutes to pack up and go.

"But where will we go?" the German asked. "Every place in Saalfelden is filled with refugees from Salzburg and Vienna. The inns are all military hospitals. There is no place for us to go. My wife and I are doctors. We are taking care of these women. There is no one else to look after them. They have come with us from Vienna. Their husbands were all killed on the Russian front."

"I'll see what I can do."

"What's eating that son of a bitch?" the Camera Killer wanted to know.

"He says there's no place to go."

"Tough."

"He says the town's filled with wounded Krauts and refugees

from Vienna and Salzburg. We can find another billet, sir. Hell, we don't have to run these little kids out."

"Bah. Raus, raus, raus!"

The women joined their children in tears. This only aggravated the Camera Killer.

"They didn't give the Jews a chance to stay home, did they?" he shouted in a voice that shook the building. "They're Krauts, and they have to go!"

"But innocent women, sir? Little children?"

"Goddamn it, soldier, quit stalling! They're Krauts. They have to go!"

"They're Austrians, sir."

"Same thing."

"But little children?"

"Goddamn it, soldier, I'm sick and tired of your backtalk. Move these sons of bitches out! The company's due in twenty minutes. They have to have a place to stay. They're staying here. They can't wait on a roomful of sniveling little Kraut bastards."

He paused for breath, and the women looked helplessly to the German officer to protect them from this violent, flushed-face man who had come to their door. The officer stepped up to the lieutenant. "Bitte . . . ," he began.

"'Bitte,' hell, you son of a bitch! You didn't give the Jews a chance. Get going!" He pulled out a pistol and waved it under the German's nose. The women gasped. The officer shrugged his shoulders and bade the women start packing.

"And make it snappy! You have only fifteen minutes. Clear this house in fifteen minutes or I'll blow your goddamn brains out!"

The Camera Killer left the apartment and started downstairs, shouting: "Raus, raus! Everybody raus! Get out, you Kraut sons of bitches!"

I stared at the little children. It was not right. I had never believed in the war until I had gone into Germany and seen what the Germans had had in mind for the world: the slave-labor lagers, the broken families, the men from Dachau; old women and little children worked to death in Ruhr factories. To me the Germans were a nation of barbarous psychopaths responsible for the first-degree murder of ten to fifteen million Poles, Russians, and Jews—innocent civilians whose only crime was to have been born. I wanted the Germans to be thoroughly punished. I wanted to help seek out those responsible for the mass murders. If I could ever catch Himmler or Hitler or Goering, I would take the greatest delight in making them die slowly. But I did not blame all Germans. I did not think it right to return barbarism with injustice, to take out on little children the crimes of their sadistic countrymen.

"I'm sorry," I said to the officer. "I didn't want to do it. But the lieutenant is an officer and I am a private, so I had no choice. I wish I could help the children. It isn't right."

The German sighed. "What can you do?" he said softly. "It is the war."

"How come the mortar squad gets stuck in the attic?"

"Third squad was on the ground floor in the last billet. They get all the good deals."

"First squad's sleeping two men to a bed. Second's got a bed apiece."

"Who picked these goddamn billets? Second platoon's got the best houses in town."

"Company Headquarters has a place big enough for forty men. We should have had it instead."

Christenson sighed. He had heard it all before: the weeping and wailing and gnashing of teeth every time we moved into new billets. Nobody was happy: Everyone else's place was better than theirs. If he put the mortar squad in a barn and the rest of the men in a schoolhouse, Henderson screamed about the hay and the horseflies. If he gave Henderson a break and put McCreary in the barn, then the whole second squad filed a protest. If the second squad got the ground floor (an important location, since it offered first crack at the meals as they were distributed in Marmite cans), then J. D., Marsh, and I stormed in to complain of persecution and discrimination. Everybody protested Hale's and Liebgott's grasping ways on the advance detail, and nobody ever saw Company Headquarters in a bad location.

No sooner did these initial rumblings settle into the disturbed earth from which they had come in fuming geysers of hate and invective (all meaningless, all part of the old army game—to claim discrimination and hold what you have) than men came by from the second and third platoons to check on the accommodations in a casual way that fooled nobody.

"Pretty good deal you got here."

"We've had better. No hot water. Goddamn Krauts took all the blankets with 'em."

"Blankets! We don't even have beds!"

The platoon leaders went to the captain and complained of favoritism, while he in turn visited them all with an eye to shifting his own people to better quarters.

"Jesus, this is better than we have."

"It looks good from the outside, captain, but it's a mess indoors. No running water, no toilets, no electric lights."

"Looks good to me."

"The place you have now is much more centrally located, sir. It's near everything. We're sort of out of the way here, captain."

Each man running down his own billet to noncoms and outsiders, each defending it from rival squads and platoons—it was always the same, all the way through Germany. A strain for the first half hour, the conflict died out as soon as another diversion came up. Billeting was a balancing of opposing forces. All a man could do was try to be fair in his assignments and then nod and talk quietly until the storm blew over. That time came at last.

The women and children had moved out, the first platoon had moved in, and Company Headquarters had evicted the dentist's son at gunpoint. Lunch had come and gone. Now it was three o'clock. Christenson was sitting on my bed, enjoying the lazy peace of a summer afternoon.

The door flew open, and J. D. and McCreary ran in with a whooping thunder. "Look out the window!" they shouted. "Look out the window!"

Christenson banged forward and swung from his chair to a standing position while the rest of us gathered around. Our window overlooked the backs of a U of houses built around an open space of small vegetable gardens. Wehrmacht trucks and tents filled the gardens and the backyards, where a hundred-odd German soldiers had made a bivouac. J. D. pointed at a house directly opposite ours.

A German girl of about twenty was undressing at a window in full view of the bivouac. She had already taken off her blouse. Now, with a born stripper's air of unconcern, she pulled her slip over her head and unbuckled her bra and let it fall. She had big breasts.

"Yippee!" J. D. bellowed, pawing the floor like a bull in heat.

McCreary waved to her. "Hiya, honey!"

"Kommen Sie hier, baby!" Chris called.

The girl started to undo the side of her army skirt. But a movement behind Christenson caught his eye, and he turned and saw our platoon leader standing in the door and called us to attention

"At ease, rest," the lieutenant said. "What's going on here?"

"Kraut broad," J. D. grinned. "Biggest tits you ever saw. Get a load of that." He pointed.

"Goddamn Krauts know how to fight a war, don't they? Bring the women along with 'em. This is a hell of a time to say it, but we're moving out in fifteen minutes."

"Oh Christ," I groaned. "When are we going to settle down?"

The girl dropped her skirt and lowered the window shade. We heaved a collective sigh and concentrated on our platoon leader and the task at hand.

"Where now, sir?" McCreary inquired. "Italy?"

"Other end of town. Start packing."

"Good!" J. D. exclaimed with his eyes still on the girl's window. "Did you get her phone number, Mick?"

McCreary grinned.

The lieutenant left, and we packed. By the time we marched out to the trucks, word of our departure had spread throughout the neighborhood, bringing the dentist's boy, the doctor, and several other evictees to the curb opposite our front door. None of the mothers was in sight.

The ride to the next billet, an old hotel by a railroad station a mile west of the main part of Saalfelden, was brief and the first impression disappointing, for the hotel was plain and poor.

We filed up the stone front steps into a dark lobby paneled with Victorian taste in dark oak. The cooks were preparing supper in the kitchen straight ahead. On our right was a small dining room, obviously the officers' mess, for it had linen on the tables. A larger dining room stood on our left. While we milled about in the lobby with its worn carpets, J. D. went to the registration desk, tapped its bell, and proclaimed in the ensuing silence that this was a clean hotel. "We're going to live YMCA style," he said. "No women or liquor." He was loudly booed. "Before ten in the morning." He was cheered. Then he reached over the counter, pulled out a picture postcard, and asked me what it said.

I translated it literally: "Anton Dick's Gasthof. Thirty rooms from 1.20 kroner up, tourists' quarters from .60 kroner up. Shady garden with veranda, billiard room. Famous for its good cooking. Advantageous junction for sightseeing trips."

"At ease, men," our platoon leader called from the stairs behind the counter. "This is going to be our home for the next few weeks, as far as we know. We have the two top floors. The first and second squads will have the third floor, the rest of the platoon the second. Cooks will sleep down here, since the hotel will also be the company mess hall. I don't want any of you men swiping food from the kitchen or the storerooms. This is also the officers' mess, so keep your fun down to a dull roar.

"We're here for a purpose. Saalfelden is now Field Marshal Kesselring's headquarters. It has four or five military hospitals and a couple of hospital trains parked outside. There are two big Kraut ammunition dumps in the woods nearby, and this station is the junction for trains to Munich. That crossroads we went through on the way over is the last big one on level ground before Germany. Our job here is to help funnel all the Krauts out of Austria. Kesselring is in charge of this movement. Krauts with armbands are on his staff and can keep their pistols. They'll be coming and going all the time, so don't bother 'em. Captain Speirs will help Kesselring coordinate his troop movements with the American army. Mortar squad'll guard the hotel and the station while the others take turns at the crossroads. Squad leaders, billet your men now. Chow in fifteen minutes. Get going!"

"We have to beat McCreary," I whispered to Marsh and J. D. "Let's run." We broke from the crowd and bounded upstairs, reaching the top floor well in advance of the second squad, but McCreary caught up with us when we hesitated whether to turn right or left.

"Thought you'd beat me to it, huh?" he panted. "Like hell, buddy, like hell. Nobody's beating McCreary. Not by a long shot." He inhaled. "Let's be reasonable about this. Our men get along good together, so let's organize the floor without any goddamn connivery. Come on."

We went on a quick tour. The rooms were very much alike in both their arrangement and accommodations. Each one had two or three big beds, simple and sturdy, high closets with drawers below, and plain white dressers. The walls were whitewashed and gener-

ously cracked, the reed rugs torn and frayed. Bits of wooden floor-
ing peeked through underfoot in the hall, which was covered by an
old red carpet. There was a china pitcher and a washbowl in each
room. The only running water was in a lavatory beside the stairs,
and the hotel's sole bathtub, we discovered, was one floor below.

We agreed that the first squad, which was Marsh's and mine,
would have the southern half of the floor and the second squad the
north. Since the hotel ran from north to south, this gave each of us
a view of the two main sights—the mountains on the east and the
railroad station on the west.

The men quickly dispersed and started to unpack. After supper,
which we ate in the tourists' dining room, we lay around until it
got dark and cold, and then we went to bed. Our day, however,
was not quite over.

McCreary, who had gone for a walk, came to my room a few
minutes after we had switched off the light, and woke up Marsh
and me. "Come on!" he said excitedly, shouting us awake. "Warehouse full of liquor!"

We ran into the hall without bothering to tie our boots or put jack-
ets over our undershirts.

"Shh," McCreary cautioned. "We don't want to spread this
around." He beckoned to Sholty and Matthews, who were waiting
near the stairs. Matthews had come up to us in Berchtesgaden after
remaining in France with the regiment's rear echelon from Holland
on. A lively, witty person, he was always welcome on a foray.

We padded downstairs, nodded to the guard at the front door,
and followed McCreary at a dead run around the south end of the
station, across the railroad tracks, and two hundred yards down a
gravel lane to a corrugated-iron warehouse on the western outskirts
of town. A guard challenged us at the entrance, but McCreary, who
had apparently spoken to him before, reassured him, and he stood
aside and let us go in.

"Second platoon," McCreary whispered. "The rookie doesn't
know what he's got in here. Cases of gin, buddy, cases of gin.
Wait'll those guys find out we've been cutting into their territory."
He chuckled softly.

Sholty stumbled on a soft bundle in the hay underfoot as we
groped toward the far end of the building, which was about sev-

enty-five feet long. Someone cursed him in German. "Krauts,"
Sholty said. "Step on their faces."

We shuffled slowly through thick darkness past oddly-shaped
machinery and over grunting, moaning, tossing sleepers until we
came to a row of wooden packing boxes along the west wall. Each
box was about a yard high and wide by four feet long.

"Come on, Matt," McCreary hissed as he bent over and shoved
his fingers under the bottom of one. "Get on the front of this son
of a bitch."

Matthews grabbed it and started backing out of the warehouse.
We followed with another. Tripping and shuffling and grunting and
straining muscles that hadn't been used for months, we moved from
one end of the building to the other, leaving in our wake a trail of
crushed hands and German curses.

The guard frowned and peered in McCreary's face as we went
out the door. His suspicions aroused by our haste, he asked what
company we were from.

"C Company," McCreary replied briskly. "First Battalion. We're
on detached service." He hurried on.

The guard's eyes narrowed, and he shook his head as if to say, I'll
have to tell somebody about this. It don't seem right.

We staggered back down the gravel road under a full moon and
stopped for a break after fifty yards.

"I sure hope it's a case of lush," Matthews remarked, panting.
"I'd hate to work this hard for monkey wrenches."

"Hardest I ever worked in the army," Sholty agreed.

I grinned. It was the first time I had ever seen Matthews or
McCreary do physical labor. We bent to the task once more and by
easy stages moved the two cases into the hotel, where we paused
again in the lobby. So far, our only witness, other than the men at
the warehouse, was the guard at the hotel steps. But now another
man hurried toward us from the back of the hotel. It was Miller,
one of the least objectionable of the cooks.

"Booze, huh?" he grinned. "Here, let me give you a hand."

"No, thanks, we'll manage."

"Why don't you store it in our rooms? The officers never come
around there."

"Ha, ha, ha."

We hurried up to the room that Marsh and I shared and, with

one man posted as lookout by the door, quickly broke open Mc-Creary's case. He and Matthews filled their arms and pockets with tall, clear liter bottles of Wacholder Verschnitt—German gin. The labels were crude, almost homemade, and stated that the gin was "nur für Wehrmacht," for Wehrmacht use only.

"You guys hide the rest," McCreary suggested. "Better keep it in one place than have it spread all over the hotel."

"OK."

"I'll pass the word around the squad for the boys to drop in any-time they want a snort."

He and Matthews left, and Marsh, Sholty, and I set to work hid-ing the remainder of the broken case, which contained forty-eight bottles. We put them in drawers, jump boots, pillows, and musette bags and on top of the dresser and under the mattresses. Each of us sipped on a liter as we worked, and though it was raw and green and smelled sickeningly sweet, we delighted in it. When all the bottles were out of the rough excelsior that had cushioned them, we carried the broken box outdoors and left it behind the hotel to fuel the washpots. The other box was covered with a tablecloth and set under our window.

Hale and our platoon leader came by on inspection the next day. Everything was fine until they reached the box. Since we had not told the second floor of our find, having little rapport with Platoon Headquarters or the squads there, we dreaded Hale's discovering our treasure. He ignored the box, however. Our platoon leader was not quite so oblivious.

"What's in that box?" he inquired.

My heart dropped to my knees.

"Squad equipment, sir," Marsh replied.

The inspection team grunted and left the room. When the door was shut, we yelled with joy.

"Buddy," Marsh said with a smile, "nobody's going to cut into our liquor."

"Have another drink."

"Don't mind if I do."

The little man lifted a white china pitcher from the washbowl on top of the wardrobe and filled the big man's glass. Almost every-body else was asleep or on guard.

"Iced tea and gin."

"I know. I'm getting used to it."

"Webster had to slip the cooks a couple of jugs to get the iced tea, but it's worth it. Not a bad drink at all. A man can't drink gin straight."

"No, he can't."

"Some party last night, huh?"

"Yep, I can still see it." I had passed out cold, and Matthews was lisping and stuttering. Marsh was bragging about how the squad always obeyed him. Winn was laughing and shouting about Bastogne. Gilmore had been pressing clothes like crazy. No one knew why Gilmore always pressed clothes when he got drunk.

They stopped talking and stared out the window, which overlooked a big stone barn, half as long as the hotel and parallel to it ten yards away, that served as home for several dozen displaced persons and refugees from bombed cities of Austria and Germany. Poles and Czechs who had once worked in the hotel still occupied dark, damp little rooms in the barn's half cellar.

A line of three sooty washpots had been set up below our window near a ramp that led to the barn's huge front door. The last late eaters were still dipping their utensils in the gray water, which had been discolored by the company wash an hour before. There was no GI can for garbage, as in the States, for nothing was wasted in Europe, where all the people were hungry. At every meal, a pathetic band of timid, bony children and quivering old women begged our leftovers before they could be thrown away. They took everything: the coffee grounds, the orange peels, the pork-chop bones.

A Wehrmacht trailer containing sleeping quarters and a fully equipped dental office was parked about twenty yards to the right of the washpots. The only other military activity was a platoon encampment of German soldiers a hundred yards farther on.

To the left, a gray brook with a charming, shaded gravel path curved toward the barn, then swung away from it and continued through small truck gardens toward the main part of Saalfelden, almost a mile distant. The ground beyond the brook was level meadowland for two miles to a row of gray, snowcapped mountains that formed the northern boundary of the valley. A picturesque thirteenth-century castle stood in the meadow halfway to the mountains.

"Been out to the castle yet?" the little man asked, blinking at its fairy-tale silhouette, now fading in the dusk. The castle was occupied by a colony of Polish farm workers brought here as slave labor by the Germans.

"Hell, yes."

"How'd you make out?"

"Think I got something lined up. She's a honey—brown hair, blue eyes, big tits."

"Got an armband?"

"I'm getting one."

"That makes it legal, huh?"

"Sure. Boys at Regiment are putting 'em on all their Krauts, and man, they got some honeys. Real high class—countesses and that kind of stuff."

"Have another drink."

"Thanks, I'll force one down."

"Stuff creeps up on you, doesn't it? Goes down like iced tea, comes up like gin."

The big man laughed and set the pitcher back in the bowl. He stood near the window for a couple of minutes, inhaling deeply, then tensed and frowned at something that had caught his eye below.

It was a cook, an object of universal contempt, and he was clad in the cook's uniform—a greasy, sweaty, long-sleeved wool undershirt and a pair of sooty, grease-splattered fatigue pants. Drunker by far than either of these observers, he had lurched out the back door of the kitchen and was zigzagging to the trailer.

"Slopshits are drunk again," the big man commented. "Sons of bitches haven't been sober overseas."

The cook pounded on the trailer's door, then stumbled inside.

"Couple of slick Krauts down there."

"Who's that?"

"Them dentists. They're cleaning everybody's teeth for cigarettes and Hershey bars."

"That's smart."

"They got women, too."

"Oh?"

The little man stood up and looked out the window. The twilight was over. It was so dark and misty now that they could barely see the trailer.

"Cooks been screwing 'em in their rooms. They're swapping chow for ass. They're living filthy."

"They always did."

"Look, look!"

Another cook staggered out of the kitchen and knocked at the trailer door. The first one came out in reply with a rather heavy, well-built woman. Watched by one of the dentists, who held the door open, a similar female followed. The dentist shut the door and turned out the light as soon as she was outside. This was the signal: The cooks whirled on the women, threw their arms around their waists, kissed them passionately, and clutched their bottoms. The women were by no means unattractive.

While the two men at the window clenched their fists, the cooks swayed back and forth in ardent embrace until the women, who appeared to be sober, wrenched free and led them into the barn.

The little man downed the last of his drink and set his canteen cup on the dresser. His eyes were sparkling. "Let's move in on 'em," he said softly.

The big man grinned.

"They're so goddamn drunk they're going to pass out as soon as they lie down. These broads know what they're doing. We just have to catch 'em before they roll 'em off and run back to the trailer. Come on."

Later they told the rest of us what else had happened. They padded downstairs to the lobby and went through the kitchen to a narrow corridor that led to the back door. A short walk took them into the barn.

They stopped in the door, which was always open, until their eyes had grown accustomed to the darkness. The snoring and grunting and tossing of the refugees in the hay sounded like a barracks after lights out. A panting came to them from the far left, a panting and thrashing, and then a woman saying, "Oh, oh, oh, ohhhhhhhh!"

"Watch it," the little man said as he started toward the sound. "Floor's covered with people." He bent over and felt ahead of him so that he would not step on anyone. He had seen these people in the daytime—the bewildered old men, the crying children, and the widows who had lost men, family, and household in the war.

He paused and, pulling his companion to him, pointed to the left, where a woman had just rolled a man off her with a German curse and was whispering to the other woman near her. The man mumbled drunkenly and shook himself, then lay still. Another man was asleep near the other woman.

"Cooks have passed out," the little man whispered. "Now it's our turn."

He crawled to the first woman and panted, "Fooken, fooken." The cook stirred drunkenly and went back to sleep. The big man was already kissing and caressing his date.

The little man unbuckled his belt and let fall his trousers and underpants, while the girl sighed bitterly, pulled up her skirt, and settled into position. Her friend followed suit, for both had become accustomed to obliging soldiers. Soon the hay was alive with a double creaking.

The steady rhythms slowly reached the cooks' addled brains, making them toss and moan and then gradually come to. When the little man in his passion accidentally kicked the cook beside him, the cook sat up and shook his head.

"What the hell?" he said thickly, blinking at the heaving figures beside him. He reached over and felt the little man's bare bottom. The little man chuckled to himself at the cook's discovery. It was too late. He had already had his fun.

The cook started yelling in the foulest language and grabbed for him, but he was too quick. He gave the cook a shove and stood up and hoisted his pants. Meanwhile the other cook came to and for a moment contemplated the big man, who was still in the act of love. But before he could do anything, his rival's body relaxed and the little man hissed at the big man to get going.

The cook lunged at the little man again. He hit the cook in the stomach and ran for the door. The big man followed, clutching his pants.

"Rape! Rape!" both cooks shouted. "Stop 'em!" But they were gone.

Our only duty was guard. The mortar squad guarded the hotel and depot, and the three rifle squads alternated on the crossroads where the main street between Saalfelden and the railroad station crossed the highway to Germany. The second and third platoons watched the ammunition dumps in the forest nearby. Elevated to the post of city manager and contact man with Field Marshal Kesselring, Captain Speirs took up residence in the latter's private train, which we raided one night for a case of Hennessey cognac, and Company Headquarters set up an information and dispatch office to handle offers of surrender, issue passes for German convoys, and arrange for deportation into Germany of the remaining enemy soldiers. While their job was interesting, ours, on the crossroads, was even more so, for it had the most movement of any post in the company.

Noncoms stood guard here once every three days, privates every other day. We wore woolen uniforms and helmet liners and stood in the middle of each road and stopped every German driver to find out where he was going and why All vehicles' passes were checked, and what with the constant procession of men and cars, the time passed very quickly. For the first time in my life, I actually found myself looking forward to guard.

German MPs helped to make it interesting. One was assigned to each of us. They were big, tired men who had seen service as infantry in the First World War and as combat MPs in this one. They wore as their badge of office a heavy neck chain bearing a brassard with the word *Feldgendarmerie* inscribed on it in raised letters, and it was a pleasure to work with them, because they were such good soldiers. They saluted with a great heel-clicking. They handled German vehicles and information seekers with cold efficiency, and they obeyed orders like robots. For all their discipline and snap, these men were, however, rather pathetic figures, having been in the army so long that they almost dreaded a return to the disorder of civilian life.

One of them was in the highway now, with his hand raised as a signal to halt. A Wehrmacht Opel Blitz truck stopped in front of him. First in a convoy of about a dozen vehicles, it was loaded like the rest with rations, bedding, haversacks, blank-faced men in German uniforms, and subdued, overworked women. The Feldgendarm clicked his heels and saluted the person sitting beside the driver. "Passkarte, bitte," he said as I strolled over with Trapazano, a slender, eager young replacement who had come in just before the Bulge.

The Wehrmacht officer on the front seat returned the MP's salute, reached in his pocket, and handed out a folded sheet of white paper. The MP nodded and passed it on to me. "Hauptmann

Ernst Meutzig has the permission of the military government at Zell am See," it said, "to transport his unit with ten trucks to Berchtesgaden."

"Soldbuch, bitte," I said to Captain Meutzig. He gave it to me, and I checked his identification against the pass. They were always correct, but it was part of our job to make sure, so I went through the routine, primarily because I did not like the captain's looks. I returned the pass and the Soldbuch with a "Gut, gut."

"Darf Ich?" the captain started to say.

"Ja, ja. Mach schnell!" the MP barked. He saluted again. Trapazano also saluted.

The captain returned the salutes, and the convoy passed through us slowly and without friendliness or greeting. None of the Germans was happy about being removed from Austria, which they had apparently come to regard as their own.

"This is the kind of guard I like," I commented as the trucks crossed the plain toward the dark, rocky pass a mile or so north that led to Germany.

"Nothing to it, is there?" Trapazano agreed. "Too bad we missed the shooting. I'd like to have seen that."

I nodded. A Wehrmacht staff car had tried to run the roadblock a few days before. It was shot off the road by a rifleman in the third squad who killed the driver and his passenger in the process. The German MPs, strong authoritarians, had approved of the action, for the driver had also disobeyed their shouts and orders to halt. They had a low regard for our discipline, muttering among themselves that they were trying to preserve law, order, and respect for authority in spite of us and not because of us, and they were pleased to see an American exhibit strength on the proper occasion.

"You don't have to salute these Krauts," I said to Trapazano. "I'd never salute anybody in another army, especially the German army. Bad enough to salute the pricks in ours."

"Oh, hell, I get a kick out of it."

"Suit yourself. Ah, the Doctor."

A sporty little tan convertible slowed down and stopped beside us. It was manned by a crew of two with whom we had already become quite familiar: a racy, fast-talking, middle-aged German who claimed to be a doctor and who talked a garbled American slang, and a quiet, decorative blonde of about twenty-five who looked expensive and said nothing.

"Good morning," I said, smiling at the blonde. "How are you?"

"OK, GI, OK," the Doctor replied. The blonde was silent. "What say?"

"Can't say it here."

"Ha, ha, very good, ha, ha. OK."

"Going to Berchtesgaden?"

"You betcha. Some fun, huh?"

I laughed, and the blonde smiled at me, warming my skin from head to toe. "Let me see your pass," I said. The Doctor handed it to me, and I studied it and frowned. "No good. I can't let you go."

The Doctor's face stiffened. "It's good," he said coldly. "I know it's good. Your Major Winters gave it to me." The blonde stared straight ahead and bit her lip.

I laughed and handed back the pass. The Doctor returned to joviality. "OK, GI?"

"Shove off."

The car spurted toward the rocky pass.

"Slick son of a bitch," I murmured. "I don't trust anybody that friendly. He's always going to Berchtesgaden, always with the same excuse. Probably organizing an underground or running messages for SS men in the mountains. He's too smooth, too sure of himself."

An elderly couple in peasant costume passed us timidly, nodding and afraid. We smiled and said good day. I left Trapazano and walked over to Janovek, who was standing at the corner where the traffic halted coming out of Saalfelden.

He was holding up a Luftwaffe convoy of four trucks while he checked the leader's credentials. "Sons of bitches are all going home," he grinned. "How about us, Web? When do we go home?" He returned the driver's pass and yelled for him to take off. The bulging, wheezing trucks went into the intersection and turned right, toward Germany.

Another familiar couple approached us. Daily visitors to the roadblock, they were a pale, quiet Frenchman and a young blonde woman. Although most of their fellow countrymen had already gone home, they apparently preferred to linger for reasons of their own. Perhaps a rope was waiting for them in France. We never found out.

"Hello," the man said. "What is new today?"

I told him what I could of the *Stars and Stripes'* latest stories about

De Gaulle, while he listened intently, pathetically eager for news from home. When I was finished, he tipped his hat and thanked me, she nodded curtly, and both strolled away, a sad, lonely couple in the land of their nation's enemies. I went on to Smith's post.

A big, sensible young man who had come to us in Haguenau, Smith had the easiest post of all. Its purpose was to stop the German traffic coming into the area from Berchtesgaden. Since almost none came in, he had very little to do for two hours.

We chatted awhile. Then he left for a few minutes' relief, and I talked with his German MP. Of all the Feldgendarmerie, he was the oldest, the friendliest, and the most talkative. In five years of war, he had once said, his outfit had been in almost every country in Europe. France was the best by far (Prima, prima"), with Italy a close second. With the exception of the Ukraine, Russia was not a desirable assignment, even for an MP.

I asked what was new, and he said that his unit was finally going to be discharged. They would leave for Berchtesgaden as soon as their captain got the transportation. "This is the end of my second war," he said. "I hope it is the last."

"What will you do now?"

"I don't know."

"Where do you live?"

"Mannheim."

Mannheim, I thought, remembering a city almost totally destroyed.

"My home was burned in an air raid. The factory where I worked was bombed. I have no home and no job. My wife and daughter are living in a public air raid shelter, and both my sons are missing in Russia. I am fifty-five," he sighed. "It is time to go home."

A horse-drawn wagon with firewood pulled up while we were talking. The driver, who was leading a team of two beautiful Percherons on foot, looked at us questioningly. Smith waved him by. I moved on to Kohler, the preacher's son who had come in at the same time as Smith and who was a bright, chatty person, selected, like the others on my relief, for his congeniality.

"Here comes that goddamn Nazi," Kohler said after we had exchanged greetings. "Sonofabitching Hitler Youth."

A boy of about fourteen walked out of Saalfelden and through the intersection toward us. A very handsome blond, he was the most poised, arrogant adolescent I had ever seen. Unlike the peasants and townsfolk and wounded Germans who passed us on convalescent walks, the boy, who wore high woolen socks, a short-sleeved white shirt, and very small lederhosen, never spoke to us, never smiled at us, never even looked at us. He moved in a cloud of hate that was more irritating than the most offensive civilian driver.

"They'll make the next war," I commented as he went by. "Snotty little bastard. Hitler filled 'em with his hogwash, and they never had it beaten out of them in action the way the soldiers did. You wait and see."

A one-legged German soldier with a pack on his back bounced out of Saalfelden and stopped by Janovek. I went over to see what he wanted. He had a thin bright face and a jaunty air that was somehow enhanced by his primitive crutches, which were olive-green saplings with the bark still on them.

"Guten Tag," he said, smiling and leaning on his crutches. "Ich bin entlassen."

"Good!" I said. Janovek frowned, and I explained that the man had been discharged. "Want a cigarette?" I asked the German.

I lit it for him, and he thanked me, inhaled deeply, and said that it was the best smoke he'd had in six years. Nodding at his right leg, which was off at the knee, he coughed and then grinned. "Granatwerfer."

"Ah," I smiled, "a mortar."

He nodded pleasantly and continued to grin. A first lieutenant, he told us that the Americans were letting him go home. "For me the war is over."

A civilian car stopped by Trapazano. "Where's he going?" I yelled.

"Munich."

"Want to go to Munich?"

The crippled man smiled. "Ja, ja."

The car came up to us as we moved into the middle of the crossroads and stopped again. Its driver, a fat civilian, appeared to be quite surly.

"This soldier needs a ride to Munich," I said, opening the back door. The driver grunted. "Get in," I said to the lieutenant.

He came up to the door, stopped on his one leg, handed me his crutches, swung inside, and sat down. I passed in the crutches.

"Danke," he said, smiling, "danke sehr."

The car drove off.

"A good man," I remarked to Trapazano, who had come up. "With a sense of humor like that, he must have been a very good officer."

We stood and watched a convoy of about a dozen GI trucks go by. The canvas tops were off, and the backs were packed tight with a picnic crowd of singing, shouting civilians wearing tricolors in their buttonholes and waving homemade French flags. Someone threw a bouquet of violets at our feet, and they were gone.

"Slave laborers," I commented. "Going home and glad to go. But I wouldn't want to return to a country as dead and beaten as France. Germany has more vitality. France just seems drained dry. They haven't even picked up the rubble from D–Day."

"Hey, Web!" Trapazano shouted. "Guy wants to trade for a 7.65."

"I'm coming."

It was a private from the 502, touring the area in a captured motorcycle. He said he'd swap a GI wristwatch for a 7.65, a small automatic pistol that would be more convenient in civilian life than a Luger or a P–38.

"You're talking to the man with the 7.65s," I said. "Let's go to my billet." I climbed on the rear seat, roared down to the hotel with him, made the exchange, and came back, all within five minutes.

There was a great commotion at the roadblock when I returned, Two German MPs were screaming at an excited civilian in a small black car, while Janovek stood by with a wide grin on his face.

"Get a load of this," he said. "They're fighting the war all over again."

The MPs turned to me with such a flood of guttural that I could not follow them. Finally I gathered that they wanted to take the civilian prisoner.

"Why?" I asked, staring at him. A thin young man in his late twenties, he had curly red hair, wild blue eyes, and a tricolor in his lapel.

"He is bad. He has been robbing the civilians. We have orders to arrest him."

The Frenchman made a remark that made both Germans turn on him, shouting and waving their fists. Their eyes were narrowed in hate, but he only smirked at them. Janovek grinned.

"We have no such orders," I said. I told the Frenchman to drive on.

"Deutschland kaput!" he yelled, racing away.

"Schweinhund," one of the Germans muttered. A corporal, he was as big and old as the other MPs but considerably harder and less sociable. Whereas the others were benign and fatherly, he was critical, harsh, and precise.

"You should have arrested him," he said. "He is a bad French man. He stole that car. He has a pistol. With it, he has been robbing the people for miles around. Your military government has issued a warrant for his arrest."

I nodded, "Uh huh," and looked at the car. I could still shoot it off the road. If it had been an SS man or some other renegade German, I would have done it, but a Frenchman? No. I would never shoot a Frenchman, especially to please a German.

I walked away, leaving the Germans to mutter at our casual airs and the lawlessness of the French. A fetching brunette in a tight blue skirt and a shapely sweater approached afoot, with two second-platoon men behind her, whistling. She tried to ignore them but finally broke down in a smile as she went by. The two GIs who had been trailing her like stiff-legged dogs stopped to chat.

"How's the fraternizing here?"

"No dice on the roadblock."

We exchanged rumors and they went on. The news was good: Pistols would be issued through Company Headquarters, the point system was about to start, and the Camera Killer had been detached from active command of any of us and put in charge of the area's Displaced Persons.

Soon McCreary marched up with the relief.

"Any special orders?" he inquired.

"No."

He sent his men to the four corners while mine formed in a column of twos and I fell in beside them. "It's all yours," I said. "We'll be back in four hours."

"See you, buddy. Anything new?"

"Nope. Just the same old routine."

Dead drunk on iced tea and gin, I had fallen into bed at about 9 P.M. and gone to sleep in my fatigues. Now someone was shaking me awake.

"Get up, Web!" he yelled. "For Chrissake, get up!"

I groaned, turning away from the bright light.

"Grant's been shot. Go out on the roadblock!"

I sat up and rubbed my eyes. "What?"

"A GI shot Grant. The bastard's loose in town. The captain wants a noncom on the roadblock right away."

Still drunk, I got out of bed, wrenched into my jump boots, shoved the laces into the tops, and stumbled out the door with my M–1 in hand.

Grant, the sunny, quiet, golden-haired boy from California, had been shot. I never knew him personally, but suddenly I felt as if I had and wanted to avenge him. An old Toccoa man, he was a noncom with a fine combat record who had knocked out an 88 in Eindhoven and been wounded in Nunen. He had made all of the Bulge and had become platoon sergeant after Guarnere lost a leg at Bastogne. How could anybody shoot Grant? I wondered aloud.

The man who had waked me up told me. Grant was forming his relief for guard in the main part of Saalfelden when a SHAEF major standing nearby saw a German vehicle rushing upon the relief. He stepped into the road and halted it. The driver, a GI, jumped out with a pistol in his hand and shot the major to death. Grant ran up, shouting for him to surrender his pistol. The GI shot him in the head and ran away. Grant was now in a German hospital, undergoing a very delicate operation on his brain, and the GI was loose in Saalfelden. The whole company had been alerted to look for him.

"Everybody up!" Liebgott shouted as I started downstairs. "Grant's been shot. Outside on the double!"

So drunk that I saw the stair well as a crazy, whirling, tilting tube, I reached for the handrail, missed it, and ran down full speed. I hit the landing, thinking it was another step, and pitched forward on my face. "Son of a bitch," I muttered, shaking my head and rising to all fours. "I'll make it yet." I picked up my rifle and went down more carefully to the second floor.

All the lights were on. Men ran from room to room and floor to floor. The hotel was seething. I smiled at the hubbub. The outfit moved fast, once it was stirred up.

Stopping on the front steps, I rubbed my face and loaded my M-1 with a clip from the bandolier that I had slung over my shoulder on awakening. Things were steadying somewhat now. I could make out individual men, forming by squads at the foot of the stairs. I ran past them to the left and down the road to the highway crossing. I zigzagged from one side of the road to the other, trying to run fast with my rifle at high port and inhaling sobering breaths of cold night air.

I staggered into the intersection with my jacket unbuttoned, my bootlaces clicking behind me, and my rifle ready. The guards were all standing together in the center like cows in a thunderstorm, fingering their weapons and whispering and watching the night for the death that might come at them any moment. I told them to break it up and scatter out, one man at each road. "Lie down in the shadows at the edge, so you can see him coming. That way he'll be silhouetted but he won't see you. Tell him to halt, and if he keeps coming, shoot him."

The guards scattered, and I ran in place and did arm exercises with my M-1 to keep warm and sober up. Gradually the gin and the excitement died down and were replaced by cold and a sense of anticlimax. Half an hour passed and then an hour. The other men had all risen and were moving about restlessly. "When's the relief coming?" one of them asked. "They're thirty minutes overdue."

I don't know," I replied. I was thinking of Grant and the GI who shot him, wondering who he was and why he had murdered the SHAEF major and shot Grant. It was a terrible thing to happen to a man who had lived through the war and would soon go home. Liquor and pistols—that was the trouble. Too much liquor, too many pistols, everybody running wild in his own vehicle. It had to end soon.

Soon a carload of riflemen came through and brought us up to date. Men were watching all the roads out of Saalfelden, they said. Mounted patrols were circling the town in German jeeps and command cars. The Camera Killer was taking a squad through the houses near the scene of the shooting. The man couldn't possibly escape. A loud, unpopular replacement from the 3rd Battalion who had seen no action, the murderer had already been identified by Regimental Headquarters, which had reported that he had shot and killed two German soldiers and stolen their car. It was rumored that the colonel did not want this man taken prisoner—his body would be enough.

The relief marched up the road a few minutes later and informed us that the man had been captured. Grant's platoon leader had found a babbling GI wandering aimlessly along a back street with a dull, unseeing look in his eye. Instead of shooting him on the spot, as we agreed would have been fitting and proper, the lieutenant brought him into Company Headquarters. He was thrown into a chair and beaten senseless. One of Grant's buddies had burst into the CP with a pistol in hand to finish him off, but four men grabbed him and held him back. Beaten unconscious, the murderer was now on his way to the regimental guardhouse in Zell am See.

We marched back to the hotel, where I had another large tumbler of iced tea and gin, went to bed, and slept restlessly for a few hours.

ACHTUNG!   ACHTUNG!
YOU ARE NOW ENTERING
THE CITY OF
ZELL AM SEE
HOME OF THE
506TH PARACHUTE INFANTRY RGT.
(FALLSCHIRMJÄGER)
WELCOME!

Christenson and I smiled at the huge billboard that Colonel Sink had had erected at the city limits of Zell. "I guess the world knows who's running this town," I chuckled. Chris nodded. Dodging duty in Saalfelden, which had become more than guard after Grant's shooting, we had hitched a ride to Zell am See for a day's outing. Our driver let us off farther in town, and we cut left and went downhill toward the lake.

It was 9:30 in the morning, and the wet coolness of the night was still rising in faint steam from grassy lawns and vacant lots where the dew sparkled like tiny drops of ice. The lake, which got choppy when the wind came up at noon, was so calm and flat that it resembled a sheet of pale-green glass. The cool, sweet, summer-morning freshness of the air made us happy and alert.

We passed a sign that said, "ANY G.I. CAUGHT WITH AN UNREGIS-TERED D.P. FEMALE WILL BE TAKEN OFF JUMP PAY PERMANENTLY," turned right at a chalet that bore the legend "THIS PLACE FOR AMER-ICAN OFFICERS ONLY," and went to a low, windowless wooden shed labeled "NUR FÜR BESITZTRUPPEN."

"What's it mean?" Christenson inquired.

"Occupation troops only," I replied. "This was a private beach club when we first got here. You should have seen the blondes! French bathing suits. Rich refugees from Vienna. The rich never suffer."

We went to the entrance and stopped at a turnstile by a counter where a GI was lounging. "Two of us," I said. "Do you have two pairs of trunks?"

"Sure, buddy. Here's your key."

We passed through the turnstile into a quadrangle bordered on three sides by the U-shaped bathhouse and the lake on the fourth. Rough brown sand filled the open space, with raised sun platforms of wooden slats laid across two-by-fours scattered about. The beach was clear except for some rowboats and canoes partially ashore. More boats were moored to a narrow pier that ran into the lake on thin piles. A twenty-foot sightseeing launch was tied up at its end.

A Victrola started to play a very old recording of "Singing in the Rain." I nodded to a German soldier sweeping out the bathhouses and went into ours.

"That Kraut used to be a captain in the 6th Parachute Regiment. A nice guy. He remembers the 101st. Fought us in Normandy, Holland, and Bastogne."

"No kidding?" Christenson studied the ex-captain, a stocky, handsome blond with an open, friendly face, and shook his head. "It sure is a small world." He shut the door, and we changed into our trunks. The little room had the damp, musty smell of all bathhouses.

"A captain policing butts for a living," I mused. "Well, at least he has a job, and that's more than most Krauts can say."

We went out, locking the door behind us, and ran across the wet sand to a couple of sun platforms and sat down on them. The sun was very warm and comfortable.

"They certainly have this place posted," I remarked, jerking my head at a notice tacked to one end of the building. "EAST SIDE OF LAKE OFF LIMITS," it said.

"Times are changing," Chris sighed. "The chickenshit is setting in."

After a few more minutes' sunbathing, Chris suggested that we go for a swim. We walked out to the end of the pier and dived in. The water was wonderfully cool and clear, as clear as glass. Loving the exhilaration and the beauty of the mountains on all sides, we swam out until Chris complained that smoking had ruined his wind, and then we lay on our backs and rested.

Soon we swam back to the beach, and rested awhile in the sun. Then we went for a row, swam once more, and got dressed for lunch, which we hoped to bum with the athletes at the Hotel Austria or at some other mess hall in town. On previous visits, I had managed to slip into alien chow lines without detection. There were lots of transients in Zell, and a quick pitch usually sufficed to get by a suspicious cook or mess officer.

A car honked at us as we walked up the narrow, cobblestone lane that led from the main road to the Hotel Austria, which was almost at the base of the Schmittenhöhe Mountain behind town. We stepped to the curb and waited for the car to pass. A black 1938 Chevrolet panel truck with rough white stars painted on its hood and sides, it stopped by us. "Off the road, dogfaces!" the driver yelled.

It was J. D. Sometime radioman, assistant squad leader, and general goldbrick, he was now the athletic noncom. We greeted him, and he opened the door and offered us a lift. "Us athletes have to look out for the working man," he grinned.

"Where's your sweatsuit?" I inquired. "Everybody else in town is wearing SS sweatsuits. How come you're in ODs?"

"Athletic noncom has to dress up. Isn't this the life? See that stuff in back?" He jerked his thumb at a net and two volleyballs lying on the floor. "Those are for Major Winters. He's the regimental athletic officer now. All I have to do is see that he has his volleyball game set up every afternoon."

"What a deal! Man, I tried to be an athlete—even volunteered for track, because I once ran the mile—but Hale wouldn't let me go. He said it was either me or Chris, so I backed out. Chris went—didn't you—but now we're both stuck in Saalfelden."

Christenson nodded. "How do you do it, J. D.?" he asked.

"Get close to the right people."

"Politics."

"You know it."

"What else do you do?"

"Make out a list of the daily softball games in the regiment. Keep score. Major Winters gave me this Shivvy to run around in—TO equipment for the athletic noncom."

"Any girls up here? There's none left in Saalfelden, now that the Krauts have pulled out."

"Got a dishwasher's wife—one of them heavy blondes. What a lay! Makes me tired to think of it. Well, here's the hotel. See you in Room 405. Have to park the car."

Christenson and I got out and went up the front steps. A crowd of loungers watched us languidly in a fly-buzzing summer drowsiness. New arrivals from the faroff distasteful world of close-order drill and military courtesy and discipline, we were obviously not too welcome at the hotel. The loungers were clad in baggy black sweatsuits with round chest patches that bore silver lightning SS insignia four inches high.

"We're in the wrong town," I remarked to Chris. "Think the boxing team needs a waterboy?"

"Make it two waterboys."

The interior of the hotel had the fresh cool pinewood smell of summer hotels in the mountains. The furniture in the lobby, which was big and high, was semirustic, while the floor was covered with cool reed rugs. Matthews was waiting for us in the hall when we reached the fourth floor. "Come down to the room, meatheads," he said. "We're all in training."

Sholty, Lyall, O'Keefe, Garcia, and two newer men, Hickman and McBreen, were playing cards or kibitzing. Matthews picked up his hand and went on with the game.

"How are things at the company?" he asked.

"Lousy. Training program has started. There's a rumor they're going to take away our vehicles soon."

"Oh?" Matthews was just making conversation. It was obvious that he was no longer interested in the company. "How's Mick?"

"He's doing all right. Got some gal in town."

"Why don't you guys come down here? It's a cinch: no reveille, no retreat, no formations, no saluting in sweatsuits. Maids clean the rooms and make up the beds, waitresses serve the chow, Kraut soldiers do the KP. Can't beat it, mates."

"Boy, I'll say," I murmured, studying the cool, clean room, with its twin beds and big windows looking over the steep roofs of Zell to the lake. "You guys really have it made." What irked me—and I knew it also irked Christenson, because we had often discussed the matter together—was that only Matthews was an old man. The others had all come in after Normandy. Half of them had seen no action at all.

"Chow!" somebody shouted in the hall.

The gamblers threw down their cards, and we started downstairs together. Christenson and I hung back with Matthews and let the others go ahead.

"Look," I said, "we're serious. We want to get up here. Can't you or J. D. fix us up? Think you can work a deal with Winters to get us transferred to one of these teams?"

"We could start a swimming team," Chris suggested.

"I'll see what I can do," Matthews said.

"We have to get out of the company. The war's over. I can't train anymore," I told him.

"You're crazy to stick with it."

"Put in a real strong plug for us, will you?"

Matthews nodded. "I'm not so sure about J. D., though. He's cozy as hell about his job. Doesn't want anybody cutting in on it. And without his help, no meathead gets through to Major Winters."

"Work on him," Chris said. "Basic training is for the replacements. We want to be athletes."

Denied the luxury of living in Zell am See, I hitchhiked there as often as possible and spent most of my time on the beach. I left Saalfelden after breakfast, thumbed ten miles south to the beach club, swam across the lake, sunbathed, ate lunch at any available mess hall, swam some more, bummed supper, and went to the nightly movie in the regimental theater. Best of all was the lake.

I loved to swim in its clear waters, so cool and invigorating that I always felt reborn as I moved across it in a steady crawl that brought me in view of the mountains, the sky, and the deep, deep water everytime I swung my head around in time with the stroke of my arms. Although the other side was off limits, McBreen, who had quit the boxing team when they had started to make daily runs ("Be damned if I'll run—I went out for boxing, not track"), and I would row across, and then I'd swim back while he accompanied me in the boat. On the days he couldn't come along, I swam across and back by myself. It was almost two miles, but I never enjoyed swimming so much as in Zell. The beauty of the lake and its countryside made me forget all distance and weariness.

One day I returned from my swim, ate supper, and went for a walk with McCreary along the banks of the stream behind the barn. His points were coming through, he said, and soon he and the others with eighty-five and over would go to the 501 in Berchtesgaden to wait for transportation home. We discussed the change that was coming over the outfit—the tightening up on private cars, the rapidly expanding training program, the mounting discipline—and agreed that it was time for us to leave. Too many noncoms were new or political or both. Too few officers had seen any action. With the replacements in charge, we no longer felt at home.

Trapazano rushed up to us when we came back in the hotel. "Jesus, where've you been, Web?" he asked excitedly. "We've been looking all over for you."

"Went for a walk. What's wrong?" I could tell that something terrible had happened.

"Janovek's hurt bad. Marsh took him to the aid station in Zell am See. He fell out of the truck and hit his head on a log."

"Oh, my God. Where'd you say he was?"

"Regimental aid station."

"I'm going there. Tell Hale. He'll understand."

I ran outside and headed for the roadblock at a fast jog. Janovek was the only person I had been close to in Holland and had known well since then. He and I shared a negative attitude toward the army, and when I had been made an acting squad leader in Marsh's absence, he had been the most cooperative man in the squad. With encouragement and understanding, he had been a good soldier. In fact, he was the one man in the squad, other than Marsh, whom I could really count on. I did not want to lose him as a friend or a soldier.

I jogged through the intersection and walked toward Zell,

thumbing the few vehicles that passed. Finally a GI truck stopped and gave me a lift into town.

The regimental medics occupied a large private home on the highway in the northern outskirts. Since the door was open, I walked in and looked for someone to help me. Major Kent, the chief medical officer, glanced up from his chair in a room that opened on the front hall. "Can I help you?" he inquired, coming out.

"Yessir," I said, smiling at him. I had always admired him for his work on the jump fields and in combat and had never regarded him as an officer but as a doctor and friend of all men regardless of rank. "I'm looking for a friend of mine who got hurt in an accident. His name's Janovek."

"Oh, yes," Major Kent frowned. "Are you a buddy of his?"

"Yes, I am."

"Come with me."

The major led me into the dining room, where half a dozen enlisted men were laughing and joking and playing cards around a mahogany table six feet in diameter. They looked up at us quickly, then went on with their game. Major Kent opened the pantry door, turned on the light, and stepped aside.

"There he is," he said quietly.

"Oh, my God." I stared down at a long figure lying still under a GI blanket on the floor. "He's dead, he's dead." My eyes filled with tears.

Major Kent shut the door. "Didn't they tell you?" he said.

"No, they didn't. They just said he was hurt bad."

"Skull fracture. He was dead when they brought him in."

The medics in the other room burst into laughter and threw down their cards. "Almost time for the movie," one of them said.

"Do you want to look at him?" Major Kent asked me.

"No sir, I don't. I've seen enough dead men in this war to last me the rest of my life. I don't want to look at another one, ever."

Major Kent stepped over to the sideboard, picked up a brown envelope, and handed it to me. I continued to stare at Janovek. I wanted to bend over and shake him back to life, to curse him for sleeping so soundly.

"These are his personal effects." He emptied the envelope. "A parachute scarf, a Purple Heart, his wings, the ETO ribbon, the Combat Infantry Badge, and his wallet. He had no money on him."

"I'll mail them home."

The major put everything back and handed me the envelope, then opened the door. Before I went out, I looked at Janovek again, hoping that he would move or cry out, but the blanket was still. Grant shot and Janovek dead and the war over: It made no sense. The army was death. Let's be done with it and go home. We should have gone home on V-E Day. If we had, Grant would be OK and Janovek would be alive. But no, we have to stay on and on and on. Come on, Janovek, get up! You're the slowest, stubbornest man in the squad.

Major Kent held the door open for me, I thanked him and walked through the medics in the dining room, hating them for their indifference. I went out the front door and up the highway.

6

WINDING DOWN

"Do you hear me, goddamn it? We're leaving in ten minutes. Get your goddamn squad out front!"

I turned and frowned at Christenson, who was watching from the door with his gear on and his Thompson in hand. It was about ten in the morning, and I was drunk already, because we were leaving Saalfelden for Kaprun, where we would start training in earnest.

"Always in a rush," I muttered. "We have to finish the gin before we go. Here, have a drink."

He shook his head. "Second squad's outside already."

"Piss on the second squad."

"You're drunk," Winn said, slapping my back. "You're drunk day and night." He laughed. One of the first athletes returned from Zell, he had helped me mix and consume a pitcher of iced tea and gin while we prepared to move out. "That's the kind of squad leader I like," he said. He lifted a tumbler and drank it down.

"Have a drink, Chris," I said. I poured the mixture into another glass until it spilled over onto the frayed reed rug. "I don't drink myself," I remarked as I lifted the pitcher, put its side lip against my mouth, and wet my face, "but I like to see other people having a good time."

"Better lay off," Chris warned. "Captain's forming the company already."

"The hell with it. Party's over. I got eighty-seven points, but I'm still in this goddamn outfit, still have to train with the replacements."

"Yeah, yeah. Now get going! Get your men out front with the rest of the platoon."

"OK, OK." I downed the full glass that I had poured for him, emptied the pitcher, and threw it out the window. "Geronimo, look out below!"

"Check the rooms for weapons and ammo," Chris said. "Step on it!" He left.

"Winn, you'd better go outside," I muttered, feeling very dizzy and barely able to separate him from his image. "I'll be along in a little while."

I went to the tall white wardrobe and got my M-1, which was standing in a corner, loosened the sling, and slipped it over my shoulder. Putting on my helmet, I staggered into the hall.

The building was empty. Feeling very much alone, I hurriedly checked the other rooms. Winn met me in Sholty's, and we both paused and looked out the window at the railroad station, where Kesselring's train had been. The rest of the company had already left in their vehicles. Only two trucks remained. Christenson, who was standing by one, yelled for us to hurry.

Shouting and laughing, we went from room to room, kicking open the doors, slamming them shut, yanking dresser drawers to the floor, knocking over tables and chairs. All we found was a box of machine-gun ammunition. At work early, the men had tidied the area very well. The extra gin had been carefully packed, the ammunition crated. Liebgott had even taken the CP's curtains and bedclothes.

"That's it," I said, slamming the last door. "We've had it. The party's over."

The trucks honked for us.

By now, the whole world was atilt. The hall rocked back and forth with tentative whirls, and it took all my self-control to keep from sinking to the floor and going to sleep. I started for the stairs and hit the wall. "Who moved the stairs?" I asked. "They were there before. I was walking straight at them."

Winn helped me in the right direction, and we started down together, careening from side to side.

A captain and a sergeant from the 3rd Battalion passed us on the way up. "What's going on?" the captain asked.

"We're moving out, sir," I replied. "Always moving out. The hotel's all yours—what's left of it."

Only one vehicle remained when we got outside. An Opel Blitz with its tailgate down, it held half the first squad.

"My squad," I said to the grinning men who were watching us. "Best goddamn squad in the regiment." I lunged for the tailgate and fell in the street. Kohler and Trapazano jumped out and pushed me in beside Winn. The truck drove off.

We arrived half an hour behind the rest of E Company, in full view of Captain Speirs. Unable to rise, I was carried indoors and put to bed. The party was indeed over.

"Retreat?" I said, opening my eyes and looking around in bewilderment. I could not recall moving into this strange, pine-smelling alcove under the eaves.

Sholty nodded. Having shaken me awake, he now stood over me to make sure I didn't go back to sleep.

"Retreat in ODs? I'll be goddamned. We haven't stood retreat in ODs since Mourmelon."

I raised myself on an elbow, wincing at the pain of a violent hangover.

"We've had it," Sholty said.

"What day is it?"

"Same day."

"Oh, God. I hoped I'd slept through till tomorrow. Why did I have to wake up for retreat?"

"Camera Killer's orders: Every man stands retreat. Class A uniform, ribbons and patches. Put on your jump wings, your Chevrolet badge, your Hershey bars, Spam ribbon, and hash marks."

"You make me sick." I jumped off the bed, ran downstairs to the toilet, and vomited.

"Retreat!" the CQ shouted. "Everybody outside in five minutes!"

I ran back upstairs and told Sholty that I hadn't even pressed my blouse yet.

"You've had it," he said as he cocked his cap over his eye and adjusted his tie.

"Retreat! Everybody out! Let's go!"

Sholty left the room, and I jerked on my pants, which had been rolled up in my barracks bag, and shouted for the squad to fall out. "I'll be along in a minute."

We fell in on the road out front, facing the slope of the mountain on the west. Captain Speirs and the Camera Killer waited till everyone was in place, and then the captain called us to attention, took a count, and told the platoon leaders to inspect their men. The Camera Killer came over to me, the first man in line, and stopped. Christenson halted behind him while Hale, as platoon sergeant, took up a position on his left, pencil poised over a paper pad to note each man's demerits.

I snapped my left hand across my stomach, grabbed the top of my M-1, and brought it up smartly across my chest at a forty-five-degree angle. Holding the weapon in my right hand, I banged the bolt handle back hard, leaving the chamber open for inspection, and then brought my left hand back up to support the gun.

The Camera Killer shot a left jab at the middle of the stock. I let go as soon as the motion started and slapped my hands at my sides. The Camera Killer glared at me: He had just caught it in time.

I ignored him and stared at the grassy slope beyond. They certainly have green grass in the Alps, I thought. Next time I'll move a little faster and make him drop it for sure.

"Too oily, soldier. Gotta keep it dry. Wipe it off and bring it to me after supper."

"Yessir."

He looked me up and down as if I were an old and unsuccessful classmate who had approached him for a loan. "Just get out of bed, soldier?"

"Yessir."

"You must have slept in them ODs. You sure as hell didn't press 'em, did you, soldier?"

"No sir." Green grass. A dead lieutenant would make it greener.

"How long have you been in the army, soldier?"

"Three years."

"Three years what?"

"Three years, *sir*."

"And you fall out for retreat in ODs with a barracks bag press?"

"Yessir."

"Don't let it happen again!" He turned to Hale, who was ready with his little pencil. "Sloppy uniform. He'll iron it and wear it after supper, when he brings his rifle back for inspection."

"Yessir."

"And put on them ribbons and medals, soldier. What the hell's the matter with you that you won't wear the Combat Infantry Badge?"

"Nothing, sir. I couldn't find it, sir!" I never wear anything but my wings, Purple Heart, the ETO ribbon with three battle stars and the invasion arrowhead. Sir.

"Find it and put it on, goddamn it! If you can't act like a soldier, at least you can look like one."

My mouth curled. I wanted to kill him on the spot. And they wondered why nobody wanted to stay in the army.

"And shine them boots!"

"Yessir." I'll chop him up and mix him with chickenshit, because that's what the army is made of, and then spread him out on the hillside. That'll make the grass even greener.

"And take off that goddamn suntan shirt and put on an OD shirt like the rest of the men!"

"Yessir."

The rest of the platoon passed inspection with a few minor complaints, and then the trio returned to the front. Hale put away his book and pencil, and the captain gave the company at ease and checked his watch. When it was 5:15, he told Luz to blow retreat.

As the last notes died out in echoes among the mountains, Captain Speirs, who had been saluting with his hand, took a breath and shouted, "Order arms!" The company lowered its weapons to the ground with a solid thump.

"Parade, rest!" We thrust our rifle muzzles out at arm's length, put our feet twelve inches apart, and snapped our left arm behind our back.

"At ease!"

Audibly relaxing, we shifted our feet and wondered what he would say, for this was the regular time for directives, announcements, and proclamations.

"The party's over," the captain said. "It ended the night Grant got shot. We're not in a summer resort anymore but a training camp. From now on, we'll stand reveille every morning and retreat every night. The training schedule starts full force tomorrow— train in the morning and compulsory athletics in the afternoon. I'm going to make soldiers out of you men again."

A groan rose from the ranks.

"Platoon sergeants will collect all pistols after supper. Each one'll be tagged with the owner's name and locked up in a strong-box in the company CP. Any man caught with a pistol after tonight loses it.

"All Kraut vehicles will be turned in to the first sergeant the same time as the pistols. That's a division order. There have been seventy-four car wrecks in the division in the past month. Sixteen men and five officers have been killed and God knows how many men injured, and the general doesn't want to lose any more. Bad enough to get killed in combat. It doesn't make any sense to be killed in a car wreck now.

"There will be no more drinking in duty hours. If I catch another man drunk in public, it'll be his ass."

He paused, and I winced.

"We have to have discipline. We have to earn the respect of these goddamn Krauts and act like soldiers. There's still a war on in the Pacific, and I'm going to get you ready for it. Fall out for chow!"

While the rest of the men whooped and ran for their mess kits, Christenson hurried over to me. "Looks like we've had it but good," he commented. "Speirs is really going GI."

"Everything's changing," I agreed.

We exchanged complaints and were about to go indoors when a familiar, slightly hunched-over figure with a long stride came down the street from Company Headquarters. It was Lieutenant Brownlow.

The 101st started a training schedule. Day after day, we did close-order drill and calisthenics, as if we had just come into the army. Organized athletics were the order of the afternoon. And late in June, the general announced that an eight-hour training schedule would go into effect July 9, in preparation for the division's move to Japan via America in January, 1946.

I had to go along with the general—and Brownlow, who had

returned from his furlough home more eager than ever and raring to get us in shape again—because my last five points hadn't come through yet. Marsh, McCreary, Luz, Liebgott, J. D., Matthews, and all the other high-point men left for the 501 in Berchtesgaden, where they slept, swam, sunbathed, shot craps, fornicated, and rode horseback all day, while we drilled, studied nomenclature and functioning, marched up and down, practiced arm and hand signals, skirmished by squads, held mess-kit inspections, and learned to read maps. Triangulation occupied a solid week before we went on the range, a week that was one of the most maddening I had ever spent, with Brownlow constantly at my elbow.

A squad leader with eighty-seven points, I was so fed up that I began to miss formations and avoid retreat by going for afternoon swims at Zell. In a short time, Brownlow transferred Henderson from the mortar squad to lead mine and demoted me to his assistant. A quiet, freckle-faced boy from New Mexico, Henderson was apologetic about the shift, but I no longer cared, because my heart wasn't in garrison duty and I wasn't a noncom anyway. The highest I ever got was PFC. I would have liked to have been a squad leader or platoon sergeant in combat, which I understood, but I didn't have the patience for this garrison business of make-work, which I hated more than anything else in the army. I could never scold Winn too severely for missing close-order drill, because I knew he was a good soldier in combat who had fought every day at Bastogne. What if he missed a formation or two? He was still a good man in the place where it counted—combat—and I thoroughly sympathized with his bored disgust.

And so I waited in Kaprun for my last five points to come through. These were the "three mission," or Bronze Star, points, which General Taylor had decreed should go to the old men to help them get home before the outfit fought the Japanese. Everybody got a meritorious service Bronze Star medal who had made Normandy, Holland, and Bastogne or who had made two and missed the third because of wounds. The idea was good, but like all the other medals in the army, this one soon found its way onto the blouses of personnel clerks and others in rear echelon who had never seen an angry German. Captain Speirs was a freethinker who believed in just desserts to all, however, and so there was no abuse of the Bronze Star in E Company. He refused to give it to the cooks, claiming that it was intended solely for fighting men.

The point system was as confused and unfair as the army's system of awarding medals for bravery, a system subject to the whim of every division commander. The Air Corps discharged flying personnel regardless of points and released men in the States who had been in the service a few months, while the infantry held everyone down. The army claimed that first release would be given to men who had seen the most arduous service, but refused to give points for the Combat Infantry Badge. Thus, the Air Corps, which was never quite in the service or even with it but always in a private world of its own, discharged men regardless of points while the infantry stayed behind to occupy Germany.

All in all, it was a pretty sorry situation that made me fell sorrier for myself than usual, but I tried to make the best of it as June slipped into July. I found a farmer a couple of miles down the road by the ruined castle beyond Kaprun who gave me five gallons of ice-cold milk for a pack of cigarettes whenever I came by, and I swam at Zell and borrowed horses from Headquarters Company for afternoon rides. In idle moments, I listened to the radio, played solitaire, and went for short walks.

The rains began in the middle of July. My milkman told me that the summers were very short in the Alps. May was nice, ja, and June and the first half of July, but from then on, cool weather brought heavy rainstorms that flooded the roads and swelled the creeks. Then came winter. In our valley, the air turned chilly in the rainy spells, and the wind bore the sweet smell of Alpine flowers, wood fires, pine needles, and new-mown hay. Although it ended my swims, the rain was not without its rewards, for it cancelled altogether the outdoor training program and forced us to conduct sleepy, apathetic indoor classes on the mortar, BAR, and other weapons—classes that quickly degenerated into poker and pinochle games or a session with the radio.

To top off a general feeling of disgust, food began to get short, due, we were told, to the French shortstopping ration trains in their zone of occupation. The 2nd Battalion promply declared open war on cattle. Bands of riflemen went out at night in German vehicles (for the program had the approval of our officers) and rustled calves and yearlings from pastures for miles around. No herd was safe. If a farmer protested, the livestock was taken at the point of a gun. Shot in the head, the animals were butchered in our basements in a crude, messy operation that left the floor slippery with blood and crawling with biting black flies. Most of the meat was wasted, because we were amateur butchers and had no means of preserving what we did not immediately consume.

The farmers finally revolted and filed strong complaints with Military Government. A division order soon appeared forbidding all such expeditions—the 2nd Battalion alone had taken some seventy-five head of cattle plus untold scores of chickens—and so Captain Speirs, vowing that no man of his would go hungry, sent his riflemen into the mountains in search of deer. A few were shot, but most of the hunters, who had taken the job primarily to get out of training, tramped through the woods so carelessly that they scared all game away.

Since I was the worst shot in the company and Captain Speirs knew it, I couldn't even work this hunter routine to escape from the platoon. The weeks went by, more and more old men left, but still I stayed with Brownlow, going nowhere and hating everything, and most of all the army.

The 2nd Battalion was assembled under a black sky on a polo field half a mile west of Kaprun in ODs and overseas caps to practice for the weekly parade that took place every Saturday morning under the new training program. Though flat to the eye, the field was actually so rutted and pitted and bumpy underfoot that it was impossible for a company, much less a battalion, to stay in step more than a few paces. The aggravation of trying to hold a line and march properly without stumbling had reduced officers and men to a seething, sweating mass.

The storm burst on us with a density that reduced visibility to five hundred yards, but Colonel Strayer ignored it. Apparently determined to get us all in step before we left the field, he made us march by once again in a column of companies.

The rain soaked through our shirts, took the crease out of our pants, chilled our backs and hands, and turned the dusty earth to slippery mud. We cursed and muttered as the water poured down our rifle barrels and the company commanders frowned at Colonel Strayer and audibly wondered why he didn't send us home. Finally he gave in to nature and ordered a retreat from the field. By the time E Company arrived at its billets, which were farthest away, every man was soaking wet from head to foot.

"Clean your weapons and stand by indoors!" Captain Speirs shouted. "Fall out."

Henderson and I rushed up to our room, changed into dry fatigues, and broke down our weapons and cleaned them with care. A rusty gun was harder to keep clean than one dirtied in firing.

"Goddamn army," I muttered, shaking the water out of my trigger group.

Henderson, who was quiet and not given to complaining, nodded and left the room. The rain had stopped, I noticed, but a threat still hung in the air.

Henderson returned in a few minutes and bade the squad assemble for an hour's discussion of map reading and the use of the lensatic compass. As soon as we were comfortably settled around a map of Salzburg province, Christenson popped in and shouted, "Everybody outside for rifle inspection!"

Livid at the thought, I jumped up, cursing Brownlow, got my rifle, and went outdoors. The air was cold and overcast, with a heavy wetness hanging overhead, waiting to fall. Thunder rumbled and banged in the mountains, and water dripped off the roofs and ran down the street in muddy little streams.

"It's going to rain any minute now," I remarked to Chris, who was waiting for Brownlow to appear. "We're the only platoon outside. Why not hold it indoors?"

"Brownlow's orders."

"He should have stayed home. Why did the one guy who got a furlough to the States come back more GI than ever? We've been wet enough for one day."

The thunder rumbled closer and closer, sending gusts of cold wind before it. A drop of rain fell on my cheek. I frowned and held up my palm. Another drop splashed into it, then another and another.

"It's raining, Chris. We'll ruin our weapons again."

"Platoon, ten *shun!*"

Christenson spun around and saluted Brownlow, who had just come up the road. "First platoon all present and accounted for, sir."

The storm burst overhead with a clap of thunder that made us cringe. A sheet of rain fell into the valley. Brownlow fidgeted for a moment, then dismissed us to our houses. I almost fainted in astonishment.

Sensing that Brownlow was in a good mood, I went to the platoon CP a bit later to ask a favor of Christenson. He was reading the *Stars and Stripes*.

"Look, it's raining too hard for athletics. Will you ask Brownlow if I can go to Zell am See and see about my points?" I asked him. "They were supposed to come through a couple of weeks ago."

Chris nodded and continued to read the paper, making comments on the more interesting stories.

I shivered and stood up, buttoning my raincoat tightly around my neck. "Cold in here. That rain's made everything cold. Summer's over—it's time to go home. Let's close up the army and go home, Chris."

"I'll see what I can do for you, Web. Come back in about fifteen minutes."

In a cheerful mood, I strolled back to my billet and killed time drying my rifle. Chris smiled when I came back to the CP. I removed my helmet liner, walked into the lieutenant's room, and stood at attention as I requested permission to go to Zell.

"Why?"

"To see about my points, sir. I've got five points due for that Bronze Star, but they haven't come through yet. I'd like to go to regimental personnel and see what's happened to them, sir."

"In the rain? It looks like more rain."

"Yessir. There's nothing much else to do this afternoon."

"Rain's slowed everything down, hasn't it? We can't follow the training schedule, go for a hike, take a run, or do anything outdoors anymore, can we? I'll be glad when we go back to France, where we can really train again. All right, go to Zell am See, if you want to, but be sure you're back for rifle inspection at 5:15."

"Yessir."

I saluted and went outside in my heavy, sticky GI raincoat, airless and hot even in winter, and walked downhill to Kaprun with my head bent forward against the driving rain. Fast gray clouds moved across the sky only a few hundred feet above my head and hung smoking against the mountainsides. The smell of pine trees and wet earth and smoke from the farmers' fireplaces made the day seem quite autumnal.

A truck shifted gears with a dry scraping behind me on the castle hill, and I stopped and thumbed a ride. An Opel Blitz in the com-

pany motor pool, it was driven by a cheerful PW who had chauf-
fered a German staff car in one of the Panzer divisions that had
overrun the British 1st Airborne at Arnhem. We rehashed the war
on the way into Zell, and he went out of his way to let me off at
Regimental Headquarters.

The lakefront hotel where it was located was warm and brightly
lit. Entering with the humility of a muddy hind at the lord's castle,
I took off my helmet liner and ran my fingers through my hair.

"Looking for somebody?" a guard asked. He was dressed in crisp
ODs and white gloves.

I stared down at my soaking wet fatigues and muddy boots while
I beat my helmet liner against my raincoat. "Where's Personnel?"

"Right-hand corridor, third door on the left. Look for the S-4
sign."

"Thanks."

Leaving watery footprints behind me, I squished down the hall
and knocked at the S-4 door.

"Come in."

A T-5 stared up from a desk behind a counter.

"This Personnel?"

"That's right. What can I do for you?"

"I have a meritorious service Bronze Star coming. The damn
thing was due several weeks ago, but I haven't gotten it yet. Five
more points and I'll be out of the army."

The corporal grinned. "I know how you feel, buddy. Everybody
wants out. We have at least fifty guys in the regiment hung up on
those last five points."

"I have to have 'em. Do you know when they'll come through?"

"Nope. The whole army's balled up on that point system. All
you can do is sweat it out."

"Could you check for me? I want to make sure I was put in for
those points."

"OK, buddy, give me your name, rank, and serial number."

I gave him the information, and he sighed and rose from his desk.
"Have a seat on the bench outside," he suggested. "This is going to
take a while."

I nodded and, crossing the hall to a wooden bench, took off my
raincoat and sat down.

Regimental Headquarters, I mused, staring around with mingled envy and contempt. They really have it made—as always. Every clerk and dog robber up here is living high and wearing all kinds of medals. I leaned back and closed my eyes.

"What company are you from, soldier?"

I blinked and sat upright. Colonel Sink! Speechless with fright, I jumped to my feet and saluted.

"I said what company are you from?"

The colonel studied me without warmth. I could read his thoughts: wet fatigues, muddy jump boots, pants not bloused, face unshaven.

"E Company, sir."

"Don't you know you're not supposed to be in Regimental Head-quarters in fatigues?"

"No sir."

"See that it doesn't happen again."

"Yessir."

"And don't salute indoors. You only salute indoors when you report to an officer in the orderly room."

"Yessir."

The colonel went down the hall, leaving me wilted on the bench, utterly crestfallen. What are they running around here, I wondered, a formal dance? No fatigues in Regimental Headquarters! Jesus Christ.

And the colonel. I always liked him. All the time I've been in this outfit, I hoped I would meet him someday and tell him how much we thought of him. Then what happens? The one time he speaks to me personally, he gives me hell for wearing fatigues in Regimental Headquarters.

I bounced to my feet and ran across the hall. "Any way you can speed up those points?" I inquired.

The T-5, who was pushing and pulling at a filing cabinet, grinned and shook his head.

"I can't wait another minute to get out of this goddamn outfit."

"Moving out, goddamnit, moving out!" Christenson kicked the bed and grinned. "Let's hope this is the last time. Next time we go home, huh?"

A whistle shrieked in the street out front, and the CQ opened the door and shouted: "Fall out for France! Everybody outside! This is it! Moving out, moving out, moving out!"

The house quaked and shook with the sudden rush of men from every room. Christenson hurried out, and I paused for a last look from the back window. It was a clear day, with big white clouds moving slowly across the green meadows and jagged mountains. The rainy weather had brought the countryside to its greatest beauty, and I looked at it with a wrenching in my heart, hating to leave it behind. If only it were raining, I thought, then I wouldn't mind going away.

"Shake a leg, Web!" Henderson called from below. "Platoon's already assembled."

"I'm coming."

I ran downstairs two at a time and trotted out the front door. The company was already formed, every man with his weapon and helmet and ammunition and a horseshoe roll lashed to his musette bag. In a jovial mood, officers and noncoms stood before each platoon as they waited for Captain Speirs and the first sergeant to start them back to the country where they had first landed in Europe a little more than a year before.

Captain Speirs came out, took the count, and then gave us at ease and briefed us on our destination.

"We're going back to France," he said, "and it isn't going to be nice, because the French don't love us anymore. They're tired of us already. They're sick of soldiers, and they don't want to be reminded of the war by seeing more of them. We're not going into France as liberators this time, men, we're going in as GIs who've worn out their welcome. We're going to be on our good behavior. The general doesn't want any friction with the civilians, and he's promised to throw the book at anybody who raises hell down there. Ten *shun!*"

The company snapped their rifles to their sides and clicked their heels together with a solid thump.

"Right shoulder . . . *harms!*"

Captain Speirs looked up and down the green mass of men with their slanting forest of shouldered weapons and smiled with satisfaction.

"Right . . . *face!* Forwarrrrd . . . *harch!*"

We marched off, counting cadence, while an advance detail from the 42nd Division stood by their jeep and watched us go. The Kaprun Valley was changing hands. The 42nd was taking over our area. German PWs had moved into the slave-labor lager below us to work on the completion of the hydroelectric station. The DPs had all gone home.

A convoy of GI trucks was waiting for us in the village square. Half a platoon in each, we scrambled aboard and moved off, "to that crummy goddamn France," as someone said.

I lifted my eyes to the great snowcapped mountains behind the upper valley to the south and rested them on a black dot in the snow of the Kitzsteinhorn, which was the tallest peak, a white jagged shark's tooth against the blue, blue sky. The black dot was a ski hut that parties of men had been going to on two-day passes the last couple of weeks. It would have been my turn soon, I thought. Now it's too late.

The truck swung around a curve and went past the castle. I had wanted to explore that place, too, I mused.

The truck hit the valley on the run and roared past the farm where I had gotten milk for the squad two or three times a week. The farmer was leading a cow into the barn. He did not see me when I waved.

We crossed the river in the center of the valley, turned right, went east about two miles, and stopped at a country railroad station.

"Everybody out!" the first sergeant shouted, coming to our truck and unhitching the tailgate. A long line of boxcars with an electric locomotive at their head stood at the station. Men were already jammed in most of the cars. A bale of hay stood beside each of the empties. Colonel Sink was walking up and down the platform, talking with the men.

"Nobody on the roofs," the colonel said as Captain Speirs saluted him. "No shooting at trees and cows along the right-of-way. Break up the straw and spread it around, so the men will have something to lie on."

Captain Speirs passed the word along and bade us climb aboard. In ten minutes we were under way.

Standing nearby in the door of the car and clinging to the frame for support, Christenson sighed, "It was great, wasn't it?"

"The prettiest country in the world. I wouldn't have missed it for anything."

The Kitzsteinhorn disappeared behind nearer mountains, and the land whipped past with mounting speed.

"Yes," I continued, "it was the only time I enjoyed the army.

Berchtesgaden and Austria were worth everything that went before."

We had slept in our clothes four days and three nights, and we were hot and dusty and sooty and itchy and irritable and unshaven. We tramped carelessly through the empty streets of the little French village of Joigny in a surly, resentful silence, hating the apathy of the shuttered houses, the tedious roughness of the cobblestone paving, the air of death and defeat and decay that lay over the whole country.

A very old village, founded in Roman times, Joigny sloped up steeply from a slow, brown river. Its narrow, winding streets and half-timbered houses lacked, in a way that we could all sense, the life and vitality found even in similar medieval villages in England. Nothing moved in the afternoon heat. Nobody waved to us or said hello or came out to watch us pass.

"France," the men muttered, wiping the soot from the corners of their eyes, rubbing the itches on their bodies, remembering the change that had come over the train as soon as it had crossed the border. In Germany, the train had traveled fast, with no delays. In France, it slowed down to a walk, with endless, mysterious stops in open fields, a wait of hours at every railroad yard and river crossing. "France" was not a country but a swear word.

We topped the hill and marched out on a plateau through the last houses of town to the high white walls of an old garrison that looked like a Foreign Legion post in the movies. The walls, about thirty feet high, were topped with vicious rolls of concertina barbed wire. A rifleman in a striped sentry box beside a pair of open iron gates saluted Captain Speirs as we marched into the compound, a glaring, dusty place surrounded by old two-story stucco barracks. A company of the 1st Battalion was drilling in the compound. Their shouts and the hot, dusty air, coupled with the barracks' smell and sounds, roused in us a terrible sense of anticlimax. "France," the men grumbled. "Let's go back to Germany."

A small band of men lounging in the shade got to their feet and came forward to meet us. The advance detail, they saluted the captain, chatted awhile with gloomy headshakings, and then went to their respective platoons and guided us to our billets.

The second and third platoons filed into a two-story barracks while we circled around to a long shed with a high roof, where Brownlow left Christenson in charge of us. He bade us go inside and pick out our bunks.

Old and stale, the air smelled musty and unhealthy. The bunks were crude, rickety contraptions, obviously homemade, with straw sacks for mattresses. We threw our gear under them and cursed France without restraint. One of the men from the advance detail moved among us, slapping backs and joking. Finally he stopped by Henderson and me.

"Welcome to France," he leered. "Civil war barracks, built in 1870, and for the first platoon, a goddamn stable with straw sacks. We've had it, mates, we've had it." He sat down, and the rest of the squad gathered around to hear what he had to say about our new home.

"Krauts used this trap for a prison in the war," he continued, raising his voice for the benefit of latecomers. "Barbed wire still on the walls. There's only one gate, and nobody's allowed out without a pass."

I groaned and threw a boot at the floor.

"The latrine's a stone wall and a hole in the floor that hasn't been cleaned for seventy-five years. There's no hot water, and you can't drink the tap water, because it'll give you cholera, dysentery, and the bubonic plague. Have to get our drinking water from Lister bags. It's all souped up with Halazone tablets. Tastes like a swimming pool.

"The town's dead. A couple of beer joints without beer, cognac, or calvados. Nothing but wine. The Frogs won't even say hello to you on the street or nod to you the way the Krauts would, and there's no women or hard liquor for miles around. No cathouses either, and no whores on the street. If you proposition a gal, she spits at you. Can't even buy a lardy cake here, Web."

He slapped my leg and smiled, and I shook my head in reply, for the atmosphere was very depressing. "This is worse than the Frying Pan," I muttered.

"Goddamn right. At least we had Columbus and Phenix City handy down there. Here we got nothing. Can't get drunk or laid or anything. Paris is ninety miles away, but the trains don't stop here, so what the hell good is Paris?"

"How about that river?" I asked. "Can you swim in that river?"

"You know these Frogs: Every river's an open sewer.

"The Frogs hate us here. They hate us everywhere in France. Save their country for 'em, and they hate you for it. But you can do business with 'em. Frog KPs are in the black market. Sell 'em your spare jump boots and fatigues and cigarettes. They'll give you a thousand francs—that's twenty bucks—for a pair of jump boots, five hundred francs for a carton of weeds or a fatigue jacket. Chow's on the blink already because the goddamn cooks are selling the good stuff to the KPs. Anybody who doesn't think Germany's the best country in Europe has rocks in his head."

"Holland's better," I said quietly. "They're Germans without the viciousness."

He ignored me and was about to continue his dissertation when someone on the edge of the group shouted for attention. The men opened a path for him, and Brownlow pushed through them angrily.

"What's going on here?" he asked. "You men are supposed to be cleaning up the barracks. We have a lot of work to do before retreat and just one hour to do it in. Sweep this place out! Get those cobwebs off the walls! Make up your bunks! Wash and shave and fall out for retreat in an hour in clean fatigues and helmet liners! This is the place where we're really going to soldier."

He spun around and stalked away with his long stride. Turning at the door, he called back, "These are dirty old barracks. God knows how many diseases are floating around in them. Bunks are jammed together too close for proper circulation. Get back here after chow and stretch shelter halves between 'em! You'll have plenty of time, because there won't be any passes for several days."

He slammed the door, and Christenson, who had come near us, shrugged his shoulders and sighed: "That's the program, men. You have to take the program. Retreat comes first, then the rest of that crap."

We began to clean our M-1s. A murmur of complaint filled the air. I'm right back where I started, I thought, suddenly overwhelmed by a feeling of futility and failure, just a lonely private sitting in a drab barracks in a hot, dead country like Georgia. I have accomplished nothing—won no medals, achieved no rank, seen almost no action. All I ever wanted to be in the army was out.

Three years have gone by, and everything is the same, nothing has changed. Retreat at 5:15, supper at 5:30, no passes tonight. Spread shelter halves between the bunks instead. Tomorrow there'll be an hour of calisthenics, two hours of close-order drill, an hour with the manual of arms. The afternoon will be devoted to squad tactics. Then retreat again at 5:15 and supper at 5:30. It'll take more than a war to change the army. Nobody ever used a rifle sling in combat, and the army knows it, but they will go on teaching the use of the rifle sling for the next thousand years, because that's the way it's been in the past, and the past is the safest guide to the future.

I thought of the army, of all the wasted lives spent in stale barracks doing over and over again things proved utterly useless in war after war. Maybe they did them because there was nothing else to do. It was all make-work in the army, putting in your time, trying to find something to do for thirty years. No matter what the outfit, the army was always the same. It was not for me.

I was still waiting for my points a week later when Christenson .thundered into the stable in the lull between breakfast and the first formation, rushed to my bunk, grabbed my hand, and pumped it up and down.

"You're in!" he exclaimed. "They finally came through."

"No kidding? Wahoo!" I sprang from my bunk, hooked my elbow in his, and whirled him around the aisle with shrieks of delight.

"Pack your bags and stand by."

"No more pencils, more more books, no more looeys' dirty looks!"

He slapped my back and left the stable.

"Peace," I sighed, reclining on my mattress, "isn't it wonderful?" I didn't know what I was going to do in civilian life, but I didn't care, because I was going back to freedom, to the place where all men were equal and there was no sirring or saluting. "Listen to those whistles. Listen to that goddamn CQ."

"Everybody outside! ODs and helmet liners. Practice parade."

"Up your ass!" I yelled. I rolled onto my side to watch the others fall out. "Have a good parade, man."

"You go to hell," Winn grinned.

I looked forward to a last, delicious morning in the sack, a lazy, sleepy morning that I would sniff and sip and savor to the final minute, when I would rise and leave the army forever. It would be like a day on Quarters, only instead of returning to duty tomorrow, I would remain on Quarters, doing nothing, traveling to the 501 and loafing with them. Tomorrow and tomorrow and tomorrow, on Quarters till I reached the States. Moaning with warm contentment, I closed my eyes and tried not to hear the loathsome sound of drilling.

"Webster!" someone yelled.

I cringed. It was my master's voice. Brownlow hurried to my bunk with a set face.

"Yessir?" I said, bewildered.

"Why aren't you out with the rest of the men?"

"My points came through, sir. I'm leaving today. They told me to stand by."

"They did, did they? Well, get out there with the rest of the men! As long as you're in my platoon, you're going to soldier. Everybody in the company has to fall out for this practice parade, including you. On the double!"

"Yessir." I started for the door. If chickenshit was money, the 506th would be millionaires, I said to myself.

I fell in with the platoon and marched off in the dust under a glaring August sun in a prickly wool uniform and a helmet liner that itched unbearably, and spent a last, bitter morning marching back and forth before Colonel Sink and Colonel Strayer on a flat brown field near the river. For three hours, we wheeled and turned, marked time in place, stood at parade rest, presented arms, passed in review by companies and battalions. By the time it was over, I was in a mood to bayonet babies and roast both colonels over small fires. I won't go into what I planned for Brownlow.

Christenson came to see me after lunch and told me to report to the supply room with my bags and bedroll for a final equipment check. The supply sergeant tried to take away a pair of new jump boots but settled for some old combat boots. Otherwise everything was all right. When we were through arguing, he went into the bins and returned with an armful of new fatigues and jump suits and handed them to me.

"Take 'em," he said. "We have a lot of extras. Good work clothes for civilian life."

I gaped at him. "A uniform in *civilian* life? Jesus Christ!" Lifting the bundle of clothes high overhead, I smashed them down on the counter. "Shove these rags up the army's ass. I'll never wear another uniform as long as I live." I hoisted my duffel bag on my shoulder and went out the door, with the supply sergeant shaking his head behind me.

Since there were still a few minutes before departure time, I went into Company Headquarters to say good-bye to Captain Speirs, whom I had always liked.

"I want to thank you, captain," I said.

He frowned. "For what?"

"For giving me a break. You're the only company commander who ever gave me a break, sir, the only one who ever made me a noncom."

"Well, hell, Webster, I tried to make a soldier out of you."

"It couldn't be done, sir," I grinned.

We shook hands and said good-bye and wished each other luck. I saluted him for the last time and went outside, where the other high-point men were waiting.

In the company area, whistles started to blow, the CQ ran from door to door like some medieval alarmist alerting a city, the men fell out noisily for squad tactics, and I felt a temporary rush of nostalgia for the outfit and the life that it led. It was my outfit, the 506th, the only outfit I had ever been in. I had cursed it steadily for three years, had avoided duty whenever possible, and prayed for light wounds every day in combat, and yet now that I was finally leaving, I was almost sorry to say good-bye. Nothing I had ever done before could compare with the feeling of belonging that I had had with the 506th.

The paratroops were life itself, life and death and the thrill of conquering yourself by jumping from an airplane. I would miss the din and clamor, the foul-mouthed good humor, the sound of marching men, the wild excitement as I went out the door and fell a hundred feet before my chute opened.

But these were minor things, now that the war was over and all purpose had been lost. The 506th was just another training camp now, and I hated training almost as much as guard duty.

Captain Speirs said a fast good-bye and shook each man's hand, then the Camera Killer, who was also going home and who had charge of us, led us at a jovial route step to an open space near the main gate, where Colonel Sink was waiting in a jeep surrounded by several dozen men from other companies who were also leaving.

On the far side of the gate, in a barbed-wire enclosure set against the high wall, inmates of the regimental guardhouse stood listlessly in the shimmering heat and watched as the colonel mounted the hood of his jeep and began his farewell speech.

He sounded mechanical and uninspired, as if he had made this speech before and was losing interest, as if he knew that none of us cared for the outfit anymore but were thinking only of getting away from it, and soon my mind wandered from his words to the guard-house. I studied the faces of the men clutching the wire. One of them waved and called my name. I started in surprise, not hearing the colonel, and waved back.

The deserter, I thought. God, he has almost nineteen years to go. He was an older man, with a wife and two children and no interest in war or the army whatsoever, and why he had joined the para-troops was a mystery that even he couldn't explain. A replacement fresh from the States, he had arrived several weeks before the Hol-land jump. When we went up the hill to Membury Airdrome, he had been so strongly affected by the tension that he swallowed a large dose of sodium Amytal pills. Thoroughly drugged, he had stumbled about the muddy tents in a blind haze, muttering. "I can't stand it, I can't stand it." But when the time came, he jumped with the rest of us. He went through seventy-two days in Holland and then he was through. "War," he had said, "is a game for vicious children. How could a mature man be a soldier?" When the outfit returned to base camp in Mourmelon, he walked out one day and never came back. The MPs picked him up in civilian clothes in Paris at the height of the Bulge and shipped him back to the regiment, where he was given the usual sentence for desertion—twenty years at hard labor.

Of course, it won't be twenty years, I thought, studying him closely to see if he had changed. It never is. They give them three or four years in a detention training center and then turn them loose. They're alive when it's all over, while the good men, the fine, brave men like Mather and Hoobler, who stuck with the outfit till they were killed, are dead forever. The modern deserter is lucky, and he knows it. In the old days, he would have been shot.

But I wouldn't trade places for a minute. He ruined his whole life because he wouldn't (or couldn't—not everybody could) take what we had taken before and had to go on taking until it was all over. I'm glad I made it, I thought, and I'm glad I'm getting out with a clean record and a clear conscience. I couldn't sleep with myself if I was a deserter.

"Good luck and God bless you, God bless you all," the colonel concluded.

A noncom called us to attention, and we saluted, then gave three cheers for the colonel. He got down and drove off, waving good-bye as he went.

I climbed into the back of one of the GI trucks that were waiting for us and took a seat where I could look into the guardhouse. I'd kill myself if I had to put any more time in the army, I thought. The army is prison with passes. Who wants to spend their life in prison?

The truck moved out of the compound, and my friend, whom I had liked and often felt sorry for, as one is sorry for a man in a totally unsuitable job from which he has no escape, waved to me.

"Take it easy, buddy!" he shouted.

"So long! Good luck!"

The truck bounced out of the gate, and I raised my eyes and smiled at the concertina barbed wire. It could hold me no longer.

They had me for three years, I thought, three years with barbed wire and armed guards and sealed transports and marshaling areas where I couldn't even cross a hedge to the next company, and they'll never have me again.

We went downhill to the river. The walls grew smaller, and I could no longer see the barbed wire. Then we rounded a corner and left the regiment forever.